7/09
06
7

HOLIDAY
S✚S

HOLIDAY SOS

Ben MacFarlane

HODDER &
STOUGHTON

First published in Great Britain in 2009 by Hodder & Stoughton
An Hachette UK company.

1

Copyright © Ben MacFarlane and Neil Simpson 2009

A CIP catalogue record for this title is available from the British Library

ISBN 978 0 340 91975 0

Typeset in Rotis Serif by Hewer Text UK Ltd, Edinburgh
Printed and bound in the UK by CPI Mackays, Chatham ME5 8TD

Hodder & Stoughton policy is to use papers that are natural, renewable
and recyclable products and made from wood grown in sustainable
forests. The logging and manufacturing processes are expected to
conform to the environmental regulations of the country of origin.

Hodder & Stoughton Ltd
338 Euston Road
London NW1 3BH

www.hodder.co.uk

To the family and friends I see too little of when I'm travelling. And to all the cabin crews who make bad flights bearable.

The Summer Season

JUNE

'Hi, I'm Ben. I'm a doctor and I'm here to help get you home. How are you feeling?'

I don't normally introduce myself to patients by my first name. But this guy has only just turned eighteen years old. His medical records show that he's not been in hospital since the day he was born so I'm guessing he's pretty freaked out by the whole thing. Especially as six days ago he was practically dead.

'I'm okay,' he says, fixing his scared eyes right on mine, his voice not much more than a whisper. Then he looks down and away from me. He reckons he's a tough, streetwise teenager, but he knows he's about to cry in front of a complete stranger.

'I just want to go home,' he mumbles as he screws up his face to try and stop the tears. 'I've been on my own here for a week and I can't stay here any more. I just need to get home.' I look over at the two Turkish nurses who brought me to the guy's bed. They're almost crying too. They don't speak any English but it's pretty clear how much they want to help.

'Cok te sekur ederim,' I say to them, desperately trying to remember the words I'd just read in my phrasebook. 'Thank you very much.' It's pretty much the extent of my Turkish but I wanted to try at least. Then, I move towards the bed and rest my hand on my patient's shoulder. I want him to know he's finally got someone on his side; someone who speaks his language.

When he's calmed down I get to talk to him a little more. I ask him about the accident, even though his file contains most of the details. We're about to have a very tough trip back to Britain, so I need him to feel as relaxed as possible with me. I can't patronise him by pretending nothing's wrong and talking about the weather or the football. But I need to hear his voice to find out how strong he is. I need him to tell me what happened.

'I was on a moped,' he begins. I wonder if he has any idea how often my consultations begin with those five words. 'We were racing about, chasing some girls, having a laugh. I'd been drinking and doing some stuff, but that wasn't why it happened. It was the gravel. I hit a corner and I just lost it.'

I'm looking at his notes. 'At least you were wearing a helmet. That saved you.'

'I know. The one thing I did right. Should have worn more than a pair of shorts though.'

I smile at him. I like this kid. I like how honest he is. 'That's the problem with mopeds on summer holidays. You're not exactly going to wear leathers to get to the beach.'

'I should never have rented it.'

I shrug my shoulders to say it doesn't matter now.

'All your mates were okay? Were you the only one to fall off?'

'Yeah. It was the last day of our trip, so they had to go home that night. I've been on my own the whole time. My mum said she can't afford to get out here, my mobile went flat and I thought I'd been forgotten. I thought I was going to die here.' His voice is ragged and again he looks down and away. But this time he's keeping it all in check. I don't think he'll cry again. I think he's ready so I stand up.

'Toby, I'm going to get you home – probably tomorrow. I'm staying in a hotel ten minutes away so I can get back here any time if you need me before then. I'm going to go and talk to the doctors myself now. Then I'm going to examine you just so I know you're fit to fly. But you have my word that everything is being done to help you. I'll have you home faster than you know it. That's what I'm over here to do.'

I drink a rich dark coffee and go over the guy's notes while I wait for the local attending physician to arrive. My patient's full name is Toby Martin Harris. He's from Newbury Park in East London and his medical record is as clean as this hospital's blindingly white waiting area. He's not on any regular medication and has no known allergies, no blood problems, no personal or family history of heart disease, cancer or strokes, no epilepsy. Not even asthma. It looks like he was one lucky teenager, until he got scooped up from a roadside out here on Gumbet Bay seven days ago. The ambulance crew did their best and got him to hospital fast. But an awful lot of Toby's skin was left on that Turkish roadside. An awful lot of his blood had flowed into the earth. His body had taken quite a battering.

Here in the mix of old and new hospital buildings he needed a blood transfusion and they grafted skin from the back of his legs to his upper arms. He was in theatre for three

hours while they pinned his right thigh and shin bones back
together with a medical Meccano set. He'd broken a handful
of ribs and when one of the splintered bones punctured his
lung they had to put a chest drain in to re-inflate it and keep
him breathing. The only good news was that the CT scans
showed his brain had survived the worst of it. Wearing the
helmet was the best decision he had ever made.

'Hello, I'm Doctor Irmak. I've been attending on Toby
Harris. You are the one sent here for him?'

I look up from my coffee and hold out my hand. The
man in front of me looks to be in his early fifties. He's
surprisingly pale and he seems incredibly tired. But having
read the notes I know how good he is at his job.

'Yes, I'm Doctor Ben MacFarlane. Thank you for
everything that you have done.'

The doctor waves the thanks away. 'He's been a brave
young man. I'm one of the few people here that speaks
English and I speak it very badly. It can't have been easy for
him. It is very sad that he has been on his own. No family.
No friends for many days. Very hard for him.'

I can only shrug my shoulders again. The only thing
worse than ending up in intensive care on a holiday must be
to end up there on your own. That, I think, is why so many
patients cry when I turn up.

'He said his mother wanted to be here. Maybe she just
couldn't get a flight. But at least you think we can move
him tomorrow?' It is my new colleague's turn to shrug.

'He's been stable for forty-eight hours. Take it slow but
you'll see that he can move quite easily. He'll need new
bandages and a final check in the morning but yes, you can
take him. If he was my son I would be happy for him to fly.
I'd want him home.'

I shake the man's hand again, thank him and head back to the ward. Then I stop and turn round but he has already disappeared through a pair of double doors. I swear at myself under my breath. I meant to tell him not to apologise for his English.

'Okay, Toby, can you lift your leg just a tiny bit for me? And this one? Can you wiggle your toes? And move your fingers?'

I'm back at his bedside trying to make sure we won't have any nasty surprises tomorrow. I've got complete faith in Dr Irmak and his team but I can't take any chances. There's a huge temptation for doctors to hide just how sick their overseas patients are. They often want to get them discharged and off their wards. Then it's us repatriation doctors who have to get our hands dirty if it all goes wrong at 35,000 feet. Which it very often does.

'Can you move your head to the left, very slowly? And the right? Now, look at me.'

I'm checking his eyes, his ears, then moving on to his pulse and his blood pressure. I listen to his heart and his lungs, check his abdomen and take a quick look under some of the bandages to see his stitching and how well his wounds are healing. His drug charts show he's taking some heavy duty painkillers and antibiotics so I check we've got enough to see us through the trip home. You really don't want to be a seriously ill patient on a flight that gets badly delayed or diverted. That's when the trouble starts. That's when Toby will really start to suffer if the drugs run out.

'Mate, you are going to be fine.' I have to say he

already looks better now than he did when I first arrived. Laughter isn't the best medicine. Feeling that your in safe hands is.

'Thank you,' he says very, very quietly. Suddenly he's looking down and away again. It's my cue to leave.

I'd been booked into the nearest hotel to the hospital and for once I got lucky. It's a business place in the town centre rather than a holiday hotel, but it has a gym and a pool in the basement so I managed to get my blood moving before heading back to my room to call the office.

'Hi Ben, how is he?'

I get through to Christine, one of my favourite colleagues on our logistics desk in Hounslow. She's the one who first took Toby's details from the travel insurance company when the case was given to our agency. She arranged my flight out, my hotel and our flight back tomorrow. She's a good person to have on my side.

'You know what, he's okay. He's not exactly an angel but he's mortified that he's ended up in hospital and is desperate to get home. He's got pierced eyebrows, tattoos running up his neck and a tough-guy attitude, but he still can't stop crying every time he looks at me.'

'Ah, bless his little cotton socks.'

'Exactly. But his charts are fine, I've examined him and I reckon we'll be good to go tomorrow. Is our transfer sorted?'

'All booked for you. The private ambulance will be there for you just after eleven. It'll take half an hour to get to the airport and your flight is at two. Groundside and the airline have been told you're coming, but don't hold your breath for any special treatment. We've reserved you extra oxygen for the flight,and got you three business-class seats to give you some extra room. There'll be an ambulance at Gatwick when you land.'

'Do I need to stay with him or can I just hand him over?'

'If he's okay then just pass him on. He's going to Whipps Cross Hospital in Leyton and they'll be ready for him. Just bring your med bag back here afterwards and you're done.'

'Are you around?'

'No, I'm on nights from tomorrow, so you'll only get me if you have some really bad delays. Camilla's got your notes for the day shift. So how's the hotel?'

'It's brilliant, you did me proud, thanks. The pool's way better than I normally get this near a city centre.'

'Well, don't thank me too fast because I've let you down on something else. I tried to swing you a great job today. It's the Maldives on Tuesday for a man with a blood clot and a seizure. The flight times mean you'd have had two full days on the beach before doing the scoop. Plus about a million air miles. I wanted to allocate it to you but Jackie snagged it instead.'

'Typical, she gets all the good ones. I still can't believe she got the Cape Town job during that dental convention last month. I've still never seen such white teeth.'

'Don't forget she got that New York job on the last week of the January sales as well. I pay more at Primark than she did for that Armani coat.' There's a silence on the line as we both work out just how much we can learn from our boss. Then Christine remembers something. 'I have got you another job for Tuesday though and it's not bad. How do you fancy a night in San Tropez?' Now she's talking.

'I think I might be in love with you, Christine. What's the story?'

'Shouldn't be too difficult. It's an old guy on a coach tour round the South of France. He's got pneumonia after collapsing and hitting his head on the pavement. He wasn't in great shape beforehand, by the look of it, but they reckon he's stabilising pretty quickly. It's all being tracked now and Camilla should be booking the flights tomorrow. You want the job?'

'I'd love it. Maybe I'll see you tomorrow.'

I hang up and walk out on to my hotel balcony. I'm on the sixth floor and I'm gazing out over the streets of this anonymous Turkish town. It looks strangely beautiful. There's that wonderful muffled buzz you hear just after the sun sets on a really hot day. A few more cars are passing and the streets down below are gradually coming alive in the cooler air. The pavements always seem really busy in an unfamiliar town. I breathe in deeply. The air is smoggy and dirty, but I love it. It's on nights like this that I love my job the most.

Two years ago I was going slowly mad. I'd been working for a few years and I was about to start another set of thousand-hour-a-week shifts. Around the same time I moved house. One of my new flatmates was a nurse who earned a bit of extra money doing repatriations for a travel insurance company. She was sent all over the world to rescue people who'd been ill or injured on holidays or business trips. When she couldn't do a job one weekend I had a quick interview and did it myself. I was hooked straight away and did another job a week later. I loved flying off and not knowing exactly what I would find at the destination. I loved meeting the doctors overseas and assessing the patients. I enjoyed looking after them at 35,000 feet and getting them home safely. Most of my colleagues said I was crazy, but a few months later I quit the hospital and signed up with my current company. I've been jet-lagged ever since. It's a real struggle to keep up with family and friends and my girlfriend Danielle dumped me because I was always away. But I still think it's the best job in the world.

'How are you feeling, mate? Now, you do know that airline food will either kill or cure you. Chicken or beef? Do you feel lucky?' It's two-thirty the next afternoon and Toby and I are having a bit of a laugh in our business-class seats, which on a European charter flight seems to mean economy-class seats with different coloured fabric. Our transfer to the airport went well, check-in and security were pretty smooth and we were able to pre-board though the service lifts into the galley, rather than bouncing Toby's wheelchair up the steps from the tarmac.

Best of all, we took off on time and the captain said that we're in for a quiet flight. I'm feeling good and Toby is practically transformed. He perked up the moment he was wheeled out of the hospital.

'I never thought I'd see the fucking sun again. I thought I was going to die in there,' he said as he looked back at the building. Now he's in an even better mood. He's tall and good-looking. A few moments ago he started flirting with one of our flight attendants. I think it's safe to say that he's on the mend.

'I want to go to the toilet. I can do that on my own, right?'

'Well I'm certainly not offering to hold anything for you, mate. Just take it slow, okay?'

It's good to see him really grinning as he uncoils out
of the seat and edges his way up the aisle. I'm offered
more coffee and get a fabulously wide smile from the
flight attendant Toby had been hitting on. I might not be
eighteen any more but maybe I'm still in with a chance. As I
daydream I start to relax. I should have known better.

'What's up, mate?'

Toby has lumbered his way back to our row and is about
to lower himself into his seat. But it's clear that something
is wrong.

'Toby? What's going on?'

The happy mood has gone. He's looking right at me, the
way he did that first moment in the hospital. But this time
instead of relief in his eyes, there's fear. He can't seem to
speak.

'Toby, focus on me. Let's get you sitting down. Tell me
what's up.'

My seat belt is off. I'm out of my chair fast, guiding
him to his and giving the cabin a quick scan. None of the
cabin crew are anywhere to be seen – and I've got a terrible
feeling I'm going to need them.

'I just can't … just can't … breathe.'

The words seem to take everything he has. His face
is pale, his forehead is wet and his eyes are scared. He's
suddenly aware that this could be it. I give him a smile.
When the shit hits the fan at 35,000 feet you always smile.
You have to make it look easy.

'Mate, we're going to sort this. Is there any pain?'

He shakes his head. His eyes close. His mouth opens
wide as he gasps for air. Out of the corner of my eye I'm
aware that people in the cabin have noticed what's going
on. People are leaning around the seats to see what is

happening. Just when I'm going to need every tiny inch of available space it's fast being taken from me. A clock has begun to tick in my brain. It's Toby's lung. It has to be. And if I'm right it could kill him.

'I need to get you on the floor.' We're a row from the emergency exits and I twist him around and half drag him towards those few precious square feet of space. A woman sitting in that row gives out a little scream. Then another. The aisles fill up with people. Where the hell are the cabin crew? This is not something that needs an audience.

'I need to see your chest.' I try to rip off Toby's T-shirt. It's cotton, but it doesn't come off easy.

'Shit. Shit. Shit.' Never, ever swear in front of a conscious patient. That's the first rule of my professional life. But today, at cruising altitude half way over Slovenia I can't keep the words inside.

Toby's chest drain has fallen out. The wound between his ribs is gaping, gasping open. It's like a tiny, angry sea anemone. It's spluttering and sucking air into the space between his lungs and his rib cage. That's a place where air really should not go – if it does then his lungs will collapse, his heart will shift to one side and he could go into cardiac arrest within minutes. The clock in my brain is ticking so loud it hurts.

'Buddy, you're not going to like this,' I say, sticking my right index finger into the hole in his chest where the tube had been. I hear another wail from a passenger inches from my face. I keep my finger there.

'Close your eyes mate. It's easier if you close your eyes. Just lie still. I won't lose you.' Then, at last, I look up. 'I need the bag from that locker back there. It's an orange medical bag. I need it right now.'

I'm calling it out to the cabin in general in the hope that someone will take the initiative. Everyone is frozen in shock. I'm about to ask again when the stewardess with the smile arrives. She has fought her way down the aisle, pushing people back into their seats. She's in control and she's going to help me save this eighteen-year-old boy's life.

'I've got it. What do you need?'

'Two things. At the bottom there's a chest drain kit. It's thin, about a foot and a half long, and it's in a white paper packet. It should be labelled "Chest Drain", but it might say something like "Trocar and Cannula". And can you throw me those gloves.' She does.

'Can someone put this glove on my hand?'

An elderly man, who appears to be crying, reaches out. He rips open the packet and pulls the latex over my left hand. He got the correct glove, first time, but still it's a struggle to pull it on, it always is. The man says he's sorry for being so slow. But he's a star.

'Is there a spray bottle of pink liquid there?' I'm shouting at my smiling stewardess again. 'Looks like a perfume bottle, it's in a pocket at the top.' She finds it and passes it over. It's the antiseptic I should have used to sterilise the wound at the start. Better late than never. The clock is ticking fast.

'Is this it?'

She's found the drain kit. It looks like a long metal knitting needle inside a clear plastic tube. My job is to push it into Toby's chest and force it through to the space that's forming inside him. Then I have to reattach the vacuum bottle that's lying, useless, at the end of the old drain. As I grab the tube I remember what my lecturer at med school said about the process: 'Inserting a chest drain is a particularly unpleasant procedure for both the operator and the patient,' he had told us in a rich, booming voice. He certainly hadn't lied about that. I don't think he'd ever thought of doing it in front of plane full of terrified passengers. Or a teenager who had just opened his eyes again.

'Toby, be cool, trust me, keep your eyes closed.' As he does, tears squeeze out of them and run towards the cabin floor. I'm breathing deeply. This is when it gets serious. I calculate we've got less than three minutes. I spray the pink sterilising liquid on to the wound.

'This is going to sting, mate, but after that you won't feel a thing,' I tell him.

It doesn't actually hurt to have a doctor poking around inside of you. It's the incision that's the problem. But Toby has his incision already there. My index finger is plugged over it.

'Okay. Take a deep breath in and hold it,' I say. I pull out my finger. There's another wail from the lady in seat 8B. I try to squeeze the wound closed and position the end of the tube in its mouth. I need to aim right over the top of the nearest rib. Go too close to the one above and I'll hit an artery. Every millimetre counts right now. This would not be a good moment for turbulence.

'What is he doing? What is he doing with that thing? Stop him.' Someone, somewhere is shouting out.

'Madam, this is a doctor. Sit down. Sit down now.' My stewardess is a lioness.

But I can see the lady's point. What I'm doing is like a magician at a circus, pushing a collapsible sword into someone else's chest. Except this sword doesn't collapse; it's very, very real. Bit by bit I push it in. I have to get it into the boy's chest.

'Yes.' I'm there. I grip the plastic in one hand, pull out the metal needle with the other, leaving the see-though tube in place. I reconnect the end of the tube to the vacuum bottle from the first drain. The seals look firm and I'm staring at the water. I need there to be bubbles. I need to see that Toby's breathing is getting back on track.

'Breathe, mate, just breathe. Slowly. Normally. Do it for me, mate.' The bubbles are there. But the job's not over. Toby's old drain had been taped to his chest in the hospital. That's normal procedure and in hospital it works fine. If it comes apart you've always got a new one to hand as a replacement. On an airplane I've only got one spare. Now that has been used I can't risk it coming loose again. I need to stitch this new tube to his body. It's going to hurt.

'Toby, mate, you're doing fine and we're making it. We've got this fixed and you're breathing okay, right?' There's a tiny, imperceptible nod of his head. His eyes are tightly closed. He wants to be anywhere but here.

'I need to stitch you up to make sure the drain stays in, okay? It's the easiest part of what we've just done, it's the last part and then it's over. It is going to hurt, though. Do you understand me? Are you okay with that?'

Another barely perceptible nod. Time to go.

'Can you see a stitching pack in there?' I ask the stewardess. 'It's flat, tin foil with a blue cover, about the size of a credit card.'

While she's looking I feel a hand on my shoulder. 'Doctor, do you want the other glove?' It's the dear old gentleman from across the aisle. 'You've been quite wonderful,' he says.

Now it's my turn to feel chocked up. The kindness of strangers makes this job worth doing.

Gloved up, I rip open the foil pack. The curved, semi-circular needle is pre-threaded with silk so I just have to click it into the long, metal stitch-holder – sharp as it is, without that extra leverage I'd never get the needle through Toby's skin. I begin to work – needle and silk through flesh, wind it tightly round the tube, then pass it back through the flesh. Tie it up and start again. Flesh, tube, flesh. More knots, then one more time to make absolutely certain it will stay put. Toby is breathing loudly now. His face is pinched tight, his teeth biting into his lips so he doesn't cry out. He is silent; it's over. I sit back up on my knees. I hadn't realised how hot it was. I'm sweating. But the job's done and we didn't spill a single drop of blood on to the plane's carpet.

'Toby, we're done now. You're fixed like new,' I say. 'Can he lie here a moment?' I ask the stewardess. I turn to face her and see she's crying.

'It's the air conditioning. Sets me off every time,' she says, wiping tears across her face and trying, without success, to bring back her big smile. 'I'll get him pillows and a blanket. And please. No more dramas till we land okay?'

The next day I'm back at my office in Hounslow to complete the standard reports I do for all our jobs. Because of the in-flight action yesterday, I've got some extra paperwork to do for the airline. It's dull, but I'm smiling because Camilla has just printed out an email from Whipps Cross Hospital. When our flight landed at Gatwick I'd seen Toby into the ambulance at the arrivals level and handed him over. The email confirms he arrived safe and well. 'He's going to be absolutely fine,' the surgical registrar has written. 'He's not the most erudite of patients, but trust me, he made it very clear that he appreciates what you've done for him. He also wants to say that he is – and I quote – "Never going on another fucking holiday again as long as I fucking, fucking live". So I think you can take it that he hasn't lost his spirit.'

This is one email I'll keep.

'So is Jackie on her way to the Maldives?'

It's late afternoon and Camilla and I are doing a tea round while the phones are quiet.

'She picked up her med bag this morning and she's on a night flight tonight.'

'Is she in a nice hotel?'

Camilla frowns. 'I've got a horrible feeling that she's not. The patient and his wife were evacuated from their island to the capital. None of the hotels near the hospital sounded very exciting, but I didn't have any choice. You've missed out on the air miles, Ben, but you're not missing out on anything special on this trip.'

We head back into the main office with a tray of teas. Camilla has promised to allocate me the next decent job that comes in. But I can hardly complain about my existing schedule. After all, I'm going to St Tropez tomorrow.

'Good morning Ben, how are you today?'

I love it when someone on the desk at one of the airport executive lounges remembers my name. A tiny part of me accepts that if I was a true VIP – or an even more prized Commercially Important Person – then they would call me Dr MacFarlane and be a little more formal. To be fair I'm never really dressed like a city slicker. Our medical bags

don't have much room for a change of clothes so I need to
wear something that will work if there's heavy lifting to be
done at the hospital. That normally means slightly scruffy
black cargo trousers and a dark blue polo shirt that won't
show too much blood or vomit. Anyway, being called by
my first name at this lounge is a step up from the lady
who checks me in to the suite at Gatwick. She always calls
me 'sweet pea'. I don't imagine that's a greeting Roman
Abramovich hears very often.

'I'm fine, Hillary,' I reply. 'How are you?'

'Well, I'm very upset. I'm devastated,' my receptionist
friend replies with a flourish, clearly bored and wanting to
talk.

'Bad day?'

'Yes it is. We were told that Enrique Iglesias was coming
through. I got up an hour earlier than normal just to do
my hair and make-up properly. It turned out it was only a
rumour. So I wasted all that time and effort for nothing. Like
I say, I'm absolutely devastated.'

We chat for a bit longer while I try to decide whether or
not I've just been insulted. Enrique Iglesias indeed.

'Now you be good,' Hillary says once I've had my free
coffee and shortbread and finally head out for my flight.
I bet Roman Abramovich doesn't get told that very often,
either.

As soon as I board the flight I know I'm going to let
Hillary down by misbehaving. The first person I see is a
stewardess I got chatting to on another flight recently. Her
name's Samantha and I really like her. I'm in a business-
class seat at the front and she's got to stand right next to me
to do the safety briefing. It's really childish but I want to see
if I can put her off her stride. I start off by pretending I'm

extremely grateful that she's explained the sheer complexity of how a seat belt works. Then we get to the speech.

'In the unlikely event of an emergency landing ...' she begins.

'Your cabin crew will be exiting first from here, here and here,' I mouth at her.

'Your life-vest is equipped with a light,' she continues.

'To help attract sharks,' I add. She still keeps a straight face. I give it one last try when we get to the bit about the oxygen masks.

'If you are travelling with a small child then please affix your mask before helping with theirs,' she says.

'And if you are travelling with more than one child then pick your favourite,' I say, perhaps just a little too loudly.

Samantha comes up to me just before take off.

'You don't deserve this,' she says, handing me a sneaky orange juice and giving me one of her fabulous smiles.

After we've landed in Nice, Samantha gave me a jokey telling off and a slap on the wrist at the plane door.

'You forgot your duty frees, by the way,' she adds. That's my favourite bit of airline code. She passes me a plastic bag with a mini bottle of champagne in it. I certainly hope I see her again soon.

The hospital in St Tropez is an hour and a half away by taxi. I pass the time by going through the file. My man was on day four of a two-week coach trip from Hove to Venice and back. He had a massive coughing fit when they got to Nice and he thinks he blacked out for a few seconds when they got out of the coach in St Tropez. After a bad night in the hotel he collapsed again trying to climb back onto the

coach. He hit his head on the kerb, needed a set of stitches
in his forehead and was diagnosed with pneumonia in the
hospital.

Looking at his medical history the only surprise is that
he reckoned he was well enough to travel in the first place.
He's seventy-four, a lifelong chain smoker with chronic lung
disease and a history of angina. He told his GP he drinks
forty units of alcohol a week, which means the real figure will
probably be eighty. I also learn that he's a widower and that
as the coach couldn't wait for him, he's been on his own in
France for four days. When I get to the hospital I'm expecting
to see a scared, fragile, shadow of a man. I'm wrong.

'If you're here to take me back to Britain then don't
bother,' are his first words when I introduce myself. There's a
twinkle in his eye but I'm unsure how to take this.

'Have you seen the food they're giving me? Cordon
bloody bleu. Better than anything I got on the holiday. I
don't think this is a hospital at all. It's more like the Ritz.
I didn't even get my own room on the coach tour. This is
bloody paradise!'

The French attending physician, who speaks great English,
is smiling broadly. 'Mr Jamieson is a very satisfied customer.
He's been very popular with our nursing staff.'

The patient calls me closer. 'It's like *Carry on Nurse* in
here. Sexiest women I've ever seen. They're even better than
the grub. I don't want to go to sleep at night in case I miss
one of them. Young man like you, you should get yourself a
job here. Like I say, it's paradise. Losing my footing like that
was the best thing that ever happened to me.'

'Well, I think we do have to work out how to get you
home all the same,' I say.

'Can't I just have another week? There's someone very

special I'm hoping will give me a bed-bath quite soon. I'm planning on giving her quite a surprise when she gets down south, if you know what I mean.' He gives me a large wink and I know I shouldn't, but I laugh.

'I'll speak to the doctor and look at your charts. But you really don't seem to be ailing, Mr Jamieson. Do you mind if I take a quick look at you?'

He makes a big fuss about it. There's lots more chat about how much he wants to stay. But there's something in his eyes as well. He's an old man in a foreign country. Bravado only lasts so long. However much he goes on about 'bloody gruel and battleaxes' in NHS hospitals at home, that's where he needs to be.

'I'm afraid to say I think you are ready to travel,' I tell him. 'Let me just check a few more details.' He's been on steroids and some powerful intravenous antibiotics and I spend a while going through his temperature charts. I want to be sure the fever has gone and we're on top of his infection. Breathing other people's air for too long on a plane won't be a great idea if he's still vulnerable. Especially as we're probably going to have enough problems with the low in-flight air pressure as it is.

'Here are his chest X-rays,' the lead doctor says as we have a little conference outside the room. Mr Jamieson's lung problems mean the X-rays aren't great, but they're good enough. He's had some useful chest physio, his oxygen levels are back up where they need to be for a flight and the antibiotics have clearly kicked in. It's time for my verdict so I head back bedside.

'Mr Jamieson, I'm going to call my travel people and check the flight times but I think we're going to be getting you out of here this afternoon as planned.'

'What about my bed-bath?' he wails.

'I'll find an old-fashioned matron to give you one back in Britain,' I say.

It's pandemonium when I leave the room. Why on earth did I use the words 'give you one'? He's laughing so much he might actually bring on another attack.

The fun continues at Nice airport. My patient flirts outrageously with the woman who checks us in. He won't actually let me wheel him off across the concourse until she has got up from her seat and let him kiss her hand. I think we're going to get arrested at security when he tries to get a petite brunette to pat him down, rather than the large, humourless male officer he was originally allocated. On the plane I swear he swaps phone numbers with one of the flight attendants while I go to the loo.

'The number's yours, for a tenner,' he tells me, with another big, theatrical wink and a tap of his big, red, cauliflower nose on my return.

'Mr Jamieson, you're a very sick man, and I mean that in every possible sense of the word,' I tell him. 'Now let me listen to that chest of yours.'

I put a stethoscope to his chest but I'm really only doing it to shut him up for a few moments. The engine noise in flight means I can't hear a thing. On a plane all a stethoscope does is identify you as a doctor in an emergency. A bit like in a hospital, to be honest. Today the state of Mr Jamieson's chest is the least of my worries. What matters more is the amount of oxygen he's got in his system. If the levels get too low he could go into respiratory failure, which would not be fun on a crowded plane at 35,000 feet.

'This little thing is going to measure the oxygen in your

blood, Mr Jamieson. So no picking your nose with this finger, okay?' I had told him when I first attached the pulse oximeter to the index finger of his right hand. It is set so that an alarm will go off if his figures go below a safe level. That will be my cue to get the plane's oxygen cylinder and try and bring them back up again.

'Fuss, fuss fuss' is all Mr Jamieson says to me every time I check the readings on the machine. He says it again when I need to top up his drugs. I slip a mask over his face and switch on the nebuliser, the box of tricks that gives him the medication in a mist.

'Are you sure that does any good?' he asks when his ten minutes of heavy breathing are up. 'I'm sure a gin would do just as well.'

Fortunately, everything stays stable all the way across France and over the Channel.

'Stop fussing. You want to relax and have a bit more fun,' he says as we make our final approach to Gatwick. He seems entirely unconcerned that the suggestion he just made when our flight attendant checked his seatbelt could have cost him dearly a sexual harassment law suit. 'I have to take my good times with the ladies when I can,' he had explained, amidst a horrendous burst of coughing. 'In a few more years I might be getting too old.'

It's a smooth touchdown, we wait in our seats till everyone else has left the plane. I lead Mr Jamieson out towards the air bridge. Then everything changes. It turns out that another passenger acquired a mysterious injury during the flight, and had demanded to use the wheelchair that was set aside for us at the gate. (Funny how often that happens when people work out how far it is to baggage reclaim.) The ground crew have been sent off to get a replacement, but my patient doesn't like to be kept waiting. It also turns out that he is a man with a mission.

'We need to stop at Duty Free after we get my bag,' he informs me.

'But we're in Arrivals.'

'There's a Duty Free in Arrivals. I don't always travel on a coach, you know.'

'Well, what do you need to get? We're going to struggle to get your luggage into the ambulance as it is.'

He twists around in his chair to glare at me. 'Are you trying to tell me what I can and can't buy?'

I look down at him, feeling strangely disappointed. It's pretty obvious what he's got in mind. 'You are still pretty unwell, Mr Jamieson. We're taking you to hospital from here so you won't be able to drink or smoke for quite some time. Why don't you take this opportunity to...' I don't get to finish my sentence.

'Why don't you take this opportunity to bloody well shut up? Don't you dare patronise me and if you don't take me to Duty Free I'll have you struck off the medical register.' By this stage I'd stopped the chair and walked in front to talk to him. How had such a sweet old face turned so ugly? 'You're probably not even a proper doctor at all,' he says finally. 'If you were you'd be in a hospital, not working in an airport like this.'

I give up and start pushing the chair again. I wheel him silently into the last-chance Duty Free shop just before the Arrivals concourse. Then I watch him. A seriously ill seventy-four-year-old man with lung disease, asthma, pneumonia – and God knows what else – buying 800 Benson & Hedges and two enormous bottles of gin. He wants some vodka as well, but he will need my help carrying it.

'Don't even think about it,' I say, as he looks in my direction. I'm busy buying Camilla a giant Toblerone and there's no way I'm risking my job by being caught buying booze for a sick patient.

'Fair play,' is all he says when he puts the vodka down and picks up the rest of his purchases. Once the job is done his former charm returns.

'Are you sure you don't want that dolly bird's number? She has two lay-overs in London every month, she told me. The number's yours for a fiver.'

'It was a tenner on the plane.'

'Well, I've decided I like you again.'

The last I see of Mr Jamieson, as the ambulance crew take over outside the airport, is him asking the young, female paramedic a question. He's clearly whispering, because she has to lean in very close to hear him. It looks like another potential law suit in the making.

Being able to wave off a patient in an ambulance is a real treat. Most of the time we have to do full 'bed-to-bed' repatriations where we travel with patients to their UK hospital. This can mean an extra internal flight, as well as a long, squashed ride in the ambulance. Plus, of course, the journey home after a very long time on the road. I get paid a lump sum for every four-hour block of time I work. If I miss the last flight home from a distant hospital I get put in a hotel and clock up a nice extra payment, but most of the time all I want is to get home. Keeping a social life going is hard enough in this job without too many extra nights on the road.

Today, I have to head back to Hounslow to get rid of my medical bag and write up my report. I certainly won't miss the bag. It's heavy and bright orange with big white,

reflective crosses on both sides. As usual I feel like I've got
a giant arrow over my head saying: 'Prescription drugs!
Syringes! Funky kit you can sell on eBay or use in some
bizarre sex game! Roll on up and grab it while the doctor's
not looking.' It's one of the many reasons I reckon we should
get danger money as well as an unsocial hours allowance.

The office is really quiet. It's a big open plan room
divided up into six different areas. Four lone figures are
manning the phones but the main logistics, travel and
accounting desks are empty till tomorrow. I like being here
at night; there's a greater sense of camaraderie. I did a lot of
overnight desk shifts when I first started doing repatriations
and the friends I made then have really stuck. One of them
is Camilla. She has two grown-up kids and she works more
shifts than anyone else in the office. Very early on she told
me that she'll always try to book better hotels for doctors
who buy her chocolate.

'That's extortion,' I told her at the time. One year on I
think I probably spend more money on Toblerone than
anyone else in the world. I put the latest bar on her desk
with the usual Post-it note saying it's from a mystery
admirer. Then I head to the desk I use when I'm on an office
shift. I check my emails, do a bit of internet banking then
start on my report.

When it's done I look over to where Jackie normally sits. It's
just before ten and I work out she probably landed in paradise
about an hour ago. I don't believe Camilla's story about a grim
hotel for a moment. I reckon Jackie will have checked on her
patient and is lying on some beach with a cocktail in her hand
by now. She's one of those people who makes a complicated
life look easy. She juggles three kids aged between ten and
fifteen, an ex-husband who lives on the same street, a full-

time job running our company and at least one long and one short-haul repatriation a month, just to keep her hand in. Plus, if there's an office birthday party, or special occasion to be celebrated, Jackie will be the first to buy drinks and the last to leave. Her enthusiasm for life is infectious and she makes everything seem possible. Actually forget the lazing in a hammock with a drink. She's probably fitting in a bit of scuba before heading up in a sea plane. Possibly as the pilot.

I get a call at home just before eight the following morning. It's Robbie, a nurse who does the occasional repatriation but is now one of our senior medical co-ordinators. He's going out with an air steward on Emirates and he's normally one of the funniest guys I know. Today he sounds abrupt and worried.

'Ben, it's about Jackie in the Maldives.'

'What's the problem? Did she forget her factor 50 or something?'

Robbie's uncharacteristic silence suggests this is no joking matter.

'It's all a bit strange, actually,' he finally says. 'She says there's something unusual about the patient, but she won't say what it is.'

'Well, what does the file say?'

'Nothing that sets off any alarm bells. The patient's at the Indira Gandhi Memorial Hospital and we've never had any problems there before. It's a good place. They're not the type to lie and say everything's okay just to get rid of someone.'

'So do you want me to come in and look at the files?'

There's another pause before he continues, 'It's more than

that. Jackie wants you to go out there and help get the man home.'

It's my turn to stay silent. We do two-person repats all the time, but almost always with a doctor and a nurse. The idea that the company's medical director would want the expense of having another qualified doctor with her for up to seventy-two expensive hours is very odd indeed.

'She wants me to do it? Why doesn't she want a nurse?'

'That's what we asked her.'

'And?'

'And, it was a bad line, apparently, but Matt says he thought she might have been crying. She asked for you, specifically. In the end she made some joke about you being so jealous of her trip and it only being fair. She said she wanted to teach you scuba diving. Matt says it wasn't very convincing.'

'So what do we do?'

'Get over here at lunchtime. We've got a med bag packed and Camilla has you booked through Doha on an afternoon flight to Malé. Ben, have you turned your mobile on yet? Jackie did say she was texting you.'

Her first message came through while I was in the shower.

'Ben, sorry to be a drama queen. Something's happened.'

A second one flashed up as I tried to think of a reply.

'Ben, this has to stay a secret. When you get here I'm going to need your help.'

JULY

Jackie had interviewed me for the job when I first started doing full-time repats. I liked her spirit right from the start. She was serious about patient care. She drilled me on my experience and on what I would do in different emergency situations. She didn't sugar-coat the long hours or underplay how exhausting the job could be. But she also made sure I knew just how important and worthwhile it was. She talked about the perks, explaining how grateful most of our patients are when they see us. She said you get a much better buzz travelling with them rather than just chasing targets on a hospital production line. Then she listed some of the places she'd been lately – and what she had done there. Concerts in Las Vegas, museum openings in St Petersburg, tennis tournaments in Dubai – she had done jobs that had got her to all of them. She also had premier or gold status in almost every frequent flier programme you could name.

'So, do you like the sound of it?' she had asked with a big smile towards the end of the interview. 'You had me at air miles,' I joked, months later, once we'd become friends.

So what the hell has happened to her now? I read her texts again on my way to the office and try to guess. Something must have happened to her patient. There must have been an accident, some crisis that a dodgy lawyer could blame on Jackie. A false negligence claim is every doctor's worst nightmare. I know exactly how Jackie must be feeling.

I'd panicked on one of my first transatlantic jobs. It had all started just before takeoff. I was in premium economy and it was clear we had a problem on the other side of the aisle. A well-dressed, middle-aged guy on his own was looking pretty rough. I watched him sweating, gripping the armrest of his seat, twisting around and looking up and down the plane, putting his seat belt on, taking it off, putting it back on again. No surprises for guessing he was making everyone around him nervous as hell. It turned out that this was just the beginning.

The seat belt signs were still on when he jumped out of his seat. 'I can't do it. I can't stay here. You've got to take the plane down,' he yelled.

Two of the cabin crew were right in front of him in the jump seats. 'Sir, you need to get back to your seat,' the steward said. He and his colleague tried to guide the man back down the aisle. They couldn't restrain him.

'I need to talk to the captain,' he shouted. He was pushing down towards the front of the plane. Like everyone else I was desperately trying to work him out. Terrified or terrorist? What could we do? As the stewards tried to push him back towards his seat I got ready to act. I had some major sedatives in my bag. I got it down from the overhead locker as another set of cabin crew tried to reason with the man at the front of the plane. Somehow they got him back to his seat. Then he started to moan.

'I said I should never fly again. I can't breathe,' he said, gasping for air.

I called one of the crew over. Her badge said she was the purser. 'I'm a doctor. I might be able to help,' I said.

'Thank you. We might need it,' she said. Even as she spoke the man lunged up and out of his seat again.

'We have to land the plane. I can't do this,' he shouted. This time he looked as if he was heading to the emergency exit aisle. Everyone's eyes were on the emergency door and two passengers got up to try and stop him reaching it. My fingers were racing as I got a syringe and drew up some Haloperidol. I needed his permission to inject him; it was time to get it. The purser let me past her.

'Sir, you're all right. I'm a doctor, you'll have to clam down,' I tried to shout over the madness. 'I'm a doctor and I can help you.'

I didn't get to say another word. The man was shoved back towards me just as a push from the crowd thrust me forwards. I injected him, right then and there, through his trousers and into his backside. He went down like a rhino. In a split second he was on his side, lying out cold in the aisle.

For the group of terrified fellow passengers the drama was over. But not for me. The crew squeezed the man into his seat, buckled him up and left him there. For the next five hours there was nothing but the occasional snort and little snore from him. Sometimes a few dribbles ran down his chin. Meanwhile rivers of sweat ran down my face. 'What the hell have I just done?' I was thinking, 'How the hell did that happen? Injecting someone without permission is assault, isn't it?' Worse still I'd done it to what sounded like an American passenger on an American airline. The legal liability would be enormous. And what if he had a reaction to the drug? What if he died? All around me people were watching films, eating, reading, sleeping. I was practising my defence in court. Could I say that I thought he had given me the permission I needed? Would I get off if I said I did it to protect the lives of everyone else on board?

We were flying to Boston and the passenger woke up just before we made our final descent. He stretched, looked around him and drank the glass of water that had been left on his tray table. If he noticed that everyone was looking at him then strangely he didn't say a word.

'How are you, Sir? Did you have a good flight?' The purser stopped for a word as she collected his empty glass. I was desperate to hear his reply but I missed it. When we landed I walked over to her as everyone else edged towards the exits.

'He said he normally gets extreme panic attacks in the air, but that this was the best flight he's ever had,' the purser told me, her voice not giving anything away.

Finding the courage I asked her the question I had been dreading, 'Did he remember anything happening to him before he collapsed?'

'As far as I'm concerned there's nothing to remember,' she said pointedly, while reaching out to shake my hand. 'I hope to see you back on board again soon, Sir.'

I won't ever forget that simple act of support. If I'd been up on an assault charge I would have wanted that lady in my corner. If something similar had happened to Jackie in the Maldives, then I'll be there for her. I look at my watch as I arrive at the office. In just over twenty hours I'll find out what's going on.

The Maldives are paradise, but it's fair to say that the country's capital, Malé, is not. I arrive in the early morning and by the time I've got through immigration and into the main part of the town it's clear that I'm in a land that the tourist brochures forgot.

I knock on the door to Jackie's hotel room. Camilla was right. It's a charm-free business-class hotel that's hemmed in on all sides by other buildings. I'm glad I'm only here for one night.

'Ben, it's good to see you.'

Jackie opens the door and we have a slightly awkward hug in the doorway. She looks pale and tired and her voice is muffled. I have never seen her like this before. Jackie's energy is legendary. Nothing slows her down. This must be much worse than I'd feared.

'Are you okay? Everyone's really worried about you back home.'

She looks down at the floor. 'That's what I was afraid of. Unfortunately I couldn't think of any other way to do this.'

There are a couple of chairs over by the window so we both sit down and I wait for Jackie to say something. She doesn't. I speak because I can't bear the silence. 'Is the patient okay? Is there a problem with him?'

'He's not okay but he's no worse than we were told. He has a straightforward PE.' That's a pulmonary embolus, the Deep Vein Thrombosis nightmare where blood clots in the leg break off and travel to the lungs. It can kill. 'I examined him, read his files, checked his meds and he has been well looked after.'

'So he's well enough to travel home?'

'He is,' Jackie says softly. 'The problem is that I'm not.'

She had begun to feel hideously unwell on the final leg of the flight out to the islands. She was nauseated and almost fainted in the hospital corridor after she had assessed the patient. Then she got back to the hotel and collapsed halfway between the bedroom and the bathroom.

'I came round and I'd wet myself. I was fuzzy for about an hour. I'd bit my tongue several times as well. There was dry blood on my face. If it wasn't for the power of make-up, you'd see I've got a black eye as well.'

'So what do you think it was?'

'I've taken sodium valproate,' she says flatly.

There is my answer. Epilepsy. I look into Jackie's tired face. Her black eye is a lot more obvious than she thinks. 'Did you have any idea you had it? Have you had an attack before?'

She shakes her head. A couple of times she looks as if she's about to say something else, but stops. Then she eases herself out of her chair, takes two steps towards the TV, then turns and sits down again.

'Ben, I've got this totally under control. Epilepsy is not that big a deal. I had the drugs in my bag and I know what I'm doing. I can get this sorted properly when I get home. It could just have been caused by tiredness, stress, a combination of all the usual things. I just need a bit of time off when I get home. Chances are it was a one-off and I'll not have another attack if I live to be a hundred.'

We sit in silence for a few more minutes. She urges me to order breakfast off the room-service menu but I'm not feeling hungry. The she stands up.

'This is the serious bit, Ben. I don't want anyone back at the office to find out about this. I knew I couldn't do this repat on my own. Maybe I won't ever be able to do any repats on my own again. I asked for you to come out because I thought I could trust you to keep it secret.'

'You can trust me.'

'Thank you. But there's a problem, isn't there? You've already told me that everyone's asking questions about this back in the office. They'll want to know why I asked for a doctor rather than a nurse.'

'We'll just say that the patient needed it. He's with his wife. We can say she had a collapse, hit her head and needed attention as well. It's a twelve-hour flight with a plane change. It's not totally unheard of to use two doctors for two seriously ill patients. You're the boss, anyway. You can approve it so there's no one else to answer to.'

'No one else apart from all the usual gossips in the office. They'll want a drama. They'll still want to know why I asked for you rather than any of the others.' Jackie's sitting totally still, staring out the window towards the office building opposite us with what looks like tears in her eyes.

'I'll tell them we're having a hot and sleazy affair.' I finally get a ghost of smile from her.

Jackie was right about our patient. He's ready to travel but he's certainly not well. He is a retired garage owner called Johnny Duncan. He's seventy-one years old and as well as the problems he's had in the islands, his records show he has prostate problems, chronic high blood pressure and a previous stroke. He was on holiday with his wife, Helen, and their travel insurance is paying for her to stay in a hotel nearby while he's in hospital. The insurance company have also bought her a new plane ticket so she can fly home with him whenever we approve the repatriation.

'I'm Doctor Ben MacFarlane and I'm going to be joining you all on the flight home,' I tell the pair when I meet them at the hospital before dawn the following morning. Then

I tell my white lie. I hadn't wanted them to think that Mr
Duncan was so ill that he needed extra help, and I certainly
hadn't wanted them to think there were any worries about
Jackie. This is my cover story. 'I've been at a conference on
decompression in scuba divers. You, sir, are in a lot better
shape than most of them. But Doctor Jackie Temple is my
boss back in London and I'm going to share the load with
her on this flight. I hope you don't mind.'

The patient's wife takes my hand. She's a slight, frail-
looking woman who walks with a stick. She looks on the
edge of a collapse herself.

'Thank you for giving up your time. I know now that we
should never have travelled so far. This is a young person's
holiday. We're very sorry for troubling everyone.' It's lovely
to be thanked just for doing our jobs. I say a few words to
Mr Duncan then move aside so Jackie can carry out the
final pre-travel checks. It's just after 6am and we're booked
on to a 9:30am flight with a one-hour stop in Doha. After
that it's about a seven-hour flight back to London. Epilepsy
or not, it's crazy that Jackie was ready to do this job on her
own at all.

The airport staff can hardly do enough to help. They let
us through fast-track security and have reserved some seats
in a private lounge for the four of us. We board the plane
first. That's always good, though it does mean that several
hundred people walk past you gawping when general
boarding begins. Then we settle down for take-off. I'm on
one side of the aisle, Jackie's on the aisle seat of the central
block, our patient is next to her and his wife is next to him
alongside the opposite aisle. I look across and can see her
holding her husband's hand. As far as medicine goes, that
might be as useful as all his drugs put together.

Jackie is keeping all her fears inside. You really wouldn't know she's worried sick. She got up before 5am and is going to be on duty for the next twelve hours straight. At the moment she's chatting away to Mr Duncan's wife. It seems their eldest grandchild is the same age as her youngest son. Jackie says she can't work out why Joe prefers to talk to his friends online rather than walking a few doors down the street and seeing them in person. Mrs Duncan can't work out why her grandson is always tapping away at his mobile phone rather than talking on it. She laughs as Jackie explains her attempt to impose a 'no phone calls' ban on family mealtimes. I can see Mr Duncan smiling as Jackie describes how horrified her kids were at the prospect.

When the fasten seat belt signs are turned off the cabin service director comes by to check we are all okay. I had a quick chat with him just after we'd boarded and he was genuinely interested in Mr Duncan's condition. That always matters. You want as many people as possible primed to help in case things go wrong. With Mr Duncan the big risk is a second embolism if another bit of his clot breaks off. At its worst we might have to tube him to keep him breathing and hope the onboard emergency oxygen supply lasts until we divert the plane and get him in an ambulance. At the back of my mind is a worry about the stroke he had a few years ago. His medical record was a bit sparse, so we don't know that much about the stroke. If it bled into his brain then the blood thinning drug he's on could trigger another one. If that happens, we'll be in real trouble.

'How are you feeling, Mr Duncan?'

Another hour has gone by and Jackie is carrying out her latest set of checks. Every hour one of us checks Mr

Duncan's pulse, his blood oxygen levels and his general demeanour.

'Are you sure you don't want to listen to any music or watch any of the entertainment?' Jackie asks when the job is done. The guy has been a real trouper. He's not a big talker and he's clearly in discomfort, if not actual pain. He's also of the generation that doesn't like to make a fuss and hates being the centre of attention.

'I'm absolutely fine,' he says as a flight attendant comes round to top up our water glasses and ask if there's anything else we need. Jackie asks for another coffee. Her eyes are starting to look strained. I take a quick look at my watch. We've got another hour on this flight and then we need to change planes for the last leg of the journey. We're still an awfully long way from home.

We had a trouble-free transfer in Doha and are three hours into the final flight. We're on a newer plane with a modern business-class cabin. It's the kind that's great if you're a single businessperson or a loved-up couple. You get more privacy, more space and fewer people sitting nearby. Unfortunately this isn't as convenient for Mr and Mrs Duncan. On our first plane we had sat in a row of three. I had sat on my own while Mr Duncan had Jackie on one side and his wife on the other. It was very sweet to watch this kindly old couple hold hands throughout the flight. Now we're divided up into two sets of two and the three of us switch seats every hour. It's heartbreaking to see how upset Mr Duncan is when his wife's not next to him.

'Doctor, I'm so sorry, but I think my husband needs your help.' Mrs Duncan has touched my arm.

'What is it?' I'm instantly alert. Mrs Duncan has been
sitting next to her husband for half an hour. His eyes are
closed and he's turned away from me so he is facing the
other side of the cabin. But I can still see a frown that could
also be a sign of pain on his face. I'm out of my seat fast
but Mrs Duncan puts up her hand to stop me approaching
her husband. She stands up and glances to her left and then
her right before speaking. It's little more than a whisper. I
lean down to hear it.

'He won't want me to say this,' she says, cupping her hand
to my ear. 'He has difficulty going to the lavatory but I
think he ought to go.' She stands aside, looking mortified on
her husband's behalf.

'Do you mind, Mr Duncan?' He's opened his eyes
and looks as embarrassed as his wife. I lift up his shirt
and look at his stomach. Oh my god. His bladder is so
swollen that it is riding right up towards his nipples. I
put my hand on it. It's the size of a football. How could
I have thought that was just the outline from all his
blankets and pillows?

'When did you last pass water, Mr Duncan?'

'Some time ago,' he whispers. I think about how much he
has drunk on our flight so far. The curse of business class
is being offered so many glasses of water. We've probably
got through a litre each. Plus a lot of coffee. I had taken Mr
Duncan to the disabled toilet at Doha airport and guided
him to the plane loo just after we got on this flight. I hadn't
thought to ask if anything had come out. When I ask him
now he admits that nothing did.

'Back in the hospital were you passing water normally or
were you using a catheter?'

His eyes flash around the cabin. This is so clearly not

the kind of conversation he ever wanted to hold. Especially when he's in a public place.

'A catheter,' he says in the barest of whispers. 'They took it out this morning just before you arrived.' He closes his eyes for a moment. 'I can't seem to go any other way. And I'm afraid it does hurt quite a lot now, doctor,' he says.

That has to be the understatement of the year. It's like he's got a watermelon in his abdomen. The poor old guy must be in agony.

'Jackie, I think I need to catheterise Mr Duncan. I'll get my bag down.'

Unfortunately for him, Mr Duncan doesn't just have to put up with the procedure itself. There are rear-facing seats in this cabin which means some of his fellow passengers will be looking right at him when his humiliation begins. This might not be all that they do. I was looking after a man who fainted in the aisle of a flight recently when other passengers started taking photos on their mobile phones. Mr Duncan deserves better than that.

'Can we get some sort of a screen up?' I ask sharply.

Jackie waves down one of the crew members and has a whispered conversation with him. He picks up one of our patient's discarded blankets.

'I can hold this out,' he says, stretching it out with both arms. Then he looks down at our patient.

'No one will see anything, Sir. I won't let anyone walk by until this is over. You'll be feeling better in no time,' he says with a smile. Talk about taking things in your stride.

I push my med bag out into the aisle and unzip it. I get a plastic pouch of antiseptic, some cotton wool swabs and some anaesthetic gel as well as the catheterisation pack. I glove up and get ready. At least poor Mr Duncan has been through this before. It's when you put a catheter on someone for the first time that they really freak out. What, that thing? Is going up where? Are you absolutely kidding me?

'All right, Mr Duncan, you know how this works. What I suggest is that you just close your eyes and leave it to me. Let me know anytime if it hurts too much.'

His wife is at his side again and she's smiling bravely at him. He gives her a barely perceptible nod then closes his eyes tightly. I'm glad about that. Maybe it really is true that what you can't see won't hurt you.

Normally catheters slide in easily, but in a patient with prostate problems like poor Mr Duncan it's a lot more tricky. I twist and turn it as I slowly move it into position. I work it a little bit at a time but it's far from smooth.

'Nearly there, Mr Duncan,' I say. 'A little more then it's all over, just bear with me.' A few more twists and the balloon-end enters his distended bladder and the waters begin to flow – fast. I click a collection bag on straight away. But I don't want to trigger a bleed by emptying Mr Duncan's bladder too fast so I clamp the pipe after about a litre. It looks as if there's a lot more to come but I can see from his face that he is already starting to feel better.

After a short wait, I unclamp the pipe and the flow begins again. The most I've ever collected from a patient is seven litres. It was a challenge for the nurse I had at my side to try and switch over the catheter bags to stop any spillages. I'm certainly glad poor Mr Duncan isn't quite in that league – though he produces a good three or four litres before the worst is over.

I give him a few moments to relax and then examine him again. His stomach is shrinking back to its normal size. The pain must have passed; his embarrassment is over.

'Mr Duncan you are going to be absolutely fine. We're getting closer to home all the time. The flight will be over soon.'

Jackie, her arm around Mrs Duncan's shoulders, is looking strong again. Meanwhile our steward is still holding the blanket up.

'All done?' he asks brightly, before taking it down. Then he turns to Mrs Duncan.

'Am I right in thinking you would like a nice cup of tea madam? Give me five minutes and I'll be back with a fresh pot. If there's anything else you want, you just let me know.'

This job is a bed-to-bed deal, so I join the couple in the ambulance at Heathrow. We've got a two-hour road trip to Poole in Dorset and with two big suitcases and a couple of smaller bags it's quite a squeeze. Mrs Duncan tells the paramedic she wants to sit with her husband so the medic takes the passenger seat up front, and Mrs Duncan and I sit sideways at the back. I check that I've got an airline sick bag close at hand just in case she needs it. Mr Duncan's fresh catheter bag is in place, so hopefully he won't need a comfort stop. Thankfully no one questions why it's me accompanying the couple to the hospital rather than Jackie.

'Will you call me, or just text me to let me know when you're home?' I had asked her as we all said our subdued goodbyes in the chaos of the airport's pick-up area. She nodded. I could see the black eye showing through her make-up. She looked like she needed to sleep for a week.

'Come on Ben, spill the beans. What was going on out there? How's Jackie?'

Damn. I'd desperately hoped that none of the regulars would be around when I finally made it back to Hounslow with my med bag. Robbie pounces the moment I walk through the security doors.

'We had bit of a crisis on the second leg. The poor bloke had a bit of an embarrassing situation,' I say, glad that this is no word of a lie. 'His wife was in a bad way as well. It was never a job for one person. I'm fucking exhausted.' I run through the worst of our patient's problems and give a commentary on the events on the flight.

'Bloody hell, Ben, you sure can pick them. So Jackie's okay?'

'She's totally fine.'

'Why did she want you out there?'

'Because she knew she would need more help with the guy. Like I say, his poor wife was on the edge of having a breakdown as well. Jackie needed someone else to keep an eye on her.'

'Well, Matt definitely thought she sounded odd on the phone.'

I shrug. 'She seemed totally fine to me. All she cared about was getting the pair of them back to Britain safe and sound.'

'But why did she want you to come out rather than one of the nurses?'

'Robbie, stop the twenty questions, okay? Look, I love conspiracy theories as much as anyone, but I don't think anything's going on here.'

'So you're not sleeping with Jackie? Can I at least believe that one?'

I'm smiling broadly. 'You can believe whatever gets

you through the day, mate. But before you tell the world give me some gossip from here. Have I missed anything?'

It's Robbie's turn to shrug. We have a handful of full-time doctors and nurses on our team and a few dozen freelancers who come in and out on occasional jobs. Almost all of us have stories to tell on our return. Robbie runs through a few of the cases that have come in over the past few days. There was a brain-damage case after a jet ski accident in the Dominican Republic, and a woman who got a fractured skull after walking into a plate-glass window at a hotel in Switzerland.

Alan, one of our other freelance doctors has hit the jackpot, though. He was sent out to pick up a patient from an island hospital in the Philippines. The connecting flight from the island to Manila was cancelled – and there isn't another one for five days.

'The patient's completely stable so Alan's kicking back on the beach. Camilla had him booked into a full-service spa place and he's left a message saying he's having a new treatment every day. He's probably going to come back looking like Brad Pitt,' says Robbie. 'That's got to be the best job we've handed out lately. Other than that I'd say your trip with Jackie had the highest embarrassment factor for the patient. If you want something a bit calmer there's a really easy Rome pick up going out tomorrow that's not been allocated yet.'

'Is it a day job or an overnighter?'

'Probably an overnight but it depends on what flights we can get. It's a gap-year girl who managed to forget that Italians drive on the right. As well as on the pavement. She got hit on her way to the Trevi Fountain.'

'How bad is she?'

Robbie heads back to his desk to check the file on his screen. 'It's not that terrible, to be honest Nothing bad internally and no brain worries. She's not very mobile and she could probably get back with a nurse. But if you want the trip I could give it to you. I don't think there'll be much drama on it.'

I'm thinking about Jackie. I don't know if she's due in the office tomorrow or when I'll next get to see her. If she's got any sense she'll go to see her GP first thing and head back to bed for the rest of the day. But doctors aren't renowned for having much common sense with our own complaints. I wouldn't be surprised to see her in at eight as if nothing was wrong.

'I'll take it. Just as long as you don't put me on a dawn flight, okay? I need a good eight hours in bed tonight.'

'With our very own Jackie at your side?'

'Jackie's nearly old enough to be my mum – but don't you dare tell her I said that. Go gossip about someone else. And try and book me on BA. I've nearly got enough air miles for Hawaii.'

My gap-year girl is called Alicia Hughes. She's twenty-three and has just graduated in Fine Art from Leeds Metropolitan University. She was planning to see the world. Europe being her first, and last, stop at least for a while.

'I don't think I've ever felt so ridiculous in my whole life. And I used to wear a red jumpsuit and a head scarf to sell baked potatoes at Leeds railway station,' she says after we've done our introductions. She's good fun, though I have to agree that she looks a little bit odd.

She dislocated her shoulder, fractured her collarbone

and her upper arm and snapped a couple of ribs in the accident. She also twisted an ankle and crushed her left knee and broke both bones in her lower right leg – what we call classic 'tib and fib' injuries. The hospital put her in a foam collar and cuffs to hold one arm up to her neck. She has a huge foam wedge under her right elbow so it points out in front of her. One leg's in plaster protecting the surgery they did on it. She's practically mummified with bandages and she needs a lot of help just getting from her bed to her wheel chair. I'm guessing she used to have long, blond hair but a patch on the right hand side of her scalp was shaved where she needed a couple of stitches. The rest looks like it's been cut back just to try and match it. I'm not sure if the Italian nurses have dared give her a mirror. I wouldn't.

'Well, at least you haven't lost your sense of humour,' I venture.

'I feel like a robot or some kind of puppet. If I didn't laugh I think I'd cry.'

'You've got a lot of flowers.' I'm looking around her bedside. She's in a four-bed ward and her little corner is a riot of colour. One vase has half a dozen sunflowers in it, another has a bunch of pink tulips and a third contains a particularly expensive-looking mixed arrangement. She's got a wicker fruit basket and a whole stack of magazines and books. Someone is certainly looking after her.

'My friends aren't carrying on with the trip till I get out of here. They've been amazing. Apart from everything else I'm getting fat because they keep feeding me chocolate. They'll probably be back in a while. You'll meet them.' There's a bit of a silence while I read her charts. 'Am I really going to be allowed on to a plane like this?' she asks, a more serious note in her voice. 'Do you carry me out if we make an emergency landing or something?'

'Of course I do. We'll probably be sitting close to the front exit so we'll be some of the safest people on the plane anyway. You're going to be fine.' Her face tells me she can't quite get herself to believe me. I clip her folder back on to the end of her bed.

'Alicia, everything I've seen and heard from the doctors says you're in better shape than you look. There's nothing wrong with you internally and your brain scans are coming up clean as a whistle. All I'm really here for is to make the journey go a bit smoother. It's going to be my easiest job of the year, I promise you.'

I ask where we're going when we get back to Britain and I spot a blush under the bandages.

'Can you believe that I'm being taken back to my parents' house?' she says. 'I'm twenty-three years old, I'm a new graduate, I was off to see the world and I end up back living with my mum and dad. I've got a horrible feeling one of them will have to help me get to the toilet. It's mortifying. All because I didn't pay enough attention when I tried to cross a bloody road.'

I leave her for a few moments and go to speak to her doctor, a tall, competent Italian woman. She seems mildly surprised that Alicia's family haven't come to fetch her instead of relying on her insurance company. She talks me through the drugs Alicia was put on after her leg surgery and confirms she didn't have any head injuries. I look at her observation charts one more time and agree that she's fit to fly. I call the office and speak to Christine. She's switched us from BA to Alitalia for the trip home as there's more availability, meaning we'll probably have more room.

There's an early evening flight and Christine has arranged for an ambulance to take us to the airport in two hours' time.

I sit in the sunshine with a sandwich after telling Alicia the good news. By the time I go back to see her all her friends are there to say their goodbyes and take some final photographs. There's a lot of laughter as they hand out her flowers and fruit to the nurses and the elderly ladies in the other beds. Then it's time to tackle Rome's rush-hour traffic.

'If you see a dark blue Fiat with a big dent in the bonnet give me a yell because I've got unfinished business with the driver,' Alicia offers as we set off.

Robbie proves to have been right about the trip. It is incident free. Our seats aren't huge, but we're first on board and have plenty of time to settle. I'm desperate for a coffee and beg for one from the cabin crew. They always say it's impossible when you're an ordinary passenger. But most crews have a pot on for themselves when they're prepping the aircraft. If you're lucky, as a doctor you can get to share it.

'Molte grazie, grazie mille,' I say as a dark-haired, dark-eyed lady hands me a cup. That's pretty much all my Italian and I hope I got it right.

Poor Alicia endures a lot of stares and finger pointing when the rest of the passengers board. Italians seem to bring more hand luggage than any other nationality. I have a few hairy moments when I think Alicia's outstretched elbow is going to get whacked by a rucksack or – bizarrely – what look like a pair of bongo drums in one passenger's bag. Italian planes also seem to be the nosiest in the world. This one is like a giant social club. Everyone talks all the time. No one pays the slightest bit of attention to the safety demonstration or the repeated calls for mobile phones to be turned off. The crew make the announcement asking everyone to get back to their seats and fasten their seat belts. Hardly anyone bothers to move. Two men are still standing up talking to friends in the row behind them when we power down the runway.

Fortunately, we still manage to take off on time, which is a huge bonus in this job. The seat-hopping, super-loud and super-fast chatting and socialising begins again a split second after the seat belt sign goes out. Everyone is fascinated by Alicia's injuries and a couple of people even ask to have their photos taken alongside her. She takes it pretty well, all things considered. I'm feeling relaxed as well. The flight attendant who came over with the coffee pot at pre-boarding offers me refills throughout the flight, while studiously refusing to make eye contact with any other passenger. Every time I look at her, I smile.

It's less than two and a half hours to Heathrow where the porters are ready and waiting for us. These are the people who really surprised me when I first started out doing this job. For some reason most of the golf carts are driven by what seem to be the coolest guys in the airport. They're normally young Asian lads with big earrings, lots of bling and massively sculpted, gelled or shaved hair. The surprise is that they're all incredibly kind and endlessly patient. My old ladies always love them. Alicia's definitely impressed – though she got a look at her hair in the disabled toilet at Fiumicino airport in Rome and says she's never going to flirt again. Her mum, dad, little sister and a few others are all waiting at Arrivals when we ride in, orange lights flashing. If Alicia's bandages, sling and foam wedges had allowed it, there would have been a lot of happy hugging. As it is I'm clearly on a roll on the drop-off stakes. Alicia's going to her family home, not to hospital, and her parents have already checked that their car has room for her. I say goodbye outside WHSmith.

I call the office to see if they'll send a cab for my med bag so I can go straight home. If I've had to use the kit on a job I like to go back with it myself so I can do a proper inventory of the contents, but after a quiet trip I can usually just hand it over to one of our regular drivers. That's my plan today.

I text Jackie while I wait for the car to turn up. 'How are you feeling? I'm waiting for a pick-up at Heathrow. Call me if you can.'

AUGUST

Jackie hasn't called by the time I get home. I pull out a few of my old medical textbooks to brush up on my knowledge of epilepsy. I'd done a quick internet search in the lobby of my hotel in Rome and I take another look online in my flat. I could get a lot more information with a proper Medline search in the office, but I'm so determined to keep Jackie's secret that I don't want to take the risk of anyone seeing.

So is it good or bad news? I check my phone for messages one more time while I try to make up my mind. Most of the good news I read online is what Jackie and I had discussed in the Maldives. Epilepsy can come out of a clear blue sky. It doesn't always have any obvious cause. You can get one attack, once, and never have it again. To be honest, if you've only had one attack and no one was there to witness it, then you can't even say you're epileptic at all.

The more worrying news is the long list of variables that come into play if you get a second attack. You can be on drugs for the rest of your life, and getting the dose right can take months. Driving is a big problem, even if you're on treatment. You lose your licence because the risk of having an attack while behind the wheel is too high. Jackie does the school run by car almost every day. Worse will be the

changes at work. She'll be desk bound. She may well go
years without another problem, but she still won't be able to
risk taking sole charge of a patient. She'll be devastated.

My phone stays stubbornly quiet for the rest of the night.
I'm guessing that Jackie will already have read all this stuff,
and more, the moment she got back from the Maldives. I'm
due in the office at nine tomorrow to pick up my bag for
an early afternoon flight to the US. I click off my computer.
Somehow, I'll make sure I grab a couple of minutes with
Jackie before I fly.

'So you're still self-medicating? Jackie you have to know
that's crazy,' I whisper as I corner her walking into the
office. It's also pretty much illegal, but I'm saving that one
for later. We're huddled in a corridor just inside the building.
Jackie looks exhausted.

'You realise I've now become a world expert on epilepsy
so I know exactly what kind of risks your taking if you are.
I also know how little you've got to worry about if you get a
proper diagnosis and proper treatment.'

Jackie finally speaks. 'Ben, just relax, I'm totally in
control of this. There's no rush now I'm back home and I'm
going to get it sorted in my own time. All I need from you
is to make sure no one else finds out what's going on. You
haven't told anyone, have you?'

'Of course I haven't. Not a word.'

'Thank you. Well if we stay here a moment longer the
gossips will go into overdrive.' She's right on that score,
and she makes matters worse by walking into her office and
closing the door behind her.

'She's had her door closed every day since she got back

from the Maldives. She's never done it before,' Camilla
tells me later on. 'Something's wrong. She's got a bad aura
about her. I've never seen her look so preoccupied. She even
snapped at Matt yesterday when he went in with a birthday
card to sign.'

I'm trying to think of something to say when Robbie
comes over. He has revived his theory that Jackie's about to
make a load of people redundant. It's the perfect cover story
for her and I leap upon it. I make some comment about how
insurance companies have started to cut repatriation cover
out of their travel policies altogether. I've absolutely no idea
whether or not that might be true. Two hours later another
rumour has taken hold. Apparently we're going to get taken
over by a giant American company that can run most of the
operation from its headquarters in New York State. I'm quite
pleased with how I got that one out there. With a bit of luck
it will buy Jackie a bit of time.

I normally ask for a few details on each new trip before
accepting it. Yesterday Matt suckered me into accepting an
American pick-up without going through the usual checks.
I'm already regretting it.

'It's San Francisco,' he had said. 'It's Virgin Upper Class. I
saved it for you especially.'

I should have remembered that in this job, 'San Francisco'
doesn't always mean San Francisco. In this case it means a
four-hour taxi journey over the Bay to a psychiatric facility
in the middle of nowhere. My night in a hotel isn't exactly
the Ritz Carlton on Nob Hill. It's more of a Norman Bates-
style motel on the edge of a suburban strip mall. Now I
think about it, there's a whiff of Norman Bates about my
patient as well. He's a slightly odd-looking sixty-two-year-
old man called William Blackall. It looks as if he has cut his

own hair. It's thick and black and there's an awful lot more of it on one side of his head than the other.

He was admitted to the hospital after the police and paramedics were sent to a diner where he had collapsed in tears after throwing all his china and cutlery onto the floor. When approached, he began hitting the side of his face with a coffee mug. His presenting complaints at hospital were simple: extreme confusion, erratic behaviour and mild self-harm. The hospital wants to get rid of him fast.

Mentally ill patients are some of the hardest to deal with on a repatriation. They make up a large proportion of all the jobs we do. Airlines don't want them on board unaccompanied in case they have some sort of breakdown and endanger the flight. As the only way to calm them down in a crisis tends to be to inject them with some sort of sedative, it has to be a doctor rather than a nurse who flies with them.

The moment I walk into Mr Blackall's room it's clear how ill he is. The stench of urine – infected urine – is intense. He is barely dressed and has a beaming smile on his face. He says he knows me. He's very pleased to see me. He wants me to meet his friends. I play along. The friends are with us in the room, even though, of course, they're not. I talk for a while and I look at his charts.

'I'll be back to see you again in a few minutes, Mr Blackall.' I head out to find his doctor and see how he has been.

'Ninety per cent of the time he's docile. He's a peach.'
'And the other ten per cent of the time?'
The doctor shrugs. 'He gets aggressive.

Back in Mr Blackall's room I decide there's no medical reason not to fly with him. He certainly can't stay in an expensive American hospital for ever. I'll just have to watch his moods and try to keep him sweet.

The traffic is terrible on our ride to the airport, so we check in relatively late for what looks set to be an on-time flight.

Mr Blackall is fine, but he's volatile. Ten per cent indeed. So far well over a third of our journey has been punctuated with some borderline Tourettes moments as he barks out random swear words. A few times in the ambulance he suddenly began a loud diatribe against former friends. His mood swings are extreme and after a few quiet moments he will lash out with his arms at some imaginary target. All things considered, I decide we're not really ready for the hush of the Upper Class lounge at San Francisco, so instead we amble up and down the long airport corridors before boarding. At one point he demands that we stop so he can have his shoes shined. They're scruffy white tennis shoes but the guy buffs them up as if they were Prada brogues.

'You gentlemen have a nice flight now,' the man says when I pay him. I wish I had his optimism.

Little more than an hour into the flight, Mr Blackall starts to lose it again. We're sitting up at the bar and I've made it clear to the steward that we can't drink anything alcoholic. Mr Blackall doesn't like being denied things. So after a ten-minute sulk he starts to poke people in nearby seats with his walking stick. Then he uses the stick's handle to pull the fruit bowl towards him from the far end of the bar. He proceeds to throw its contents across the cabin.

'Mr Blackall, let's go back to our seats. Maybe we can watch some television?' I say. After a lot of sulking and struggle I get him there.

'Let me just strap you in.'

'Take your hands off me.'

'We need to have our seat belts on, Mr Blackall. It will only take a moment. I can help you.'

Then he really starts to go for it. 'Rape! Rape! This man is trying to rape me! Help me! Somebody get him off me.'

'Mr Blackall, please. Let me help you. Let's just keep the noise down.'

'I need help! I'm being attacked.' He stands up just as I'm about to click his seat belt around him. Then he slumps back into his chair and starts to moan incredibly loudly. The cabin crew are gathering around and I know I need to act.

'I'm going to give you a quick sedative, Mr Blackall,' I say. I get my med bag down from the overhead locker as he kicks out toward the seat in front of him.

'This really won't hurt at all, Mr Blackall,' I tell him as I give him the quick jab.

I should have known he wouldn't take it very well. He screams with the full force of his lungs. He yells 'Rape!' yet again. Then he starts to cry. I hold his hand while the drug begins to do its job. Two minutes, three minutes, five. At last his docility comes back. He starts smiling again. He starts to chat happily, partly to me, partly to himself, partly to his imaginary pals.

I decide there's one other thing I can do for him. I'm guessing that his urinary-tract infection is partly to blame for his confusion and volatility. If we had a microbiology lab tucked between the business and economy cabins I could get some tests done and work out exactly what strain of nasty is affecting him. Without that I can simply take a punt and give him a shot of general purpose antibiotics. Chances are they'll hit the target and start getting the infection under control by the time we land. That might not help his aggression but it will stop his confusion. So it's worth a try.

'One more quick jab, Mr Blackall. You're going to start feeling better really quickly,' I tell him.

'I don't like you,' he says, though he doesn't pull his arm away.

'How are you both getting on? Can I get you anything?' The steward from the bar is at our side.

'Could we both get some water and can you keep us topped up?' I ask.

Then Mr Blackall has his say. 'This man tried to rape me. He should be arrested,' he declares.

So much for his docile state. I won't be able to risk even going to the loo unless I'm certain he's asleep.

For the next eight hours Mr Blackall calls out to almost every flight attendant who serves us, and to every one of the passengers who walks past on their way to the loo or to the bar. At regular intervals he simply shouts, 'Rape! This man is trying to rape me!' to all and sundry. I've never been so glad to land at Heathrow. There's one last bit of embarrassment ahead. A lady comes up to me as we all collect our bags and prepare to leave the plane. She gives me a kind, sympathetic smile.

'You've had a very difficult flight,' she says. 'I do hope your father gets better soon.'

Jackie's door is closed when I drop my med bag off after the trip and do my paperwork.

'She's said she mustn't be disturbed,' Camilla says when she sees me looking across the office. 'I'm guessing that she's been having conference calls with the new company in America all morning. Everyone's going spare with worry. This job could be your last, Ben. You'll never get a mortgage and buy your own flat now.'

I shrug it off as she hands me a few printouts. Straight away I'm confused. I'm off to Ibiza to pick up someone who's had a heart attack after a bad reaction to Ecstasy. On a party island like Ibiza in the summer that's a pretty standard job. But this patient is a seventy-eight-year-old grandmother.

'What the hell was she doing taking Ecstasy? What is this, Saga louts gone wild?' I ask Camilla. She shrugs.

'We've not got any more details. The poor dear's been in a bad way, it seems. Luckily she's got her granddaughter with her. They're from somewhere just north of Edinburgh. We're ticketing you up there with them on the way back.'

The hospital on Ibiza has got a good reputation and we deal with it fairly regularly. It's got plenty of English ex-pats, as well as English-speakers amongst the staff. Unfortunately, my latest patient wasn't lucky enough to be seen by any of them when she was admitted in the early hours last Sunday morning. She had been found walking half-naked through her hotel reception, confused, incoherent and agitated. The notes say she was sweating profusely when an ambulance arrived. Her granddaughter couldn't be found and the lady didn't respond to anything that was said to her. That's the curse of falling ill somewhere you don't speak the language.

I reread her past medical history. Until relatively recently she's been very fit and well. Three healthy kids. No major problems. No allergies or issues. It's only in her seventies that things have taken a turn for the worse. She's had some blood pressure and cholesterol problems and had her first angina attack about six years ago. The rest of Mrs Walsh's file explains what happened on the night she was admitted. The doctors diagnosed a trop-positive event – a minor heart attack that showed up on her blood tests. They made the decision to keep her under observation for two or three days. It was then that her lead doctor tox-screened her urine for drugs.

'We see a lot of things on this island,' he tells me when I meet him. 'If this lady had been eighteen then we would have said right away that it was drugs. She's seventy-eight, but everything else is the same.'

'What were the test results?'

'They were what I expected. The lady had taken Ecstasy and her heart did not like it.'

'Have you told her?'

'We are not the police. If we were, there is someone I would speak to.' He pauses for a long time, looking at me carefully. 'The lady has a granddaughter. She is eighteen. If I were the police I would speak to her.'

'You didn't change your medication before the trip or take anything unusual during it, Mrs Walsh?' I ask casually when I examine my patient. She's pretty spry now. She also looks the model of respectability, the very last person you would think to be in this situation. Her mouth closes firmly and she looks at her hands. We've been chatting easily until now. Suddenly our conversation is over. Interesting.

In the hospital waiting area I meet her granddaughter for the first time. Her name is Emma. She's tall and slim with straight blond hair and wide, watery eyes. She looks distraught and is rocking slightly in her chair.

'Did you notice that your grandmother was feeling unwell

before this happened? No warning signs, nothing you were worried about?'

She says she can't think of anything.

'Your gran takes an aspirin a day for her angina, doesn't she?' I ask. 'But the doctors think she took an Ecstasy pill. That's what triggered her heart attack. You were sharing a room weren't you?'

Emma looks tortured.

'Could she have gone through your bags looking for aspirin? Can you think how this might have happened?'

Emma closes her mouth just the way her grandmother had done. It must be a family characteristic. After a few more unanswered questions I let it go. I reassure Emma that her grandmother will be okay and that we'll be flying home the next morning. Our local doctor is right. We're not the police. Emma knows what must have happened. Her gran probably knows as well. This is something the family will have to discuss between themselves.

It's been surprisingly hard to get us booked on to a flight off the island, so I have a free evening in Ibiza town. I head up the cobbled streets to the castle and eat on a terrace overlooking a little square. There's a little festival going on in the cathedral and the locals are all dressed up to the nines. This is the one big downside of this job: I get to see great things every week, but always by myself. I don't think I want to add up the number of solitary dinners I've eaten in the past year. There's no language in the world where 'table for one' doesn't sound desperately sad. I'm always reading newspaper articles saying you should take a book to a restaurant to remove the stigma of eating alone, but I read enough books waiting out delays in airport terminals. The last thing I want is to read even more over dinner. Instead, I pick my restaurants with care. Silent, half-empty places are a disaster: too often you get seated next to the only other people there, which feels awkward even if you don't speak their language. Very busy places are just as bad: you get the worst table and the staff ignore you because they know groups spend more money. Tonight I've got it right. It's a casual place and there's plenty of distraction outside. I feel part of things and there's no pressure to get the bill and go as soon as my plate has been taken away.

The next day I head back to the hospital after breakfast to assess my patient. She's ready to travel and a still nervous-looking Emma is at her side, all packed up and ready to go. Our local doctor shakes both their hands as we leave. Emma can't get herself to look him in the eye and I actually start to feel a bit sorry for her.

'Your gran's going to be fine,' I repeat as we get to the airport. But I'm soon having second thoughts. Our flight is delayed by an hour and a half and the terminal is hot, crowded and airless. By the time we finally get to board Mrs Walsh has started to turn pale. Just before take-off she begins to look clammy. I'm at the very last point before I can ask the crew to have us taken off the flight to get her back to hospital. Around 150 passengers will be very pissed off if I get the plane sent back to the gate now. But if my patient is in trouble it has to be done.

'Mrs Walsh, are you feeling okay?'

'I just feel a little bit sick,' she says, her voice quiet and slurred.

'I just need some air. I'm going to be fine.' Emma and I point the air jets in the lady's direction and get rewarded with a weak smile. 'That's much better. It's already passing,' she says.

All I can do is take her word for it. As a repat doctor
you're on your own once the plane doors are closed. There
are specialist, twenty-four-hour, medical information centres
that airlines can call from the air if crew members or doctors
don't know what's wrong with a passenger, but all they
can offer is advice. At this stage I'm the only one who can
decide if Mrs Walsh is fit to fly. I look at her again and
weigh it all up. Taking her off the flight may make her feel
she's more vulnerable than she really is and if she doesn't
fly today she'll have to go through it all again tomorrow. I
make the call that we go ahead. If she throws up all over me
when we reach cruising altitude then so be it. It won't be the
first time that's happened.

We taxi towards the end of the runway before waiting for
what seems like for ever. We edge forward and stop again.
Meanwhile, the hot Ibiza sun is pouring in through the
windows, seeming to suck ever more air out of the plane.
There's nothing the crew can do. Window blinds have to
be kept open on take-off and landing. There are two main
theories about why this is. One says it's so the emergency
services can see in to check for survivors after a crash. The
other says it's so the cabin crew can shout out a warning if
one of the engines catches fire. I'm not sure which is worse.
I put both out of my mind and start to fan Mrs Walsh with
a safety card. She's still giving weak smiles. It worries me a
bit that they're getting weaker by the minute.

The cabin temperature finally falls when we get airborne.
'Is that feeling a little easier, Mrs Walsh?'

She finally gives a far more convincing smile. 'Call me
Margaret,' she says. 'You're an angel. I feel just dandy now,
though I would like a glass of water.'

That's when she throws up in my lap.

'It is okay, Margaret, it's okay. This happens all the time. Now you just hold on to this bag if it happens again. I'll get some others for you as well.'

Her granddaughter passes me the bag from her seat back pocket and I'm handed one from an elderly Spanish man across the aisle as well. The cabin crew are absolutely nowhere to be seen. I'm in dire need of a few napkins.

'Take a few deep breaths, Margaret, and you'll feel better. We'll get you that glass of water in a minute as well.'

Her eyes are closed. She retches again, though this time precious little comes out. It looks as if the worst is over so I take the sick bag out of her hands. She opens her eyes and looks across at me.

'Doctor, I've ruined your clothes.'

'That doesn't matter at all. They'll go in the wash the moment I get home. I just want to be sure you're okay.'

She nods and keeps on looking at my shirt and my lap. 'I'm so sorry, Doctor. I'm so embarrassed.'

One of the crew has finally arrived and is offering Margaret a microscopic face wipe.

'She might need another,' I suggest, before turning to Margaret. 'Are you okay for a minute if I just dash to the loo to clean up?'

I take my shirt off in the lavatory and try to rinse it through with hand soap. I do the same with my trousers. The soap is labelled as 'Tuscan breeze' but I'm not sure it's strong enough to cover the scent I want it to mask. I wring my clothes out, pull them back on and head back to our row. I'm steaming, ever so slightly, as I sit down. Margaret has a glass of water in front of her and is dabbing her face with a full-sized hot towel.

'Am I going to be all right?' she asks me as I sit down.

'You're going to be fine. I think that was just the heat
and the lack of oxygen up here. Plus the hospital food. I
saw what they were feeding you back on the island and I'm
surprised you weren't sick days ago.'

That's a line I use all the time when patients throw up on
me. Sometimes it raises a smile. It doesn't work today.

Margaret sits in silence for some time. She takes tiny sips
of her water and keeps on dabbing her face. That's when
I realise that it isn't over. Something is happening to her
breathing. She's starting to pull in short, shallow, dangerous
breaths. That's very different from how she was breathing
before. This could get serious. I turn slowly towards her, not
wanting to scare her the way she's scaring me.

'Margaret, are you feeling sick again? Can you relax for
me?'

Her eyes flash out a warning. She swallows deeply and
tries to say something but stops herself. Her hand reaches
out to my arm. She is scared now. It's written all over
her face. 'I don't feel well, Doctor. I can't seem to breathe
properly. I've got palpitations. Something's happening to my
heart.'

I turn her arm over and count her pulse for ten seconds.
I do the sums to get the reading. In the hospital and earlier
in the flight it was around eighty. Now it's close to 200. No
wonder she's gasping for air. No wonder she's scared.

'Margaret, it's going to be fine,' I say. I'm cursing myself
inside. Why didn't I get her off the plane while I had the
chance? Even if I can get the captain to do an emergency
divert now we'll have to fly back out over the Mediterranean
to dump our fuel before starting our descent. It will be an
hour until she's in an ambulance. I'm not sure she's got that
much time left.

'I feel dizzy, Doctor. It hurts.' She's got her hand on her chest. 'It really hurts here, Doctor. What's happening to me?'

'What's going on?' Emma is out of her seat now and starting to panic again. Other passengers are starting to notice. One lady across the aisle lets out a low moan and starts jabbing at her flight attendant call button. That's all we need.

'Just give us some room. Your gran's going to be fine,' I tell Emma.

Truth is I'm not so sure. I count her pulse for another ten seconds. It's going even higher up and off the scale. I know I need to move fast. She's in SVT or Supraventricular Tachycardia. If I don't put the brakes on her heart then her blood pressure will drop like a stone. At that point her brain could get starved of oxygen or her lungs could fill with water. Both could kill her – and putting the brakes on an old lady's heart is easier said than done.

'Give me some space.'

I'm out of my seat now and I've got my right hand on the left-hand side of Margaret's neck. My fingers are kneading Margaret's skin. I'm working that area to the side of her windpipe. One way to re-set her heart rate is to massage the vagus nerve that runs from the brain to the heart. It's a tricky manoeuvre and it doesn't always work. It isn't working today.

'Come on, come on, do your job,' I'm silently telling Margaret's vagus nerve. I pick up her hand and check her pulse again. I know instantly that I haven't saved her. I'm back at her neck, massaging the other side. She's moaning in fear now. I'm rubbing hard but I'm not getting anywhere. I check her pulse once more though there's no point. Even before the sum comes out at 220 I'm moving on.

'I need my medical bag.' I shout out at Emma. 'In the locker, up there.' She's frozen and won't move.

'Emma, I need the bag now.' Finally it's in front of me. The cabin crew have arrived as well. They've chosen to stand close enough so that they can help if they're needed. But they're not so close that they're getting in the way or adding to the drama. One of them has even managed to calm down the woman across the aisle who pressed the call button. That helps everyone.

I let go of Margaret's hands and zip open the bag. An injection of adenosine might bring her heart rate back down to earth. I find the drug and prep the syringe. Margaret has a cannula in her arm – the easy gateway for an injection like this. I get the syringe in and press it but nothing happens. I press again. Nothing. The cannula's blocked. Bugger, bugger, bugger. Her eyes are even wider with fear. She can tell from my face that something's gone wrong. I need to inject into a vein now and I've got a feeling it's going to be very hard to find one. The doctor on Ibiza said they'd struggled when Margaret had been admitted. That had been in a well-lit, well-staffed hospital on the ground. On a bumpy charter flight at 35,000 feet things are set to be a little harder.

'Okay, Margaret, I'm going to give you a normal injection now. I just need you to hold your arm out for me. Turn it just a little for me. That's exactly right, here we go.' There isn't a vein. My fingers are pushing, kneading, just as they had been on her neck.

'Any minute now, Margaret, I'm going to give you that injection.' There's nothing. No way to do this. And even without a proper count I can tell her pulse is still at the top of the range. Emma has started to cry, Margaret is gasping for air and we're running out of time. I've got one more plan. The dive reflex. I've read about it, but never done it. Much less in public. But I've no other choices. Margaret needs this to work.

'I need a big bowl. Like a washing-up bowl. I need some litre bottles of water. And ice. As much ice as you can get me.' I yell out at the cabin crew. The steward and stewardess get moving fast. One heads to the front galley, the other to the rear. They both get back to me at almost the same time.

'We don't have a bowl,' one says. 'But we have this.' It's the tray that's usually clipped on top of the drinks trolley for all the bottles and juice cartons.

'It's perfect,' I say, even though it isn't, really. I slam the seat-back table down in front of Margaret and put the container on it. I tip half a bag of ice into it. Then I slosh two litres of water on top. A whole load of ice cubes fall out and a river of freezing cold water pours out over Margaret's bare legs. Her thin summer skirt is soaked through. She lets out another cry but I'm not done with her yet.

'Margaret, you're not going to like this. I need to get your head in this bucket of water. I need your face in there. It's like bobbing for apples, can you understand that?'

'Bobbing apples? I can't do it,' she says, staring at me as if I've gone mad.

'Why do you need all the ice?' Emma shouts at me.

'It has to be cold. There are nerves running down your face and neck and the shock of freezing water can re-set the heart.' I turn back to Margaret. 'Did you hear that? Are you ready, Margaret? I know there's not much room but I need you to get your face in this water. I'll hold your head. You have to trust me.'

She looks at Emma then gives the barest of nods. She's ready.

'Can you take a deep breath? I'll do it on the count of three.'

When Margaret gulps in some air and I get to the end of the count I do it. I push her face into the bowl. That's when Emma goes wild. She screams and lunges at me, hitting my shoulders with one hand, trying to pull me away from her grandmother with the other. I barely notice. I'm counting to three then pull Margaret back up by her hair. She's gasping for air, shaking, shivering, too upset even to cry.

'Margaret, I'm so sorry about that. You were amazing. I'm going to check your pulse right now.' My hands are on her wrist as I speak. I give her one more moment to calm down. Then I count the beats. Ten seconds. I do the sum. It comes out at just over 100. I'm breathing as loudly as she is now. I wait a few moments then count it again. Please can it still be okay. Please can this lady be safe. She is. The second count is below 100. We've made it. We're there.

'Margaret, listen to me, you're going to make it, you're going to make it,' I repeat, trying to smile, trying to get her to look at me. Her eyes are full of tears and full of fear. I don't think she's taking anything in. But she must know the panic has passed.

'Blankets. She's going to need blankets.'

The crew run to get some, but Margaret's fellow passengers beat them to it. A young girl from the row behind takes off her sweatshirt and tries to wrap it round the old lady's shoulders. I've got my fingers on Margaret's wrist and I'm counting her pulse yet again. It confirms, thank God, that we're over it. We're low and we're staying low. As the blankets arrive I'm suddenly laughing at the sheer horror of what I've just done to this poor old lady. No wonder she and all the other passengers are in shock.

Margaret closes her eyes while the crew take away the water, mop up the seat area and wrap her in blankets. By the sound of it she's starting to sob, quietly. I feel terrible about that. But I don't have time to worry about it.

'Excuse me, Sir.' The stewardess touches my arm and points across the aisle. I've got another patient. Emma is hunched forward in her seat. She's deathly pale, sweating and rocking backwards and forwards. The stewardess hands me a sick bag. This lady is way ahead of me. She's good.

'Emma, you're having a panic attack. I need you to breathe in and out of this bag. Just keep blowing the same air, in and out, just use the bag, breathe it in and blow it out. Seal it round your mouth, breathe really deeply and it really will work, it will make you feel better.'

Emma won't make eye contact with me. But at least she is doing what I tell her. I can understand, perhaps, why she doesn't want to listen to me. But at least she's not too proud to ignore me. Fortunately, the old 'breathe in the bag' trick does the business. We've re-set Margaret's heartbeat, now we've re-set Emma's breathing. The panic is over, so is her panic attack. The flight crew have been busy moving passengers around so Margaret can have a dry seat. We lead her, swathed in blankets, to her new row.

'Can you bear to have me sit next to you?' I ask as we settle in.

She pats my arm and says she's very glad I'm there. Then she shows she is a true Brit by asking for some hot sweet tea. Once she's drunk it she really does seem to be on the mend.

'As if the shock wasn't bad enough you soaked my skirt. I think the whole plane saw my bare legs and petticoat. I was quite mortified,' she says with a flash of her old spirit.

'Margaret, I've got a confession to make,' I tell her. 'There was one other way to try and get your heart back to normal. It sounds unlikely, but some medical books recommend getting a patient to do a handstand. For future reference, would that have been better or worse for you than the iced water?'

'I think I you were right to choose the water,' she says drily.

We touch down at Heathrow and there's a rare ripple of applause from some of the passengers near us at the front of the plane. We have bonded amidst the drama of the flight. Everyone wants to do their bit to keep Margaret's spirits up.

Cabin crews sometimes let frail passengers leave planes first but today we've elected to leave last. Margaret, Emma and I stay in our seats till everyone else has left. Lots of people want to shake Margaret's hand and wish her well. The old Spanish man who gave her the sick bag gives a courtly little bow. The girl who had handed over her sweatshirt leans down for a hug. When they've all gone we make our way to the exit door. The two crew members who had helped us the most are jealously guarding the wheelchair that's waiting for Margaret.

'Do you need anything else?' the steward asks as we settle her down and put a new blanket on her knees.

'I think we all want a double vodka' I reply, relieved the worst is over.

After going through fast-track immigration I wait with Margaret while Emma gets their luggage. Then it's off to a place few other passengers get to go. The pair's final destination is Edinburgh and we've got three hours before our flight. We're going to wait at Heathrow's onsite medical centre. The old one was in the Queen's Building sandwiched between Terminals One and Two. I always quite liked that place. It had the feel of one of those Sunday night medical shows set in a 1950s hospital – though the collapsed drug smugglers and the drunks scooped up each day from the various terminals tended to give it a slightly more contemporary edge.

Today the medical centre is in an office block alongside the multi-storey car parks of Terminal Three. There's no full-time doctor, but a small team of nurses are there from dawn till dusk. A lot of the time they're dealing with people sent over for medical checks from the border staff at immigration. Most other people who might need a bit of medical advice probably get lost along the way.

We get to go in one of Heathrow's private ambulances and take for ever getting round the one-way systems. Fortunately, we're pretty much the only people there when we arrive. I run an ECG to check Margaret hasn't had another heart attack. She's fine. I take the opportunity to put another cannula in her arm just in case there's a drama on our next flight. But after that I leave her alone. She's still incredibly weak and she's probably exhausted after the events of the flight. She knows she's close to home, so she's just trying to keep it all inside until she gets there. Small talk is the last thing she needs.

On the other side of our tiny waiting room Emma seems to have her own issues to deal with. I'm guessing she's a little worried about facing her parents. I won't be the only one to put two and two together and work out how an old lady ended up taking an Ecstasy pill on holiday. Maybe Emma is a bit embarrassed about the panic attack on the plane, as well about lunging at me with her fists when I was trying to help her gran. Either way she's not up for much of a conversation.

I find myself a chair close enough to Margaret to keep an eye on her, but not too close to intrude. Apart from the traffic noise it's totally silent in the waiting area and we've still got well over two hours till we board our next flight. I don't think I've ever been so keen to have a Tie Rack or a WHSmith to wander around. I think I could even face a Claire's Accessories.

I open my bag and start the paperwork on the repat. On an uneventful job you only need to fill in the factual boxes on the forms - where you picked the patient up, what you were told about them by their attending physician, how you transferred them and who you handed them over to at the end. When you've had vomiting, a major problem with heart rhythms and a panic attack, you need a few extra pages. The forms are done in triplicate. One copy goes to the patient's doctor, one to the insurance company and one to the office. I deal with all our incidents then put the files back in my bag.

'Margaret, if you're still feeling okay, I'm just going to head outside to make a quick phone call,' I say. I want to speak to Jackie but I don't feel it's a conversation I should have with other people listening.

'Take as long as you need, I'm going to have another wee doze,' Margaret says with a tired smile. I get my mobile and stand amidst the traffic fumes outside the medical centre. Jackie picks up her phone on the first ring.

'You sound like you're at a race track,' she says.

'I'm at Heathrow, at the medical building, waiting for a flight up to Scotland. How are you feeling?'

'A lot better, to be honest. You'll be pleased to know I've got an appointment with a neurologist in a week.'

'That's brilliant.'

'It is. My only problem now is keeping it all under wraps till then. I feel under siege here. Everyone seems to have guessed that something's up. I've been in my office with the door shut for so long now I'm too afraid to leave. What am I going to say to everyone?'

'Don't say anything,' I say. 'I'm staying in Edinburgh tonight but I'll be on the first flight back tomorrow morning and I'll be in the office just after ten. By then I'll come up with some way to distract everyone.'

There's a bit of a pause.

'It won't be a strippergram will it?' Jackie asks eventually.

'You've got a dirty mind. That's why we all love you. But no, it won't be a strippergram.'

The Autumn Rush

SEPTEMBER

My flight back to London leaves Scotland over an hour late and Jackie isn't in her office when I arrive just after eleven. I find a desk I can use and kill time checking my email. There's one from Jackie: 'The neurologist can see me this morning! All should be well by this afternoon. Cancel the gorillagram.'

I try to think of a funny reply but can't. To be honest I'd struggled to think of any new way to divert office gossip from Jackie's strange mood. Hopefully, I won't need to by the time Jackie gets her proper diagnosis and treatment options. She'll probably break the news to the team straight away. Then we can all stop walking on eggshells and help her through it. I'm crossing my fingers for good news as I leave the office and head home for a shower and a quick change of clothes. I normally try and have at least one night at home between jobs, but we're busy at the moment so I've agreed to do an extra one to help clear the backlog.

I call my mum while I heat up some soup. She and Dad are off to Cyprus at the weekend and have just booked another holiday in New England for the fall. It's not hard to see where my love of travel comes from.

I'm on the phone to them both for about half an hour. Then my car arrives to take me back to Heathrow. I'm booked on to a flight to the United Arab Emirates and I'm about to get a very pleasant surprise.

'You're in 3A now, Sir,' the lady on the check-in desk says, tearing up the first boarding pass she had printed out for me and handing me a shiny new one.

'Is that an aisle or a window seat?' I ask.

'It's both,' she says.

Fantastic.

I'm heading to Dubai to pick up a forty-two-year-old businessman from the West Midlands. He slipped on the shiny floor of a restaurant and fell head first against the corner of a table. The blow knocked his eye socket back into his skull – what's known in the trade as an 'orbital blowout fracture'. He'd needed some careful neurological examinations, plus some fairly extensive plastic surgery to rebuild his eye socket. He's been in hospital for ten days and is now desperate to get home. We've agreed for a local doctor to discharge him from hospital and take him to the airport by private ambulance. I'm due to meet him there to check he's as fit as we've been told. If so, and if all the flights are on time, we've got a two-hour wait before I get back on board with him and do the whole trip in reverse.

This kind of airport pick-up is relatively rare, because there is always the worry that we've been misled about the patient's condition. If so, and if they're not well enough to fly, then we have to send them back to hospital, which racks up ever bigger bills and wastes everyone's time. In Dubai, though, we've got a good relationship with this particular hospital and trust the doctors not to let us down.

In the meantime I'm treated like a king for the whole

flight. There are just eight seats in the first-class cabin and
only three of them are occupied. We have six crew members
on call at all times. Plus our own chef. Just after take-off he
comes over to chat. He wants to know what I might like to
eat and when. I then get a stream of hot snacks while I wait
for the first of his creations to arrive. When I go to the loo
I find there's a window (with a window blind, just in case
someone is really paranoid about being overlooked).

A few hours later, when I feel like a snooze, I recline
my vast seat back in my personal pod the way I would on
any other airline. Big mistake. The crew pounce on me.
This is their job and it needs all six of them to sort it out
and bring sheets, big fluffy duvets and full-size pillows.
Just wonderful. I've got used to flying business and Upper
Class since doing repatriations full-time. But the personal
attention you get in first on one of these oil-rich airlines is
off the scale.

The fun continues on the ground. Surprisingly for the
Middle East there's no air-bridge for us to get straight off
the plane so we all need to be bussed from the tarmac to
terminal. I head down the steps and walk towards the
big bus that's parked in front of us. One of my six crew
members comes to get me – a look of horror written all over
his face. It seems first-class passengers have their own bus,
even when there are only three of us.

Inside the terminal I ask for help tracking down my
patient. A ground service agent takes me though a maze of
corridors and back to the tarmac where a private ambulance
is waiting. It's desperately hot outside, but when I open the
back doors a rush of wonderfully air-conditioned air blows
over me. I climb inside and hold out my hand. 'You must be
Mr Hammond?'

He returns the greeting with a hearty, double-handed grip. 'Yes I am, and I'm so very pleased to see you,' he says. 'I know I look as if I've been in a plane crash already, but I do hope you agree I'm safe to travel.'

He's not wrong about the way he looks. It's ten days after his little spill and his face is still swollen and bruised. The skin around his left eye is so puffed up he can barely open it.

'May I?' I ask, touching his face and looking around at his wounds.

'I'm having all the colours of the rainbow on my face, doctor,' he says. 'I seem to have entered a green phase now. You should have seen it when it was purple. The doctors assure me that this is all part of the healing process. They say it won't last for ever.'

I carry on examining his face, check his general health and take a look at the notes he was given when the local doctors discharged him. Nothing leaps out as a potential problem.

'So can we fly?' he asks, almost childlike in his enthusiasm.

'I don't see why not. I think our plane is waiting because I just came in on it.'

It's a new crew, of course, but the service is seven star just like before. The only bad thing for my patient is that the injury on the side of his head means he shouldn't really use earphones to watch a film. He says he's more than happy for me to watch one and that he'll nudge me if he needs me. He soon dozes off and I watch three films back to back. Two are new and the final one is an oldie – *Fight Club*. I pick it partly because I vaguely remember it from first time around but mainly because the warning message in the in-flight listings magazine makes me smile. 'Passengers of a nervous disposition should be aware that opening sequence of the film includes graphic images of a plane crash.'

It's an uneventful flight and I say goodbye to Mr Hammond at Heathrow when he climbs into a pre-ordered taxi. I get a cab of my own back to the office with my med bag. When I'm there I compare businessman stories with Bilal, one of our other regular doctors. He just went to Atlanta where a man was offered a tablet so he could have a little help with a prostitute.

'It might have been blue, but it wasn't Viagra,' says Bilal.

The guy went out cold, had his cash, cards and computer stolen from his hotel room and then had a heart attack.

'He'll have a lot of explaining to do now and no safe haven. When his wife's finished with him I'd imagine his boss will want to have a go,' Bilal says. He's heading home for a few days off.

I've got another job lined up, leaving from Gatwick the following afternoon. It sounds like one of the saddest pick-ups I've done in months. A mum of two dived into the swimming pool on the first morning of her holiday on the Costa del Sol in Spain. Her husband was standing on the edge of the pool with their kids to take a photograph. No one had noticed that it was the shallow end.

'They've scanned and stabilised her and we're waiting to see if it's spinal shock or if she'll be permanently paralysed from the neck down, poor love,' says Christine as she passes me the file. 'The family have all been in a really bad way as well. The little boy's only five but apparently he jumped in to try and help his mum. Somehow in the confusion he ended up gashing his head on the side of the pool and then fainted and fell back in again when he saw the blood. He could have drowned if one of the other guests hadn't spotted

him. Later on it got bad again. Once they got the mother
to hospital and realised how bad she was, the dad and the
older girl both collapsed and needed sedation because of
the shock. The mum's been in hospital for over a week now.
They must all be in pieces.'

I sit and read the full reports in silence. We've been told
that the woman's parents have flown out to Spain to be at
their daughter's side and to help with their grandchildren.
The rough plan is that they will all fly home on one plane
while mum and I go on another. She's going to have a bad
enough journey as it is without having to put on a brave
face for her kids.

I head to the storeroom to make sure I've got absolutely
everything I might need for this job. All our medical kit
is kept in a secure room at the back of the office. We've
got several choices of bag. They start with a 'nurse bag'
with a basic first-aid kit and they go up to the silver metal
suitcases that tend to be used on air ambulance jobs. Today
I go for a mid-sized medical bag that can be kitted up like a
mobile A&E department. I pull open the zips and go though
the contents. Other people could check it all for me but
wherever possible I like to do it myself. It's a bit like packing
your own parachute. I want to know I've no one but myself
to blame if something's wrong.

First I check all the drugs are in date and in place.
Standard kit includes everything: adrenaline, adenosine,
bretylium, atropine, lignocaine and all the other things you
need a dictionary to re-order. On the hardware side I want
an intubation kit so I can get a tube to the patient's lungs
and ventilate her artificially if necessary. I also want drips,
disposable cannulas and all the other bits of equipment that
could save her. When it's all in I try and leave a bit of room

for some spare clothes at the top of the bag. Airport staff normally make an exception for working medics if they are doing a one-bag rule at security. But even if you get lucky in London you might not get waved through on the way back. So I always make sure I can squeeze everything in together if required.

I head back into the main office. Christine's not around but Robbie calls me over.

'Don't ask why, but we were all talking about you earlier on. We want to know if you've rung Danielle recently.' He never does beat about the bush.

'I don't think she'd take my call.'

'Well, we've all decided that you should try. We liked her.'

'It's been too long. It's been months now. She'll have moved on.'

Danielle and I had split up in the spring after nearly a year together. She's a physio from my last hospital. She'd come to our office Christmas party and got on brilliantly with everyone. The problem was she wanted a boyfriend who was around every night. I was always on a plane.

'She's probably seeing someone else by now. Some nine-to-five guy who never misses a dinner party. Anyway, wasn't it you who allocated me the trip to The Gambia when I was supposed to be at her dad's birthday lunch? That was the final straw that got me dumped.'

'So your entire, disastrous love life is my fault?'

I think about it for a moment. 'You know what, Robbie? I think it is. So it's your job to find me someone new. I'm off to Spain tomorrow night. Try and get me a date by the time I get home.'

My Malaga flight is delayed by nearly two hours so it's nearly eight in the evening when I get out of the airport, and gone nine by the time I reach my hotel. Normally I'd say that's too late to visit a patient. Tonight I decide to go anyway. A full stretcher repatriation like this is tough. The sooner I see what kind of condition Mrs Wallace is in the better.

Her hospital is in a modern, medium-sized building on the outskirts of the town. The lights are warm and strangely welcoming in the night air. I explain who I am at the reception area and an orderly leads me through deserted corridors to my patient's bedside. An older man is sitting in the half-light. His eyes are red, his head is resting in his hands.

'I'm Doctor Ben MacFarlane. I'm over from Britain to help Mrs Wallace get home.'

'It's Fiona, Fiona Wallace. She's my daughter,' he says, matching my whisper. He looks so strained he might break.

I look at his daughter. She's lying semi-flat on the other side of the rails of the big, white hospital bed. She looks tiny and very precious. She has a halo brace – a metal support cage – screwed into her skull and attached to a plate around her collarbone and shoulders. It's there to stop any extra movements that could make her dire situation even worse. I can see blond hair pulled back beneath it, and a few scars and stitches on her forehead. It looks as if she might have broken her nose and there are deep dark shadows around her eyes. Both her arms are lying outside her blankets and her right hand has a cannula in it, though right now she's not attached to any drip or machinery. I can see her chest rise and fall silently under the sheets. This somehow makes everything seem strangely peaceful. She is one unlucky woman. But at least she can breathe unaided. My notes say she can eat as well, as long as someone feeds her. Small mercies, but important ones.

'I don't want to wake her. I just wanted to make sure someone knew I was here. I'll be back to examine Fiona when she's awake tomorrow morning. We're hoping to fly her home in the afternoon.'

Her father nods and tries to smile. He looks at his watch. 'My son-in-law will be here soon. He's due at ten and I know he would like to see you.'

There are four chairs on the other side of the room. I sit there with Fiona's father.

'How is everyone bearing up? How are the children?'

He shrugs. 'I think we're all trying to hide how we feel from each other. Nobody wants to let go in case we lose control. It's like walking a tightrope every day. I'm a sixty-five-year-old man, doctor, and I've never experienced anything like this in my life. I hope I never will again.'

It's clear this proud, strong man is finding it hard to talk. So I don't push it. We sit in silence from then on. Ten minutes become twenty. Fiona's quiet breathing is all we can hear. Almost on the stroke of 10pm, a young-looking man in his forties walks silently into the room. He stands at the edge of Fiona's bed and slowly looks over every inch of her body. He's tall but hunched, somehow. He turns around. Fiona's father stands and guides him over.

'Gavin, this is the doctor who's here to bring Fiona home. I'm sorry I can't remember your name.'

'Ben. It's Ben MacFarlane. You must be Fiona's husband?'

'I'm Gavin. Yes. Thank you for coming.' He turns back to his father-in-law. 'Has there been anything? Any change?'

'None at all, son. But she's hanging on in there. She's a fighter, son, you know that.' With that he gives Gavin an awkward half-hug, blinks hard as he nods in my direction and steps towards the door.

'Rose will be here at eight sharp,' he says. 'Call if there's anything at all.' Then he's gone.

I only stay a few more minutes. It's clear that Gavin isn't up to talking. I leave him my number, tell him I'm only half an hour away and get a cab back to my hotel. I've got a mini-kettle in my room and a sachet of hot chocolate in place of coffee. It's not your normal late-summer Spanish drink, but I find it surprisingly comforting. I'm desperate to ring Jackie and find out what her doctor said, but worry that it's a bit too late. I watch CNN instead then turn out the lights. I'll try Jackie from the airport tomorrow, if I can.

Gavin is still at his wife's side the following morning. Nothing has changed, he tells me, as Fiona's mum arrives. She is a small, strong-looking woman with stylishly cut grey hair. Her eyes are bright, alert – and very worried. It's the eight o'clock switchover and Gavin says that Rose will now sit with her daughter until her husband takes over after lunch. The kids come for half an hour mid-morning and mid-afternoon every day. Then Gavin's shift begins again at ten in the evening. That's how they've all worked it for a week. It's quite a family.

'How are you and your children bearing up? I know your little boy had a bad time as well at the start. Your daughter has taken it badly as well?'

Gavin and I have gone to get a coffee. His tired face picks up the moment I mention the kids. 'They've been amazing. Louis needed six stitches and he nearly drowned, for God's sake. He's been a little hero, though, and Sasha's dealing with it now. It helps that they've got their gran and granddad here. I suppose that makes it all feel a bit more normal, somehow.'

'So how are you?' In the flurry of medical detail it is so easy to forget to ask the patient's partner how they're coping.

Gavin gives the smallest of shrugs. 'I'm just trying to keep it all together now. I don't know if you're told these sorts of things, but I lost it at first, which I shouldn't have done because of the kids. They had to put me on Valium to calm me down. I'm ashamed of that. I was so scared we'd lost her.' His voice suddenly speeds up and gets louder. 'Fiona can't move, you know that? Not her arms, not her legs, just her face, her mouth and her eyes. She's always on the go at home. Now she can't move. She's the best mother in the world. This can't have happened to her. It just can't.'

He's breathing hard now, huge gulps of air as he tries to do what he promises and keep it all together. I stare at the floor to give him as much time as he needs. In the end he doesn't lose it. He's holding on to the arm of his chair much tighter than he probably realises. Then he shakes it all off.

'What happens now?' he asks.

It's clear we've moved on from the emotional stuff. From now on I think he wants to deal in hard facts.

'I'm going to examine your wife, talk things through with her and speak to her doctors. Then I'll call my office and make the final arrangements for the journey home. That's when your wife can really start to get better.'

A little later Fiona's mum introduces me to her daughter. I crouch a bit and look down into her warm, dark eyes. 'Gavin says you can get me home today,' she says. 'That's what I want, please.'

'Well, that's the plan. I just need to check a few things and then we can get the flight sorted.' I take my notes out of my bag.

'I'll leave you to it. I'll be back in five minutes,' her mum says. I turn to smile goodbye as she leaves the room. When I turn to look back at Fiona her eyes are tightly closed. Her voice, when she speaks, is angry.

'You know, apart from childbirth, I've hardly been in hospital my entire life. I only ever go to the GP with my kids. I am so sick of being examined by doctors.'

I can see her point. I also know my examination is going to seem invasive in the extreme. Every nerve from each spinal vertebra serves a different area of the body. I want to touch each area to check what, if anything, Fiona can feel.

'Can you feel this?' I say, tapping the top of her right shoulder very lightly. 'How about this? And this? Now this?' The answer, as I move around her whole body, is always 'No'.

'I'm going to check your reflexes now. The doctors have probably done this already so you'll know how it works.' I tap her just below the knee cap – and her leg jerks up. It's an irony that people with spinal injuries can have overly pronounced reflexes. I hope Fiona gets some comfort from the fact that some part of her body can still move.

I listen to her chest and check her body for bed sores. First thing this morning her doctors had shown me her CT scans and talked me though everything that's happened since she was admitted eight days earlier. She certainly did well to end up in this hospital. Spain was always infamous for dodgy deals between medical clinics and British tour reps. Bad hospitals paid big money to reps who brought clients to them. I've no idea if that still goes on. I do know that Fiona has had excellent care.

'Mrs Wallace, I'm going to call the office now and check we're still booked on to a flight this afternoon. Are you okay, Fiona?' Her eyes are closed again.

'I just can't bear this,' she says. 'I want this to be over.'

'It will be. We're aiming to get you back in Britain this evening. Last night I heard your dad tell your husband that you're a fighter, Fiona. He said you can get through this.'

Her eyes are open, suddenly. 'My dad said that about me?' she asks. 'To Gavin?' She's looking directly at me. Her eyes are filling with tears.

I only get to see her children, Louis and Sasha, for a matter of minutes. They're booked onto a late-afternoon charter flight with their dad and granddad. They come in to say goodbye to their mum, all smart and serious and subdued.

Three hours later I have a final talk with Fiona's doctors and get ready to discharge her. The crucial thing is to keep Fiona's body as still as possible throughout the transfer. Her head is still locked in the halo brace and we take it very slowly as we roll her from her bed to a trolley, strap her in and make her safe. Then we wheel her through the hospital and down the lift into the waiting ambulance. The same trolley gets lifted into it and we drive slowly towards the airport. Security staff meet us at a perimeter fence and after a lot of paperwork and some searches we're waved through towards the tarmac.

'We'll have a lift to take us right into the plane,' I say as we reach our destination. It's the lift that takes the food carts on board and it's not very big. Fiona's mum Rose is determined to stay at her daughter's side so we squeeze on to it alongside the two men from the ambulance.

'We're going to take this slowly. Are you ready?' I ask.

Rose nods, Fiona mouths a yes and one of the

ambulance staff presses the button. The lift edges its way up until we're alongside the door at the rear of the plane next to the galley.

Three flight attendants are waiting for us. They're dazzling in their bright charter uniforms and stand aside nervously as Rose and I step into the cabin.

'We've never had a stretcher on board before,' one of them says while the ambulance crew get ready to manoeuvre Fiona's trolley into the plane.

'Is she really going to fit back there?' I can see why he's asking. We have reserved three rows of seats at the back of the cabin for Fiona. The crew have pushed the seat backs forward, rather than back, which makes them go flatter. Fiona's stretcher will lie above the seats, attached to some metal supports that have been fitted alongside the cabin walls. We can screen the area off with some curtains to give Fiona some privacy – creating what's known as a Patient Treatment Compartment or PTC. It will be claustrophobic and cramped. Fiona's face won't be much more than a foot from the overhead bins. But at least she'll get decent air to breathe. In the past, the last few rows of a plane used to be the smoking section. Having a stretcher there must have been a total nightmare.

'They're bringing her in,' the flight attendant says as I finish checking that the PTC is ready. Fiona is lying on a scoop-stretcher on top of the trolley and the ambulance crew are lifting it off and guiding her very carefully through the galley. They help attach the stretcher to the supports and check it's secure. Then it's time for them to go. They shake my hand, then say goodbye to Rose and Fiona with little salutes that are really touching. Then they head back down the lift to their ambulance.

I make sure that the special mattress under Fiona is laid out as smoothly as possible. Bed sores are the last thing she needs right now.

'Are you comfortable, dear?' her mum asks her as she fusses with one of the other blankets. There's an awful silence. Fiona is paralysed. Comfort doesn't matter that much to her. The older lady flushes bright red when she realises what she has said.

'Well, I'll make you comfortable, my love,' she says defiantly, tears sparking in the corners of her eyes.

'Where's everyone. Where are Louis and Sasha?' Fiona asks suddenly.

I look over at her. 'They're with their dad and with their granddad. They're fine. They're probably home by now. They flew a couple of hours ago, remember? It's just me and your mum with you now.'

Fiona's eyes are wild, wary. 'I don't remember,' she says.

Her mother edges me aside gently and looks down at her daughter. 'Fiona, love, everything is okay. Louis and Sasha are with their daddy. They're going to paint you a lovely welcome home sign for when we get you to hospital. They're going to be there to meet us. Oh, don't cry, love. You've been so strong so far, my love. Please don't cry.'

But Fiona can't stop. A huge almond-shaped tear forms in the corner of her left eye. Another builds up in her right. Both trail down her pale, drawn face. The tears trace their way round her cheek bones, the one on the left leaving its salty residue in a wound by her ear. All I can think is that she must be able to feel that. Maybe that gives her hope.

'Mum I don't know what to do. I don't know what to do.' Fiona is gasping now, her still, calm face suddenly transformed by panic and fear. Whole huge sobs rack her face, her eyes are blinded now by tears. 'Hold me, please can you hold me.' She's shivering. Her teeth have started to chatter and she's letting out wild, awful cries as she gasps for air. 'Hold me, mum.'

Her mother isn't tall enough to reach around her daughter. 'I'm here my love, I'm here,' she says, desperately trying to climb up on the seat backs. She's trying to climb on to the stretcher. I don't know if it can handle the extra weight and we can't risk jerking Fiona's body by as much as an inch.

'Rose, stop. We have to be careful,' I say but Fiona's mum won't turn away. I grab her shoulders and half push, half lift her back into the aisle. She stands there, distraught and frantic, looking at me without seeing me. All she can see and hear is her daughter. She lunges forward, ready to fight her way back to Fiona.

'Rose, calm down. Right now. You'll hurt her. We can't move her spine.' I grab her again and force her to look at me. I can sense the cabin crew watching the drama unfold. Finally Rose catches herself. Her eyes are locked on mine. Her face is wet and for a moment she stands totally still. Then she's back.

'It's okay. I'll be careful. I understand the danger,' she says.

We still need to do something to help Fiona. A floodgate has been opened. Maybe it's being out of the hospital. Maybe it's knowing that for now at least she doesn't have to put on a brave face for her children or her husband.

'What am I going to do? What can I do?' she keeps screaming, ever louder, ever more tormented.

'Fiona, it's okay, it's okay. I'm Ben, I'm your doctor, remember. You can let it all out and say whatever you want but I will need you to calm down in a few moments. We can't fly if you're upset like this and we do want to get you home. Do you understand me? Can you breathe a little deeper for me? Fiona, can you focus on your breathing, just for a few moments?'

Her eyes are still flashing and thrashing around. Her face, the only part of her body she can move, is still twisting and jerking. I'm stroking her forehead and brushing her hair away from her tears.

'I need my babies. Why aren't they here?' she shouts out, suddenly.

The three flight attendants are hovering nearby. 'Can we do anything?' one of them asks.

'We're fine. Fiona's going to be fine soon,' I say.

Her mother pushes past me again. She's gently stroking her daughter's hand. I can't bear to remind her that Fiona won't be able to feel it.

'Love, you mustn't get so worked up. You've been so brave so far. We've been so proud of you. It's only the flight home now. That's all you have to get through. You'll make things worse if you keep on like this, my love. Can you hear me? Can you please be strong again, my love?'

Fiona still isn't listening. With one more deep breath she crosses the line into hysteria. Her screams are bouncing off the plane walls. One of the flight attendants touches my arm.

'Sir, the captain has told us we're ready for boarding. The passengers are on their way from the terminal. Can we do it?'

'Can you give me two, maybe three more minutes?' If we need to take Fiona off the flight we need to do it now. If I'm going to calm her down I have to do that now as well.

'Fiona, Mrs Wallace, are you listening to me? I know

how hard this is but if you don't calm down you're going
to put yourself under too much strain. You've been doing
so well and it could push your recovery backwards. I can
give you something to calm you down if you are okay with
that. Do you want me to, Mrs Wallace? I think it's a good
idea.'

'I want my babies. I need to see my babies. Why aren't
they here?'

The tears and the screams are going on. Fiona's mum
is almost beside herself now. We're all crammed into this
awful, tiny space at the back of the plane. Fiona's face is
pushed right up against the overhead bins. It's hot and it's
horrible and it's inhuman.

'I can give Fiona some diazepam. It will calm her straight
away. It'll get us through the flight.' I'm half speaking to
myself, half to Fiona and her mum.

'Is it safe?' Rose asks.

'Absolutely. And I'll be at Fiona's side the whole flight.' I
open my med bag and give the injection.

'You're going to feel better straight away, Fiona, straight
away,' I say.

She does. It's mainly the sedative, but maybe it's also that
her nightmare has run its course. She's let out everything
she has kept inside since the accident. Slowly the loud
heart-breaking sobs are replaced by more muffled ones. Our
crew allow our fellow passengers to board, though one of
the attendants stands near us and puts her fingers on her
lips to try and keep the ones closest to us quiet. That's a
nice touch. I barely take my eyes from Fiona. Her chest is
still rising and falling. It looks the perfect, regular rhythm. It
needs to stay that way.

'Sir? We've put the fasten seat belt signs on now. We're

about to leave the gate. We need you to sit down if you can.'

The flight attendant is back at my side. I've got an aisle seat right next to Fiona's stretcher. We haven't put the curtains up around it yet so I can sit and watch her as we taxi to the end of the runway then lift up into the air. With all the turbulence of take-off it's impossible to really see Fiona's breathing. The moment they click off the seat belt signs I'm on my feet and all is well. Fiona's eyes are closed. She might be asleep, she might just be trying to shut us all out. Either way is fine. Rose is at my side and I give her a smile. She grips my hand.

'This is better, isn't it,' she says. 'It's not like my daughter to make a fuss.'

The crew help us give Fiona a bit more privacy with the curtains and as the meal carts are brought out a middle-aged lady approaches us. She's a nurse and she says she can watch over Fiona for a while if her mum or I want to eat or take a break. Rose doesn't say a word but she hugs her. Then, embarrassed, she turns back to her daughter and we continue with our vigil.

Fiona's children are waiting at the hospital in Stoke Mandeville when we arrive. It's late and they look exhausted. They've got a little home-made banner saying: 'Welcome Home Mum'. They're both good, strong kids. I've got a feeling they'll need to be.

It's gone ten by the time I say my goodbyes and head back to my flat. Once again I think it's probably too late to call Jackie so I send a quick text. She replies straight back. 'Textbook self-diagnosis. Well done us. Doctor only confirmed what I knew. Treatment a bore but I'll live. Taking next week off. Let's have dinner when I'm back. Pizza's on me. Jackle.'

'Who is Jackle and why are there pizzas on her?' I reply with a big silly smile on my face. If Jackie's really dealing with this then she's going to be fine. I still can't quite believe she took over a month to see a doctor, but better late than never. I open my front door just after midnight and realise I've not really eaten anything all day. All I can find in my kitchen is a packet of dehydrated potatoes, a tin of tuna and some tomato ketchup. I'm so hungry that they seem to mix up surprisingly well.

I sleep till gone ten the next morning. Lately I've got into a routine of doing two jobs a week, though if we're busy or they're all short-haul I sometimes fit in three. In general I reckon I sleep in my own bed three or four nights out of seven. It's not so bad, as long as I can mix up the early starts and the late-night finishes. Jackie's been great at showing me how to stop the job taking over my life entirely.

'Just accept that your mobile phone bill will be huge. Ring friends every time you're stuck on the Piccadilly line or sitting at the departure gate at the airport,' she says. 'Meet up with people even if you're too jet-lagged to stand. It's better to go to the pub and just stay an hour than not to see anyone at all. If you don't have to fly somewhere till the evening then meet your friends at lunchtime. It's not easy, but it's not as hard as it sounds.'

Today I'm taking her advice. I'm heading to my old hospital at midday to join some of my old colleagues in the canteen. Then I'm doing a big shop so I've got more food in my cupboards next time I get back on a late flight. I'm also tackling my laundry. All things considered I'm feeling pretty good when I head back to the office in the early evening.

I fly out of Stansted at ten. It's a no-frills charter
flight, which isn't great, but the job itself promises to be a
breeze. I'm going to Skiathos in Greece where one of the
lecturers on a Mediterranean cruise ship is recuperating
after a nasty fall on an island excursion. Her boat had
to sail on without her and after two nights in hospital
she's been moved into a local hotel. The reports we've
had suggest that she is still too frail to make it home on
her own. I've got to say I'm glad I'm meeting her in a
hotel. The last time I went into a hospital on one of the
Greek islands I got the shock of my life. My patient was
a twenty-two-year-old girl who had suffered a series of
seizures. She was literally shackled to her bed. The whole
scene was part medieval, part *One Flew Over the Cuckoo's
Nest*. If anything like that had happened in Britain the
press would have had a field day. Out on the island no one
apart from me seemed to think there was anything even
slightly wrong about it.

This time around my patient should be in a lot better
shape. The accident wasn't particularly dramatic. She twisted
her ankle, fractured her right wrist, damaged her elbow and
took quite a blow to her nose. I'm guessing she'll have two
big panda eyes – and probably won't be happy about them.
Her wrist has been set in a whole arm plaster cast and she
can't walk unaided but she should recover well once she's
home. There are a few complications in her medical history,
which is why I've got the job rather than a nurse. She's had
a heart valve replacement three years ago and is on lifelong
blood thinning medication. That means there's an outside
chance she could have a cardiac problem on the flight. The
only unusual thing about the job is the way Robbie hands
me the file. He gives me a giant comedy wink and tells me

I'll get the surprise of my life when I get there and meet the patient.

'Why? Is it your mum? My mum? A celebrity? A drag queen?' I ask. Then I remember Robbie is supposed to be finding me a new girlfriend. 'Even you wouldn't set me up with someone in her seventies. What's going on?'

Robbie just smiles. 'Be ready for a life-changing experience,' he says.

My flight isn't much fun – and not just because it's charter hell and indescribably cramped. You get a strange feeling when you're the only working person on a plane full of holidaymakers and families. There are a few big groups of people all travelling together and making a lot of noise. Everyone else boards two-by-two, or with their partners and kids. Everyone is relaxed and looking forward to a week or so away from reality. I always worry that if they knew what I was flying out for they'd run back to the terminal and stay at home. Being a repatriation doctor makes you the biggest party pooper in the air.

Today, I get lucky. I'm sitting next to a teenager who's plugged into his music from the moment he sits down and doesn't want to talk. Like all doctors I can sleep instantly almost anywhere. I get in a couple of hours then stare out of the window trying to spot the island's lights as we approach. I don't think I'll ever lose the thrill of flight or the excitement of landing.

It's late September and the Greek island air is wonderfully warm when we troop down the plane steps and walk towards the terminal. It's two in the morning and I'll be back here in less than twenty-four hours to head back to

Britain. In the meantime I'm being paid to look out across the dust of a warm Greek island and into the blackness of the Aegean Sea. No one could complain about that.

I've got a wad of euros in my pocket. Sometimes you need to spend quite a lot to make a repat go smoothly and claim it all back later. Other times pretty much everything is already covered. Tonight it's just the taxi into Skiathos Town where Robbie has booked me into the same hotel as my patient.

Everything is quiet when I climb out of my cab. A bored-looking guy is sitting on the hotel reception. He's got my room key ready, gives me the briefest of smiles then turns back to his computer game. Then I walk into a mini-paradise.

From the outside the building hadn't looked very exciting. Inside it's lovely. My room is big, white and cool. The bed is huge and seems to have dozens of pillows as well as crisp, clean sheets. A tray on the table in front of it has a plate of bread rolls, fruit, meats and cheeses. There's a jug of coffee being kept warm by a set of tea lights and a little note saying there is fresh orange juice in the fridge. Best of all, there are two French windows leading out on to a terrace that's almost as big as the room itself. It's right on the water. Soft waves bubble up and fall back a few feet beneath me. I can see the outlines of boats out in the distance and while there's no moon, the sky is alive with stars. I sit out there with my coffee and feel as if nothing in the world can ever go wrong again. This is the kind of hotel you dream of finding for a holiday but hardly ever do. It's the kind of place you almost never get when you're travelling on business. I don't know if it's Camilla, Christine or Robbie who tracked it down. But I'll need to buy more than Toblerone to thank them.

I tear myself away from the terrace around three and

snuggle up for the best and deepest sleep I've had in ages. The late nights and early starts of this job do catch up on you. I hadn't expected to pay off any sleep debt on this quick trip.

In the morning I head down to the front desk where last night's bored young guy has been replaced by a fresh-looking older man.

'Hello, I'm Doctor Ben MacFarlane. I arrived in the middle of the night. I'm here to help bring one of your other guests home, a lady called Professor Frances Ashworth.'

The man holds out his hand. 'My name's Bill. Welcome to Skiathos. Was your room okay and did you sleep well?'

'I slept incredibly well. And thank you to whoever left the food and coffee. That was really thoughtful.'

He dismissed it with a shrug. 'Now, you want Frances. That could be a problem.'

'I'm sorry?'

He's smiling. 'Because we're not sure we want to let her go.'

'What do you mean?'

'She's quite a character. In fact she's a complete riot. You're her doctor, aren't you?'

'I'm the doctor who's been sent to help her home. I'm not her GP and I haven't met her before. What's the big mystery?'

My host takes a quick look at his watch. 'You'll have to wait and see. In the meantime we can bring breakfast to your terrace or you can have it on our roof. I can't imagine that Frances will surface for a while. To be honest, you probably only missed her by half an hour or so when you arrived last night. Like I say, she's quite a character.'

I head up to the hotel's roof for breakfast. It's even more beautiful than my terrace. There are tall plants in huge earthenware pots and several teak steamer chairs are pointing towards the early morning sun. Around one corner there are amazing views over the Aegean. Around the other there are rooftop views of the town. It looks as if Skiathos is only just shaking sleep from its eyes. When I look towards the town I see a scattering of people putting up parasols, setting out chairs and tables and laying out breakfast. It could hardly feel more relaxing.

The commotion begins while I'm pouring myself a second cup of strong, dark coffee.

'Steady, boys, steady! To the left, young man, to the left. Watch for that step. I won't be dropped, I'll tell you. I'm fragile enough as it is.'

Fragile, I soon decide, is not quite the word for Professor Frances Ashworth. No wonder the ship's doctor deemed her capable of looking after herself on the island as they all headed on down towards Istanbul. She is being carried on a sort of makeshift sedan chair by Bill from the front desk and another man. My first impression is that if anyone suits being carried around like a Pharaoh it's this lady. She's wearing a wildly eccentric silk kimono. I get a waft of her perfume and she's still twenty feet away. She has a 'Harrods helmet' hairstyle that looks as if it could survive nuclear war. Huge dark sunglasses cover most of her face – I guess I was right about her being embarrassed by her panda eyes. But it's not just my patient's looks that set her apart. She acts like a grand old lady from central casting as well. I get a regal wave as she approaches. She's like a memsahib from imperial India. The kind of no-nonsense character who helped Britain win an Empire and never really accepted the fact that it had been lost.

'You must be my doctor. These are my boys,' she booms grandly as she is carried to my side. Bill and the other man give wry smiles. 'Set me down here. No, not there, set me here in the sunshine. No sense in wasting it,' she says as they try to settle her. This is clearly someone who wasn't brought up to worry about skin cancer.

She settles herself on a lounger. Her right arm, supported in its sling, is held up towards her neck. She holds out her left in greeting. I get an awful feeling that I'm supposed to kiss it. I make do with a handshake and have a sudden feeling that I have failed my first social test.

'I am Frances Ashworth. As you can see I've had a little bit of trouble with my wrist,' she says. 'That is the bad news. The good news is that I've been having a far more marvellous time in this hotel than I ever did with on the cruise ship. So if you want to lie to my insurance company and say I need to stay here till the end of the season then I'll remember you in my will.'

'Frances, you said last night that I would get the lot,' says the second of her 'boys'.

'Last night, as you know full well, I was as drunk as the proverbial skunk. Now go downstairs and get me my breakfast.'

'I told you she was a riot. Good luck telling her what to do,' Bill says before heading down the central stairway with the other man.

'Marvellous young men,' she breathes as they disappear. I like the way she talks in short, staccato bursts. 'Now, I expect you want to know how foolish I was and why I've ended up here at all?'

'You had a nasty fall?'

'I certainly did. I'm quite mortified by it. I'll have you

know that seven years ago I did a parachute jump to
celebrate my seventieth birthday. I raised eight thousand
pounds for my local hospice and I didn't so much as break
a fingernail. I have photographs showing I didn't have so
much as a hair out of place. Then I walk on to the marble
floor of an old church and end up in a wheelchair. You
won't want to see what I look like behind these sunglasses,'
she adds. 'I asked one of the boys to buy me the largest and
darkest pair he could find. I told him to think Jackie Onassis.
I fear he was edging closer to Roy Orbison. I shall take
them off and reveal my face to you once I know you a little
better. Now, could you be an absolute darling and pour me a
coffee before I fade away with thirst?'

I do as I'm told. She has more to say. 'Now you can see I
am keeping my spirits up by enjoying my time in this hotel
but I have to tell you I'm very disappointed in myself. I have
no idea how I shall explain it to my friends at home. They'll
think it's the beginning of the end for all my travels.'

'Do you mind if I take a look at your injuries up here? Or
we can go to your room if you prefer?'

My patient dismisses the idea of going back downstairs.
'I'm not leaving the sun for a single second,' she says with
spirit. 'Examine away.'

I look at her cast, check her pulse and listen to her heart
and chest. 'And the sunglasses?' I say.

'If you insist. But I'll warn you it isn't pretty.' She takes
them off.

'Well, I've certainly seen a lot worse,' I tell her as I
examine her face. It's all just superficial bruising, made
worse by her blood thinning tablets.

'So will I live?'

'To be a hundred, I'd imagine.'

'Well, I'll settle for that. Must I really leave this little
corner of paradise? No chance of even a tiny little white lie
on my insurance form? I'm sure I could fly home unaided
in about a month. Wouldn't that be cheaper and easier all
round?'

'It wouldn't be very good for me if it got me struck off the
medical register.'

She calls me a spoilsport as Bill returns with her breakfast
tray.

'I think this would be a good moment for me to leave you
to your little corner of sunshine, Miss Ashworth,' I say.

I head down to my room to read through the lady's notes
one last time. The local hospital has sent her X-rays over on
a disc, which is pretty impressive. There's nothing unusual
about any of her fractures and her blood results all look fine
as well. I call the office and confirm we are fit to fly.

'We're aiming to get you on a flight out at 9:15 this
evening but we'll confirm it within an hour,' says Robbie.
It's not even midday and I've got the whole of the afternoon
and most of the evening to while away on the island.

'Been sunbathing at the hotel yet?' Robbie asks,
mysteriously, when he calls back to confirm our
reservations.

'No, why?'

'No reason. Just don't forget factor 15 for your white bits,'
he chortles before hanging up.

It's not till late afternoon when I finally find out what
the joke is all about. I've spent a lovely few hours walking
around the old town and had a rich green Greek salad for
lunch on the edge of a tiny cobbled square. Then I get back
to the hotel. I pick up my book and head up to the roof. As
I step out on to it I hear the now familiar boom of a laugh

from Frances. I head round towards the back of the deck where the sun loungers are. Bill nearly bumps in to me as he heads down the stairs back to the reception.

'Up for a bit of sunbathing?' he asks. What is it with sunbathing in this place?

'No, I thought I'd just read a bit in the sun. I've not actually brought any—'

'Swimming trunks?' he finishes as my words fall away.

I've turned the corner and am looking at an extraordinary tableau. Frances is in the middle of the roof terrace, all draped in silk and propped up on a bed of cushions. She is surrounded by no less than seven men lying on sun loungers. Seven completely naked men. Robbie has booked me into a gay, nudist hotel. No wonder he's so keen to know how I'm getting on.

The night flight home could have been dull in comparison with the riotous conversations we'd had on that roof terrace. Frances makes sure that it's not. She simply won't stop talking. She steamrollers complete strangers with pure charm so she's got a new little gang of followers in the departure lounge. In the air the natural assumption seems to be that the entire cabin crew are there specifically for her and need only pay passing attention to the other 150 or so other passengers.

For all this ebullience it's interesting to have seen one other side to the remarkable Frances as we had approached the airport terminal just after seven in the evening. It gets dark relatively early on the island and Frances clearly hadn't wanted to take off her crazy sunglasses.

'Call me a vain old fool but it's bad enough having an

arm in a cast I don't want complete strangers to think I'm
the kind of doddering old wrinkly who walks into doors,' she
said.

'Frances, do you want me to tell you a secret?' I told her
about the last lady I took on a flight with huge, black panda
eyes. A glamour model who had complications after flying
to Brazil for a boob job and a face lift.

'So if I take these off people will assume I've had a boob
job? How bloody marvellous,' she roared. She handed her
sunglasses to a young girl who happened to be standing
near us. Then, once we had checked in and gone through
security, I found us a couple of seats where we could wait
for pre-boarding.

'Frances, if it's okay with you, I'm not going to take your
pulse every ten minutes or do anything silly like that on
the flight. You let me know if you feel unwell at any point.
Other than that no one need know that you're a patient and
I'm your doctor.'

She gave me a grand, imperious look and puffed out
her not inconsiderable chest. 'You're not my doctor,' she
declared. 'Ever since I gave away those blasted sunglasses
I've been a glamour model. You, young man, are my toy
boy!'

OCTOBER

I get back to base just after midnight and put a yellow Post-it note on Robbie's computer screen.

'Very funny. But if I were you I'd check your brakes before driving your car down any steep hills from now on. And no, you can't see my white bits.'

When I see him the next day he has a bit of a laugh when I tell him what happened. But my story isn't the big news of the day. We've had a call about a woman whose first name is Catherine and whose much older husband has had a water-skiing accident in Barbados. It's a private job and they're paying for a top spec air ambulance to take them back to South Wales.

'It's Catherine Zeta Jones. It's Michael Douglas. It has to be. I'll kill to get this job,' Robbie's saying. Apparently no one has been as excited since Jackie was told 'The Palace has approved you' when she got allocated a repatriation from the Caribbean in the late 1990s. She was convinced it was a repat for Princess Margaret who had just slipped and fallen at her house on Mustique. That job was cancelled the morning Jackie was due to fly so she never found out the truth.

We don't get to meet Hollywood royalty this time around

either. Bilal does the pick-up. He discovers that there is a Catherine, there is an older husband and there is a private flight to Cardiff. But no one on board has ever won an Oscar.

'They were a nice couple but he's something very high up in the tax office and she's a lawyer,' he tells us when he gets back four days later.

I'm catching up on my expense claims when our post gets delivered. I've got a postcard from Alicia Hughes, the gap-year girl I'd brought home from Italy. We rarely hear anything about our patients once we've dropped them off so it's great to get some feedback. Alicia has certainly recovered well. The card's from Australia.

'I'm not going to run a marathon any time soon but I'm mobile again and I've joined the rest of the gang on this part of the trip. Sydney is fabulous. Thank you so much again for seeing me through Rome airport and beyond. Happy travelling.'

I pin the card on the wall and pop into Jackie's office to see if she's finished work. She's back after her week off and we're off for our pizza tonight. We head to an Italian restaurant in Hounslow. It's somewhere the team go to now and then for birthdays or leaving parties. Fortunately, there are no familiar faces there tonight. We talk about business until our drinks arrive. Jackie looks tired and strained and all of a sudden I forget about Alicia's postcard and all the jokes I've had with Robbie and the others back in the office. Suddenly everything feels very serious. I can't avoid the subject any longer.

'So how did it go with the neurologist?' There's something ridiculously evasive about Jackie's answer. I try again. 'Did you see him at Queen's Square or did you go private?'

I still don't get a direct answer. Jackie won't meet my

gaze. We order our food and sit in silence. Something is very clearly wrong. My mind is working overtime as I try to work out what it could be.

'There's something else, isn't there,' I say eventually. 'Will you tell me what it is?'

'I haven't told anyone yet.'

'Well, you know you can trust me. I won't tell a soul. Maybe I can help.'

There's another endless pause. Then Jackie takes a deep breath and goes for it. 'Ben, it's not about the seizure in the Maldives. I've found out something else since then.'

'What is it?'

There's another long silence. I have no idea where this is going and Jackie clearly doesn't want to talk.

'Give me a moment,' she tells me as our food arrives. We both play around with what's on our plates for a while then she puts her knife and fork down.

'I found a lump in my breast a few weeks ago,' she says in a rush.

'So you think you've got breast cancer?'

A very weak smile. 'I know that I have. I know something else as well. Why do you think I had that seizure out in the Maldives? It wasn't tiredness or stress and it wasn't epilepsy. I've been thinking about it every day. It must have been triggered by secondaries. The cancer has already spread to my brain. It caused the fit. So it's too late. There's nothing anyone could do even if I were in hospital right now.' I'm looking at her in shock.

'So you've not seen anyone about this? Not the fit, not the lump, nothing? Jackie, you have to get this checked out. There's always something that can be done. You should be in treatment right now.'

'Ben. I'm a doctor, I know what I've got. I know what can and can't be done.'

'But you know better than to do nothing. You can't ever make assumptions on things like this.'

Jackie holds her hands out to me, trying to calm me down. 'Ben, listen to me. I'm a single mum. I have three children. Joe is only ten. I've spent my entire career seeing what serious illness does to families. I won't put my children through that.'

'But this is crazy.'

'It's crazy to you. Not to me.'

We sit in silence again for what feels like for ever. But I can't keep it all inside.

'So does Martin know?'

Jackie's on good terms with her ex-husband. He looks after their kids when she travels.

'I'm deciding who to tell right now.'

The waiter takes away our uneaten food. He looks about to ask us if there's a problem but stops himself. It must be clear we're not there for the food. My mind is racing as he walks away, trying to keep up with the implications of what Jackie has said. She's sitting opposite me, looking broken, lost and vulnerable. But I know, suddenly, that this is not the time to be kind. In medicine you need to talk tough sometimes to get your message across. This is one of those moments.

'How can doing nothing about cancer be the best thing for your children? What if you die, Jackie? What if you die before you get the chance to speak to them? Or what if doing nothing means you have less time with them than you could have done?'

'That's exactly what I'm weighing up right now.'

'But it's been months since the Maldives. This is crazy.'

'Well I only felt the lump a few weeks ago. I am dealing with it. I'm talking to you, aren't I? I've worked out who I need to see to get this diagnosis sorted, and I'm just getting ready to make the calls.'

'You don't need to make any calls. You can get to a walk-in clinic within twenty-four hours. You can sort this out this week.'

'Look I am going to do something. It's been a shock and it's been one thing after another but you have to trust me, Ben. Now, tell me about your love life. I'm well overdue a good laugh.'

To be honest, I can't remember what we do talk about for the rest of the evening. I'm still in shock that a medical professional – my medical director – can bury her head in the sand about something so important. The self-diagnosis and denial is crazy. But it is ridiculously common in doctors. I read somewhere that denial is our biggest killer, after suicide. That's not something they teach us in med school.

'Jackie, I don't want to hound you, but you know I have to, don't you? You need to go and see someone. Is there any real reason why you shouldn't go to see someone tomorrow?' I ask as Jackie gets into a cab.

'Tomorrow, Jackie, see somebody tomorrow,' are my last words as she sets off. I can't hear her reply.

I'm not in the office for long enough to see what Jackie does the next day. We've got a new recruit, a twenty-four-year-old nurse called Rebecca and I'm heading to Morocco with her in an air ambulance. I've got two reasons for looking forward to the trip. First, it's a nice change to do a job with someone else. Secondly, everyone says Rebecca is going

to be great company. She's spent the past two weeks on
the logistics desk and gets on like a house on fire with the
whole team. Camilla and Christine both like mothering her
and Robbie wants her to be his new best friend.

'She's brilliant,' he told me at the end of her first week.
'When we went to the pub none of the men could take
their eyes off her. She's going out with some builder from
Southfields, but we spent the whole night holding hands
and pretending we were a couple. You should have seen all
the guys' faces. It was hilarious.'

Camilla, though, has spotted something else. 'You will
have to look after her,' she says when she hands me the
latest case notes. 'She's not as confident as she looks. She
says she wants to travel but she's nervous about looking
after patients on her own. So far she's only done one job,
bringing a broken bones case back from Porto. I thought it
would help her to do a job with someone else. You can show
her how easy it is.'

I promise to take care of her. This Morocco job has us
there and back in a day, so even if Rebecca's freaked out by
it she'll be back in her own bed tonight. The wild card will
be the air ambulance itself. She'll either love it or she'll hate
it. I know I made a total fool of myself the first time I flew
in one. No one had told me that the really basic planes don't
have fully pressurised cabins. I hadn't had time for lunch so
I'd picked up a couple of packets of crisps in the terminal.
The bags exploded when we got to our cruising altitude.
Forget the patient. I thought I was the one that was going to
have a heart attack.

Things picked up on my second trip. That was the one
that really got me hooked on life as a flying doctor. It was
in a six-seater Gulfstream jet. I was working with one of

our older nurses, a lady called Denise who had been doing repatriations for more than twenty years. We were picking someone up from Durban in South Africa and the whole experience had been incredible. Our plane left from a tiny little airport in Kent. The terminal wasn't flash, but I felt like a millionaire when I looked out the windows and saw all the private planes. I felt like a billionaire when I headed out and climbed into one. Ours was lavish. The seats were basically armchairs made of rich, soft brown leather. The floor was covered in thick, pale cream carpets. Forget ancient stains on plastic meal trays. All the surfaces on the plane gleamed and we had freshly cut flowers in crystal glass vases on every table. I seem to remember that there was even an oil painting on the loo wall.

'I think I could get used to this,' I said to Denise as we nosed about before take-off. It kept getting better. Our pilot joined us for a bit of a chat before disappearing into the cockpit.

'Good choice of seat, by the way,' he said to me as he walked away. He mentioned the name of one of the most famous supermodels. 'She was sitting in that seat yesterday. Though sitting is probably the wrong word. She was having very noisy sex with one of her photographers. You enjoy your flight now.'

Denise and I cracked open the mini-bar once we were airborne. Maxi-bar would probably be a better description. There were full-size bottles of every type of booze you could imagine. We looked through some amazing vintages, drank out of crystal glasses - and then got our sandwiches out.

'Talk about being brought back down to earth with a bump,' I said. 'I bet no one else ever brings a packed lunch on a plane like this.'

We refuelled twice and got to Durban after about eighteen hours in the air. Denise had been great company. She had a thousand funny stories to tell about different jobs she had done over the years. She was also the queen of office gossip. I don't think I'll ever be able to look at some of my colleagues in the eye again. Or use the shower beside the lifts.

It was all a lot quieter on the way back. Our patient was a twenty-two-year-old man from Northern Ireland who had been in a car accident just outside Durban. Among many other injuries he had ruptured his aorta – the biggest artery in the body. He'd had major surgery and two weeks in intensive care. He could just about have got back on a stretcher on a commercial flight, but even if we'd found an airline that would have taken him it would have involved two plane changes with two long layovers. In the end his insurance company had booked the private plane.

'Are you comfortable, Mr Reid?' Denise had asked just before we took off on the way home.

He had nodded, but he hadn't said a word. In the hospital we had judged him to be stable, but still almost catatonic with shock. He had barely spoken when we had assessed him as ready to travel. He remained silent for the entire flight. He didn't close his eyes, let alone sleep. He simply lay there, surrounded by extraordinary luxury but lost deep within himself.

'That poor, poor boy,' Denise had said downing a glass of vodka in one after we had dropped him off in Belfast. We were on our own in the plane again as we headed back to Kent. On the way down to South Africa we had joked about getting blind drunk on this last patient-less leg of the journey. When the moment came neither of us were in the mood.

Today I've got my fingers crossed that Rebecca's first time in a private plane goes well. But it looks as if it might be touch and go. She really is nervous about the job and looks as if she'll need as much hand-holding as the patient.

'All I've done so far is look after an old lady with a plaster cast,' she says in the taxi to Luton Airport as we look at the case notes for our job. 'This one's in a different league. The guy's seriously ill, Ben. I don't know if I'm ready for it.'

'You'll be fine and the patient will be fine. There are two of us so we'll watch each other's backs. Even if something goes wrong it's a whole lot easier to deal with in a private plane than on a normal flight. We've got the right equipment and we'll have plenty of room to move. There really isn't anything to worry about.'

Unfortunately for Rebecca, that isn't quite true. Our patient's name is Warwick Cadogan. He's a fifty-four-year-old businessman from South London. He had been working in Morocco for nearly a month when he had a cardiac arrest. He has been on the coronary care unit of a hospital in Rabat for four days. In normal circumstances we would leave him there a while longer to stabilise. This, however, is a private job. The client is paying for his own repatriation and wants to get home as soon as possible. I can veto the trip if I assess him as unfit to travel. But I'll need a very good reason.

We're not booked on a Lear jet or Gulfstream today. Mr Cadogan has hired a full-spec air ambulance, the kind of airborne ICU ward that can transport people out of war zones.

At Luton I stand aside on the tarmac so Rebecca can board before me. That was probably a mistake. If she was scared before then she's terrified now.

'Oh my god, Ben, this is pretty hardcore, isn't it?'

In our cab out to the airport I'd told my supermodel story and described some of the other super-flash planes I'd been in recently. Poor Rebecca had obviously been expecting something similar. This isn't it. The cabin is tiny. You can almost reach both sides by stretching out your arms. You can get from front to back in about six paces. The ceiling curves above and around us so you can only stand upright in the middle of the plane. Today there are no big chairs, thick cream carpets or oil paintings in the loo – though at least we've got a loo, which isn't always the case. What we do have is a mass of hard edges, electronic monitors, wires and machines. There are defibrillators, ventilators, cardiac monitors – everything you need for a critical care flight. What make me smile are the yellow triangular 'No Smoking' signs. You would have to want a cigarette really badly to consider lighting up in here.

'There's not much room, is there?' Rebecca says as we try and find space for our medical bags.

'There's the bed. It's a long trip, you could grab forty winks on that,' I say.

Rebecca looks at the white stretcher bed that takes up around half the space in the cabin. 'Ben, that is way too creepy. It would be like sleeping in a coffin.'

We settle for the pull-down jump seats.

'I don't exactly feel like a rock star,' Rebecca says.

I tell my exploding crisp packet story to try and put her mind at rest a bit. That was a mistake as well.

'How low does the air pressure go?' she asks, horrified.

'What does that mean for the patient's heart or breathing when we get him on here? Ben, I should never have put myself up for this.' She looks around her again. 'You need someone more senior for this. I don't think I know what half this equipment does.'

'Rebecca, it is going to be OK. This all looks a lot worse than it is. I can talk you through some of the kit when we get going if you want. But I bet we don't need to use anything more than a vomit bowl on the way back. We'll only need that if we hit turbulence. Otherwise it'll just be an easy four-hour flight. You'll get a job in a Lear jet next time, I swear.'

She does her best to smile across at me. It's not that convincing. If our patient does anything more than vomit on our return journey then I've got a feeling this will be the last job she does.

My worst fears are confirmed when we get to Rabat and visit our patient in hospital. He really does look too weak to move.

'You've been in the wars, Mr Cadogan,' I say. 'How are you feeling?'

He attempts a shrug. 'The staff here have all been pretty decent. They've patched me up as best they can. Now I want to get home.'

'That's why we're here. We just don't want to move you till you're ready.'

He's not too weak to frown. 'I've been through this enough times with your company, doctor. I accept your opinions as the medical experts but I do know my own capabilities and my limits. I also know that I've got a baby

119

daughter at home who is growing and changing every day.
I didn't spend any time with my first kids. I don't want to
make the same mistake again.'

'We're really only talking about a matter of days till
you're much stronger. An extra week at the most would
probably be our recommendation.'

He dismisses the idea with another half shrug. 'Can you
just check me over and then tell me if I'm safe to fly? I've
been out here for a month already. Every day does matter
to me, doctor. I'll let you drug me into a coma and fly me
home in a box of ice if that's what it takes. I want to be with
my family. I want you to make it happen.'

I do my usual examination. His pulse seems regular, if a
little weak. His blood pressure is okay. There's possibly a bit
of fluid in his lungs, which is quite common after a heart
attack. I don't really want to fly him home, but I can't put
my finger on any specific reason to refuse.

'The plane is here?' he asks when I give him my verdict.

'We flew in on it this morning.'

'So let's fly home this afternoon. If you'll excuse me I
want to call my wife.'

If he hadn't been so pale already I'd say Mr Cadogan went
even whiter when he was stretchered on board. Maybe he
had been expecting a corporate jet, just like Rebecca. He
gets a shock when he sees his new surroundings. He stays
silent as we strap him on to his bed. I can see his eyes
taking in all the medical equipment around him. Depending
on your level of squeamishness, being so close to all of this
kit can either reassure or terrify you. With Mr Cadogan it
seems to be the latter.

Rebecca tries to take his mind off it by asking about his baby girl. His eyes soften. His whole face becomes warmer. It turns out he's recently got a new, and much younger, wife.

'I promised her that if we started a family I'd work less and spend more time at home. Then I go and get a contract in Morocco and have a heart attack at the end of my first visit.' He starts to talk about his baby again but stops abruptly. 'I'm tired, now. Let's talk later,' he says. This really is a man who knows his own limits.

We're cleared for take-off, thunder down the runway and fight our way through the clouds to our cruising altitude. It feels a bit of a battle, to be honest. We're buffeted quite badly and it seems a lot noisier than it did on the way out. Rebecca and I have agreed to take it in turns checking our patient's vital signs, though as we're both on jump seats no more than three feet from him we're unlikely to miss anything. She still looks tense and strained. I see her checking her watch all the time. She's clearly as keen as our patient for the flight to be over.

One hour into it and Mr Cadogan is breathing clearly and his pulse is regular and as strong as it's likely to be. An hour and a half in he's calm and starting to look a little bored. Two hours in and he's still doing fine. It's almost exactly half an hour later that it goes wrong. It's my turn to stand up to check him. I can tell straight away that everything has changed. Our razor sharp, straight-talking businessman is looking glazed and muddled. In a heart patient that's a very bad sign.

'Are you all right Mr Cadogan? Sorry about all this turbulence.'

All I get in response is a blank look and a strange, sickly

grin. That's very bad. I flash a look at Rebecca and get my second fright. She's well aware of what's going on. She looks as bad as our patient.

'Stay with me, Rebecca, we're going to be fine. Mr Cadogan, are you hearing me? Are you still with me?'

The same blank look and sickly grin. His face looks as if it's made out of wax. We need to check this out fast. I grab the red, yellow, green and black leads of the cardiac monitor, reciting the old 'ride your green bike' mnemonic in my head to hook them all up in the right order. I look at the spikes on the screen. I want to see a narrowly spaced, regular pattern. I don't. Mr Cadogan's spikes are widening in front of my eyes. In seconds they become a chaotic, wiggly line.

'He's in VF.' I shout at Rebecca, even though she's right next to me. I think it's the very last thing she wanted to hear. Ventricular Fibrillation means the heart's normal activities have gone awry. 'It turns the heart into a useless, quivering blob,' was how a lecturer at my med school had always put it. 'If you're going to get it back you need to act fast.'

Before doing anything else I lean over Mr Cadogan to deliver a precordial thump. A heck of a pre-cordial thump. I bring the side of my clenched fist down hard on the man's breast bone. The idea is to generate a low-grade electrical shock in his body. It can be enough to bring the heart back to order. It's something you can only really do once and it isn't enough today. I feel for a pulse in Mr Cadogan's neck; I already know I won't find one. At that moment the plane suddenly lurches to the left. After half an hour of relatively smooth air the last thing we need is more turbulence.

'We've got problems back here. We need it smooth', I yell

at our pilots. 'Come on, Mr Cadogan. Come back to us,' I shout to his unconscious body as I check the ECG monitor. It's still not showing what I want to see. Now I look to my right. Rebecca is standing with one white-knuckled hand gripping the stretcher rail and the other clamped to her mouth in horror. She looks terrified. Her eyes are sweeping around our tiny cabin, looking at the walls of equipment as if she has no idea why she's here. Thank God we talked through all the kit on the way out here. I'm praying that her training will kick in any moment. Emergency medicine is about instinct as much as anything else. If this man is going to survive we don't have time for much else.

'There's no output Rebecca. I need you to start chest compressions. Are you ready for that? Rebecca? Look at me.'

Finally she snaps herself alive. 'Chest compressions. Yes, I'm ready,' she says.

I try to smile at her but I can't. I don't have the time. She leans over Mr Cadogan's chest as I flick the switch on the defibrillator. I want it charged to 200 joules for our first shock. Rebecca begins the compressions. They aim to do the job of the heart, to move blood to the patient's brain and vital organs. They're hard work. Rebecca pushes down on his chest and gets the rhythm going. The deal is simple: one beat a second, a touch faster if you can. Don't worry about breaking ribs, just get that blood where it needs to go.

While Rebecca works on Mr Cadogan's chest I need to get him oxygen. I hold a mask to his face, sealing it over his mouth and nose. Then I deliver four short bursts of oxygen deep into his lungs. Rebecca's compressions should help deliver that to his brain and all around his system. Now it's time to shock him. I rip open his pyjama jacket. I tear open the foil pouch containing the defibrillator's jelly pads.

They're two cold pink squares. I slap one on the centre of his chest, the other on the left-hand side of his ribcage. As I do so Rebecca and I both need to brace against another sudden dip in altitude. What the hell has happened to our flight? 'Can you get us some smooth air?' I yell again.

Every time we take a dip I hear another cry from Rebecca. Her face is pale and tears have suddenly appeared in her eyes. She's coping but she's still on the edge.

'Rebecca, we're in control of this but we've just got to keep working.'

At that moment the defibrillator's whining reaches a crescendo. It's fully charged. But there's a problem.

'His arm,' I yell at Rebecca. It's pressed against the metal rail of his stretcher. She moves it and wedges part of the blanket alongside it to protect him from skin burns. Now we're ready.

'Stand clear,' I yell, purely out of habit. Under the low curved ceiling of the plane fuselage there's nowhere for either of us to go. I press the paddles to Mr Cadogan's chest, depress the buttons and his body lurches as the electrical charge surges through his body. We both stare at the monitor as the trace comes back on screen. He's still in VF.

'Carry on cardiac compressions,' I shout. I put the mask back on him and give him another burst of oxygen. I flick the charger to 360 joules. Whilst it's recharging I click the top off a phial of adrenaline and inject it through his cannula. Rebecca looks as if she could use some herself. Her eyes are going from the guy's chest to the ECG display every second. She's pumping the guy's chest with everything she has. Sixty beats per minute. Hard and deep and strong. Don't miss a beat. Just get him back.

'You're doing a great job, Rebecca, keep it up. We're going to get there. Next time we'll get there.' The defibrillator is charged. I put the paddles back on his chest. He lurches again as 360 joules power through him. This time he has to be back. I look at the monitors. He's still in VF. Bugger, bugger, bugger. I mask him and give him more oxygen.

Then Rebecca cries out. 'Ben, I'm so sorry. I need help here. I'm losing it.'

She looks wiped out. I'd forgotten how exhausting cardiac compressions can be.

'I'll take over. On the count of three.' We try to switch places fast, just as we hit a mini air pocket and take a lurch towards the back of the plane. Thank God Mr Cadogan is strapped in. I take a deep breath and begin pumping. Get the rhythm. Make him feel it. Forget about the ribs. As I pump his chest Rebecca masks him and gives him more oxygen. But we're still nowhere near getting this man back. We're also running out of time.

'Give him another shot of adrenaline,' I say.

'Ben, I'm not covered for IV injections.' Rebecca sounds distraught. She sounds as if she's crying.

'Rebecca, there's no one else here. Just do it.'

No more time to be nice. Our patient needs this now. Rebecca draws the meds up in a syringe and jabs it through the cannula in his arm. The defibrillator is fully charged. I move fast to get the paddles on his chest for the third time. 'Clear.' He gets the full 360 joules. This third shock runs through him. This time we've got it. We're both looking at the monitor. Yes, yes, yes. The spikes are coming back into a regular rhythm. My hand is back at Mr Cadogan's neck to feel a pulse. He's got an output. But I know this isn't over. His heart is pumping but his chest is still. He can't breath unaided. So we could still lose him.

'I'll have to tube him,' I say. It's not a pleasant or easy thing to do on solid ground. Right now I'm praying for some smooth air till the job's done. Rebecca reaches into the med bag and passes me a laryngoscope. It looks like an ice pick and it's what we use to guide a tube into a patient's windpipe. I lean over Mr Cadogan and push his head back. I slide the laryngoscope over his tongue. The scope has a light on the end and I'm using it. I'm peering down, trying to keep myself steady to see where the tube has to go. That's when the plane does another little lurch.

'This is hard,' I hear myself say.

'You can do it, Ben, I know you can. You're so close.' Rebecca sounds almost delirious.

'Just a little bit more. Come on, just a little. Come on. Where are you?' I'm talking out loud. Suddenly, it's there. I can see Mr Cadogan's vocal cords, like two half-closed lift doors. They're the big signpost I need on my route. I hold out my right hand. Rebecca places a clear plastic endotracheal tube in it. I pass it alongside the laryngoscope and guide its tip through those lift doors. I'm in. It's there. I'm breathing fast now. I remove the laryngoscope and connect the oxygen supply to the end of the tube. Mr Cadogan has been short of oxygen for some time. Now he can at least begin to stabilise. I quickly inflate the balloon to hold the tube in place and Rebecca helps me tie it in position with a long strip of gauze. His heart is beating. Now we need to breathe for him. On the ground we'd do it with a ventilator. Up here my right arm will be the ventilator for as long as he needs it, squeezing the oxygen bag every five seconds to give him another burst.

'We should set up a lignocaine infusion,' I say.

Lignocaine is used as a local anaesthetic and should stop Mr Cadogan's heart going back into fibrillation. Rebecca gets going. She does it. Then she looks at the heart monitor. Then at me.

'Ben, he's going to be okay, isn't he?' She's holding on to the stretcher rail so hard that I can almost see veins popping out of her arms. She's still a coiled wire of tension. I'm so glad I can finally tell her to relax.

'Rebecca, he is going to be okay. We did it. We really did it.'

It's freezing but I realise I've been sweating. Rebecca's face is just as flushed. She's breathing fast and is too hyper to sit down. So am I.

After our bumpy flight we at least get a smooth landing back at Luton. Mr Cadogan had regained consciousness about half an hour before we came in to land. He started coughing and gagging on the tube in his throat. I withdrew it carefully, gave him some oxygen then watched as his lungs rose and fell on their own accord. He could breathe unaided. He really was back. What a brilliant feeling. I told him very briefly what had happened, but it was hard to see if he had taken it all in. Like every patient, at this point he just wanted the drama to be over.

Rebecca and I watch him get stretchered out of the plane and lifted into a private ambulance. This whole job must be costing him tens of thousands of pounds. He has a doctor and a nurse to accompany him to a private hospital in West London where his wife and baby daughter are waiting to greet him. I step out of the plane and talk the doctor and

nurse through what had happened in the air. Then I wish Mr
Cadogan well and shake his hand. He isn't looking great, but
he is conscious.

'I don't know exactly what you did up there but thank
you. Both of you,' he says.

Back in the plane Rebecca is slumped in her seat. I tell her
we're free to go but she doesn't move.

'Are you okay?' I ask.

She shakes her head. 'I think I need a moment to get
myself together,' she says.

Behind her I can see our pilots shrugging their shoulders.
They must have been trying to speak to her while I was with
Mr Cadogan. A minute later Rebecca stands up. She picks up
her bag and smiles weakly at the pilots. 'Sorry about that, I
don't know what came over me.' We say our goodbyes and
head to terminal to clear immigration. When that's done I buy
Rebecca a can of Coke. I'm guessing she could use the sugar.

'Feeling better?' I ask when she's finished it.

She finally gives a weak smile. 'Not really, no. I'm still
shaking. I'm just so glad that's over.'

We climb into a taxi to take us back to the office and she
curls up on the back seat.

'I don't know what to think about what just happened,'
she says. 'We saved that man's life, which was incredible.
But it was also the most terrifying experience I've ever had.
I can't believe we had to do all that on our own. It was just
the two of us. If we'd done something wrong at any point
that man would have died.'

'But he didn't die. We did everything right. You're a
professional and you did an incredible job, Rebecca. You
should be so proud of what you did today.'

She looks across at me. She really does look exhausted.

'I think I'm going to close my eyes for a few moments,' she says.

She sleeps for the next half-hour or so and wakes just before we head into Hounslow. The doze seems to have done her a bit of good.

'Do you remember the flight out?' she asks suddenly, a touch of the old Rebecca back in her voice. 'You said that the worst thing would be a bit of vomit. Instead the guy goes and has a cardiac arrest and then he needs ventilating. A bit of vomit would have been a pleasure compared to all that. You and Robbie and Camilla are always going on about how great this job is but I think it's a giant lie. It's a conspiracy to give me a nervous breakdown.'

'You'll change your mind once you've had a proper night's sleep at home.'

'I don't think I'll change my mind after I've had counselling. I've joined an office full of absolute maniacs. Trust me, it will be a very long time before I go on a plane like that again.'

Jackie is just about to leave for the night when Rebecca and I arrive back with our bags. I put my head around her office door.

'Any progress? I ask her.

It seems that there is and she's ready to talk about it. She has had her shock; she has had her extended time in denial. Now she is attacking the situation with the precision and the focus of a military strike. She shows me a list of the specialists she is seeing.

'My God, Jackie, they're stellar. The Queen doesn't get to see all these people.'

'The Queen doesn't have my telephone manner. I've found the best and I haven't taken no for an answer.'

'So what have they said?'

'I'm only halfway down the list and I want second opinions as well. I'm on top of this. It's the best challenge I've had in years. I've made one very simple decision since we spoke that other evening. I'm going to face this down. I will not roll over and let it beat me.'

'Well I'm pleased you're going for it. Have you told anyone else yet? What about Martin?'

'I told him and he supports me absolutely. He agrees I'm doing exactly the right thing. He's ready to let the kids stay with him for as long as I need. We're all just waiting to get to the next stage of this now. I don't think this could have been handled any better or in any other way.'

Jackie's enthusiasm has always been infectious. She could carry all of us along with her if she wanted. She makes it impossible to believe that she won't beat this.

'What are you grinning about?' Camilla asks when I leave Jackie's office.

'Nothing. I've just got a very good feeling about the next few months.'

The next day I've got a quick overnight job to pick up a thirty-year-old man who forgot to duck at a vital moment on a learn-to-sail holiday in Croatia. Fortunately, the boom didn't hit his skull, but it did break his collarbone and dislocate his shoulder. He also broke his nose and cheekbone when he hit the deck.

He's great company, using his one free hand to show me all the photos on his camera and laughing away at his own expense over the accident. He's totally relaxed about the journey and we don't have a single problem on the flight. Why didn't Rebecca get a patient like this?

Straight afterwards I'm assigned another short-haul European pick-up. It's a dementia job, a confused old lady who had a bit of a breakdown in Portugal but is incredibly easy to manage. I stay in an amazing hotel in Faro with a four-poster bed and a vast wet room. The trip home goes smoothly from start to finish. I tell Rebecca about both jobs and about the hotel when I'm back in the office but I've got a feeling she doesn't believe me.

'If I'd been there they would have gone wrong somehow,' she says. 'Maybe the plane would have crashed. Or the wet room would have flooded. I swear to you I'm thinking of tearing up my passport. If working on the phones is good enough for everyone else then it's good enough for me. Just add me to the list when you're buying fancy chocolate and I'll be happy.'

Across the desk I see Camilla shake her head in exasperation. It's nice that she wants to bring Rebecca out of herself. But I've got a feeling this is one battle she might not win.

I'm about to say something when Jackie comes out of her office and heads over towards the coffee area. I've not had a chance to speak to her for nearly a week and I want to know how she's getting on with the specialists.

Jackie is pale. 'Sorry I didn't get the chance to reply to your texts, it's been madly busy in here,' she says. 'Now, I'll be quick. I've got very good news on the CT scan. There is no tumour. Whatever else caused the seizure in the Maldives it wasn't secondaries. That's one nightmare I can lay to rest.'

'That's wonderful news.'

'It is. But there is something else that's a bit more serious. I only found out yesterday so it's all a bit of a rush. I'm about to make an announcement to the whole office. I don't want to tell anyone else about the CT scan because you're the only one who knows about the seizure. But I need to share the rest of it with the whole team at the same time. I owe it to everyone to do it that way. I can't just send an email or ask someone else to pass on the news. Now, let me go back in first and wish me luck. I've made enough medical lectures in my time. I'm telling myself this is no different.'

I'm pretending to drink my coffee when Jackie makes it to our finance desk. She claps her hands and asks for quiet in the office. No one has ever done this before. I feel my heart start to thump. The news from the CT scan is brilliant. But what else is there? I'm trying to read the expression on her face. For a moment she almost looks as if she's smiling. I've no idea what that might mean.

'If the phones ring then answer them. Otherwise I've got an announcement to make,' she begins. 'Some of you might have been concerned about the way I have been acting lately. It's nothing to do with the company or its future. I'm going to keep this as brief and as factual as possible. A few weeks ago I found a lump on my breast. I had a mammogram and ultrasound scan and a fine needle aspiration. It was cancerous. I had a wide local excision and had samples of my lymph nodes taken. It seems that they removed the complete tumour. They contained all the cancer cells in it. The lymph nodes were also free of cancer. I don't need more surgery. I'm very pleased about all of this, as you can all imagine. I am going to have chemotherapy, however. I begin six cycles of treatment at the end of next week. It will all take around eighteen

weeks. I may well be able to come into the office for much
of this time, but I have chosen not to. I'll be doing some
work from home and I will be back.' She finally looks up
from the floor. I've never heard her speak with so little
emotion before. But here it comes.

'However bad this sounds it could have been so much
worse. I'd built it up in my mind to be much worse. I am
so sorry to have kept this from so many of you for so long.
You are all my friends here as well as my colleagues. I feel
better already for having spoken to everybody. Thank you.'

Jackie heads back into her office. She's not alone for
long. Camilla, Christine and several of our other old-timers
rush in after her. Through the glass wall the rest of us can
see a lot of hugs but no tears. They only start later, when
Jackie has left for the day. Christine is the first to need a
handkerchief. We all carry on answering the phones and
doing our jobs. But in every spare moment all everyone
talks about is Jackie – and what might happen to her now.
We deal with illness and injury every day but we're just as
lost as everyone else when it hits one of our own.

NOVEMBER

I ring my sister Lindsey to ask what she thinks I should buy Jackie for her last day in the office.

'A plant,' she says without a moment's hesitation. 'Flowers are for celebrations or commiserations so they're out. Chocolates are a bad idea if she's starting chemo. Books or DVDs would be good but you don't know what she's already got. So get a plant. You can't go wrong.' I love that my sister always makes decisions so quickly. She runs a catering company and could probably run the country.

I hand over the gift on Jackie's last day. She likes it so I probably ought to buy Lindsey one as well to thank her for the idea. Everyone else is taking Jackie out on a goodbye lunch but I'm on an early afternoon flight to Tunisia so I can't make it.

'If you want to moan or talk it through at any time just give me a call,' I say just before I leave. 'Ring in the middle of the night if you want. I'll probably be up with jet-lag so it will be nice to hear from you.'

Jackie gives me a quick hug. 'I'll bear that in mind,' she says. 'In the meantime you go out there and enjoy every minute of your next set of jobs. I'll be getting stir crazy at home without any travelling. I'll want to hear all the details and I'll be living through you so don't mope around and miss anything.'

I head out to my taxi trying to feel good about it all. I'm on my way to Tunis, which Jackie says is lovely. She's written down a few places I should see and I'm determined to make time for all of them. Better still, Camilla has booked me into a hotel with a pool on the roof. It's late afternoon when I arrive and I'm not due to see my patient and her doctor until the following morning. So I head up for a swim to get my blood moving after the flight. There's no one else there and the water is as still and reflective as a mirror when I dive in. Then it comes alive. The waves dance in the sunlight as I pull my way through the water. Every time my hands reach forward they seem to touch diamonds. I lie out in the sun for ten minutes or so after the swim. It's not that warm but it feels so good to have this place to myself. I feel like the king of the world.

I head down to change and get Jackie's list of sights. I take a mellow walk around the old walled town and grab a beer in a café she recommended. Some streets in Tunis seem dusty, silent and forgotten; others are alive with noise and smells and colour. It's a complete change of pace.

I get up at six the following morning so I can have another swim. Then it's back to business. I get my bag, check out and head to the hospital to meet my patient.

'Bonjour. Ahalan,' I say at the main reception desk. My guidebook wasn't clear if I should say hello in French or Arabic so I decide to try them both. Then I continue in English.

'Hello, my name is Doctor Ben MacFarlane. I'm here to meet one of your patients, an English lady called Carole Harman.'

After a lot of tapping away at her computer the lady at
the desk tells me very falteringly that there's a problem. She
promises that a doctor will be with me soon to explain. I
take another look at the case notes while I wait. Mrs Harman
has had a tough time. She'd been staying in a resort an
hour's drive along the coast and had been mugged going
to a bar with her daughter. The mugger had grabbed her
bag and her daughter told the tour rep she'd fought like a
tiger. That turned out to have been a mistake. By refusing
to let go of the bag she had been swung off her feet and
dragged off the pavement. When she hit the roadside she'd
cracked bones from her skull on down. She'd briefly lost
consciousness. She hadn't even saved her bag. Someone
else had grabbed it from her when she lay on the ground.

The ambulance staff had pumped her full of painkillers
on the way to the hospital. Their initial assessment had
been that she'd fractured her jaw as well as broken her
hip. A little later they discovered that Mrs Harman had
also had a heart attack in the ambulance that night. It had
probably been triggered by the heavy internal blood loss she
had suffered when her hip bone shattered. Its effects had
probably been masked by the painkillers. After assessing
the damage to her heart on the ECG the doctors had gone
ahead with the surgery and added pins and a plate to hold
her hip together. It was a big operation but the X-rays
show they did a decent job. They also took care of her as
she recovered. Her internal bleeding meant she couldn't be
given the usual clot-busting drugs you would expect after a
heart attack. Nor can she expect her heart to ever be quite as
strong again. The medical report faxed to us for translation
in London said that the doctors would normally have got
their patient up and walking two or three days after the

hip operation. They had waited a couple more to be on the safe side. Ultimately this seems to be the story of one very unlucky lady who had been incredibly lucky with her medical care. I'm about to discover that she doesn't quite see it that way.

'Hello, you are Doctor MacFarlane? I am Doctor Hadhri.'

'Bonjour. Ahalan. Nice to meet you.' The attending physician is a greying middle-aged man with a very direct gaze.

'You are here for Mrs Harman,' he says, raising his eyebrows quizzically for reasons I don't yet understand.

'Yes I am. I gather she has had a tough time but she's ready to be taken home?'

'I'm afraid I can't confirm that to you. You see, Mrs Harman is no longer in our care.'

'What do you mean?'

'I am not sure how this should be said. Mrs Harman is a difficult woman. She has a daughter and a granddaughter with her. They too are difficult women.'

This doesn't sound good.

'Where is Mrs Harman now?'

'She's outside,' the doctor tells me. 'She was told that someone was coming to take her home today so she discharged herself. She has wanted to leave for many days now. She wanted to be ready to leave just as soon as possible. If you go through to our smoking terrace you will find her. You will find the three of them.'

'Was she well enough to discharge herself?' As soon as I say it I wish I could bite the words back. I didn't mean to suggest he had let a sick patient leave his care. 'I'm sorry. I mean, is she well enough to be out there on her own?'

Fortunately, no offence has been taken. The doctor sits opposite me and puts a thick file on the table between us.

'I can talk to you about her case now. It is okay to do it here?'

'Absolutely. I'm sorry you seem to have had so much trouble with this case.'

I always feel responsible for my patients' behaviour overseas. It's crazy, but I worry that everything they do or say will tarnish the way their carers think of every other Brit they ever meet. Dr Hadhri has clearly kept everything in perspective. In confident English he runs through the original injury in the street, the treatment and drugs that were given in the ambulance. He moves on to the examinations and tests that were carried out when she arrived in the hospital and all the treatment she has been given since then. He has the X-rays, the ECGs, the obs charts and drug charts so I know everything there is to know about the patient. There is a lot to say and he is thorough, professional and in clear command of the facts. If I'd been scooped up on a Tunisian street with a broken hip and a weak heart I'd have wanted this man on my case. What on earth is going on in this lady's head?

'Doctor MacFarlane, I can get someone to direct you to the smoking area where we believe your patient and her family to be. I shall say goodbye to you here, however. I don't feel my being present will help anyone.' He grips my hand tightly. 'Good luck with your journey, doctor. I think you will need it.'

It's not hard to spot my patient when I get to the smoking terrace. She is sitting on a plastic chair in the centre of a very distinctive trio. On her left is a thirty-five-year-old version of herself, and on her left a teenage incarnation. All three have the same blond hair tied back sharply in single ponytails. All have deeply tanned faces. All are dressed in pink and white. All seem to be wearing enough gold to bail out a bank. I also spot the fact that they don't travel light. Six suitcases are piled up in front of them. About half a dozen plastic shopping bags are stacked up on top of those. All three women are talking so intently, and all at the same time, that none notice my approach.

'Hello, are you Mrs Harman? I'm Doctor Ben MacFarlane.' I offer to the oldest and loudest of the trio.

'About fucking time too, Doctor fucking Doolittle,' she says blowing a lungful of smoke towards my chest and making no move to shake my outstretched hand. I withdraw it, feeling a little foolish.

'About time too,' adds the lady's daughter.

'Doctor fucking Doolittle,' says the teenager. I keep my focus on the patient.

'Mrs Harman, the doctors tell me you've discharged yourself? Could you explain what's been going on?'

'I'd fucking love to explain Doctor whoever you are. Have you any idea what it's been like for me in this place? I've not had a fag for a week now. I've not had a telly, I've been stuck on a ward with God knows who and you've taken a week to move your arse and get yourself out here. I don't know what the fuck the point of paying for my insurance was. As far as I'm concerned I've been abandoned and mistreated ever since that bastard grabbed my bag.'

Her daughter takes up the story. Her sense of outrage is so extreme it could almost be funny. Almost. 'Do you know that none of the nurses here speak English? Not one. It's a fucking disgrace. That fancy doctor with a rod up his arse is the only one who can speak to my mum properly and I'll tell you, his attitude is unbelievable. He should be arrested for talking to her the way he's talked to her. Telling her what she can and can't do. And the things he's said about my daughter? Laying down the law like he owns the fucking place. How dare he? I'm having him reported the moment I get home, I can tell you that. Causing trouble indeed. How fucking dare he?'

The youngest of the trio then decides it's her turn.

'You should see the crap they serve as food here as well. Pigs wouldn't eat it. I threw up the first time I just looked at it. I don't know how they can call this a hospital. It's disrespectful. It's just—'

'A fucking disgrace,' her mother interrupts.

She seems ready to go off on another one so I turn to my patient and try to talk over the noise. 'Mrs Harman, this is all something we can perhaps talk about later. You know I'm here to help get you home, don't you?'

'Of course I know it. What do you think I am, a retard?'

Well, that's it. I'm over the shock now. Time for the rules.

'Mrs Harman, I'm going to have to ask you to watch your language. That means all of you. If we do the journey home I'm your doctor and that's the way it has to be.'

The teenage girl mutters something, stubs out her cigarette and flounces off towards the other end of the terrace.

'Mrs Harman, let's start again, shall we? I'm here to make sure you get back to Britain safely and get you admitted to hospital there. There's a flight we could use later this afternoon but before we confirm it I need to talk through what's happened to you and examine you to ensure you're fit to fly. That's normally something we would do in the hospital, which is why it's not ideal that you've already discharged yourself.'

'If I'd had to breathe that air for one more minute or put up with those foreign so-called nurses one more second I'd have...' there's a long pause and another lungful of smoke, 'I'd have exploded.' A whole sentence without the f-word. The granddaughter has rejoined us and the three of us look a little shocked. Maybe I'm getting somewhere.

'Well, let me talk you though your condition and you can tell me if there's anything else I need to know.'

I have to let a few expletives pass as we stumble though the story. Florence Nightingale and Mother Theresa could have looked after this patient and she'd still have had them up in front of the Royal College of Nursing for negligence. It seems incredible that she can be so dissatisfied in the same breath that she describes the most amazing free care she has been given.

I score a mini-breakthrough when I start on my examination. I check her heart rate – it's regular. I listen to her heart but don't hear any worrying murmurs. Her lungs sound good, her pulse is fine, I check her ankles aren't swollen – if they are it's a sign the heart's not pumping properly. I pass on my verdict. The family seem to like it.

'That's what those nurses should have been doing. Speaking in English. Why can't they speak fucking English?' the daughter shouts out.

Maybe I shouldn't, but I let that f-word pass. At least I seem finally to be viewed as someone who knows what he's doing. I talk for a little longer then make the decision that Mrs Harman is good to go. It's a bit annoying, to be honest. If I'd flagged up a problem I could have left her here a few more days and persuaded Camilla to send Robbie over to do the transfer. That would have paid him back for booking the nudist hotel in Skiathos.

I leave the angry little trio chain-smoking on the terrace.

'Get three cans of Coke from the machine for us, would you?' the youngest yells at me as I head into the hospital.

When hell freezes over, love.

I seek out Dr Hadhri. He is smiling broadly and I cover my face with my hands in mock shame.

'You have met Mrs Harman and her family,' he says.

'Please readmit them and let me go home on my own,' I say. 'You deserve a medal. I don't think I can ever say sorry enough.' Dr Hadhri grips my hand in both of his. 'It is you who will need the medal, my friend. She is your patient now.'

I might not like Mrs Harman personally, but as my patient I still worry about her. This is a woman who had major surgery just nine days ago. A woman whose general health was far from good beforehand. She is dosed up on beta blockers, a statin and painkillers. She has low mobility and a nasty wound on her side. Just as worrying is the state of her heart. I checked the charge levels on the defibrillators before leaving the hospital. I also make sure I explain how this works so all three know what to expect if I need to use the kit. If they think serving bad food in hospital is tantamount to assault then God knows what they'd think if I slapped those jelly pads on and yelled 'clear' without any warning.

'Mrs Harman how are you feeling now?' I ask as our private ambulance approaches the hospital entrance to pick us up.

'Just get me out of here.'

I sit in the passenger seat, leaving the trio to sit sideways in the back with all their luggage. They don't approve but it's relatively easy to tune out of their complaints. When we get to the terminal someone from the airport's ground staff brings us a wheelchair. I push Mrs Harman over to check-in.

'Hey, what about her suitcases?' her daughter shouts after me. I resist the urge to tell her where she should put them. Or that I suspect there will be room.

No surprise that no one really likes the airport. Too foreign, apparently. Nowhere decent to smoke. A disgrace.

'Hi there. I'm a doctor, I'm in charge of the repatriation of the lady next to me in seat 7B. Her daughter and granddaughter are further back in the main cabin. She's had hip surgery and a heart attack but she's certainly well enough to travel. I think my London colleagues had called to pre-order an extra oxygen cylinder. I just wanted to check it was on board?'

I'm at the front galley with the cabin service director. In theory I do want to check that the oxygen is here for us if we need it. But my real intention is different. I want to make absolutely clear that the crew know I'm the doctor in charge of Mrs Harman's repatriation. The last thing I want is for them to think she's my mother or – worse – my wife.

As it turns out there are no medical emergencies during our three-hour flight. There is, though, a minor crisis when trays of sandwiches are served. It's a vegetarian selection. A fucking disgrace, apparently. The tea doesn't get a great review either. Mrs Harman demands to know why foreigners don't understand how to make a fucking cup of fucking tea.

'Mrs Harman, there are children just behind us,' I say a

little later when something else has annoyed her and the swearing gets out of control again.

'So?' she asks.

Back at the office Camilla calls me over the next day.

'Come and make coffee with me, I need a word,' she says. We huddle around the kettle and try and find the least grimy of the office mugs. I worry about drinking too many expensive Costa and Starbucks coffees at airports but out here in our industrial park I really miss them.

'What's up?' I ask Camilla.

'It's Rebecca.'

'Oh God. Don't tell me she's still traumatised about the Rabat job?'

'It's not a joke. She talks about it all the time. She's proud of it, but she's terrified of going through it all again. If we don't get her out on a job soon I think she'll stay in this office for ever. She only took the job here because she wants to see the world. I like her, Ben. It's all such a waste.'

Just for a split second I see a shadow pass across Camilla's eyes. Did she ever want to do more than work at a desk in Hounslow? Does she want more than Duty-Free chocolate and the occasional postcard?

'I'll talk to her,' I say.

'You know, we should go out for a drink sometime. It's ages since we did that.'

We bring a tray of coffees back to the desk and Rebecca is the first person to pick one up. She and Christine are arranging my next job. Maybe talking about that will inspire her to get back out there. I'm on my way to Cairo. It's my first time and I want to follow Jackie's advice and make the most of it.

'This time tomorrow I'll be on a camel looking at the Pyramids,' I say. Out of the corner of my eye I can see Camilla smiling at her end of the desk. 'I'll be cruising up the Nile and taking pictures of the Sphinx and being paid for it. Best job in the world.'

Maybe that was a bit over the top but this does promise to be great trip. After looking through a guidebook in the office I've asked Christine to cancel my reservation at a business-type hotel near the airport. Now I'm booked into a backpacker place, in the middle of the city, where Michael Palin once stayed. Better still, she's having difficulty getting seats on a direct flight back to Britain so I might be in Cairo for two nights, not just one.

'If you don't want to stay the extra night we can send you out a day later. It just seems to be the inward-bound flights on Wednesday that are fully booked,' Christine says tapping away at her computer.

'You're joking, right? I'd go today and stay three nights if I could. It's Egypt. I might discover a priceless mummy or something. The longer I get to stay there the better.'

'I had a feeling you might say that,' Christine says. She clicks on a few more airline sites then shrugs her shoulders. 'You can fly out tomorrow, you can spend a whole extra day digging for treasure then come back on Thursday. I think you really do have the best job in the world.'

I daren't meet Camilla's eye as I head back to my own desk. I've got a feeling she'll be laughing.

Cairo doesn't disappoint. Nor does Mr Palin's hotel. It's exactly the way I'd imagined it. A dusty, dark hallway, a wide grand central staircase with a gorgeously decorated wrought-iron lift running up the middle of it. I get a fifth-floor room with a vast high ceiling, a metal bedstead, shuttered windows opening right out on to the noisy city streets and a bathroom that hasn't been updated in thirty years. It's shabby, impractical, hopelessly dated and exactly what I'd hoped for. Stay in too many anonymous business hotels and every city seems the same. Here I only need to breathe in the traffic fumes at my window to know I'm somewhere exotic. I love that the paint is peeling off the ceiling over my bed. I don't care that there's an extended scampering noise when I turn on the bathroom light. Or that smoke from a very interesting cigarette seems to seeping up through the wobbly floorboards from the room below. This is Egypt. I've been up since four in the morning, but I've got enough energy to light up a small town.

I shower with the cockroaches then head out to meet my patient. She turns out to be an absolute blast. Her name is Sandi Simmonds. She's a forty-four-year-old dental receptionist from a village just outside Cambridge. The headline issue is renal failure and she's been on dialysis since she was admitted. But it seems things started to go wrong for her long before this. She's on her own and she has been in hospital for five days. She is clearly relishing the chance to tell someone all about it all. It turns out to be quite a story.

'I can call you Ben, can't I? I don't have to call you Doctor do I?'

'No, Ben is fine.'

'Well, before you get me ready to fly home let me tell you just a little bit about what you're taking on here. You know all about the problems with my kidneys?'

'I know what your medical report says and I'll want to examine you shortly to confirm it all.'

'Well, we can get on to all that in a moment. I'm trying not to think about it, to be honest I'm still in shock about what happened beforehand.'

It turns out Sandi was in Cairo for a romantic holiday. She was with a man she had been dating for just four weeks.

'I wanted a holiday, he wanted a holiday, we'd been getting on like a house on fire. It seemed like a great idea. If a relationship's going to work then you need to be able to cope with each other twenty-four seven and you only find that out when you're on holiday, right? We thought we might as well just go for it.'

'So, what happened?'

'My bowels happened. "Don't eat food that's been kept warm all day in a buffet", the guide book said. What the hell, I thought. What's the point of living if all you do is worry about things? We'd just got off the plane and I was hungry. It was a fancy hotel so I dived right in. Oh God, Ben, why did I do that? Why?' She starts to describe the most explosive case of vomiting and diarrhoea I've heard in years.

'It was coming out of both ends like a tidal wave. Both at the same time. How do you deal with that in a hotel bathroom the size of a postage stamp if you're not a bloody contortionist?' she asked me.

'That poor man. He thought he'd got this perfect, demure new girlfriend. Then he saw the real me. And you know what, Ben? Turns out the vomit bug and chronic diarrhoea were only for starters. The next day, for the main course, I thought I'd follow up with a sudden case of thrush with a side order of the world's most painful cystitis. The thrush was so bad I couldn't wear any underwear. I had a day in bed trying to get over the vomiting and diarrhoea and thought I was ready to finally see the Pyramids. We go down to the hotel reception and we're asking about a trip down the Nile when I had this massive, overwhelming urge to pee.

'You don't need to pee. Relax, girl, you know it's just the cystitis, I told myself. So I relaxed. Guess what? I only went and peed all over the marble floor in the lobby. The poor, poor guy. I don't think I've ever seen anyone so bloody mortified in my life. Should he mop it up, ignore it, or run a mile? I could see the thoughts go through his mind. That bloody dating agency. The very least he deserves is a full refund.'

'So did he run a mile?'

'You know what, Ben, he didn't. Well, not straight away.'

'Don't tell me he mopped up your pee?'

'He wasn't that much of a gentleman. But he got me back up to our room so I could change. That was when I needed another contortion effort in the bathroom when I threw up and got the runs yet again. I don't think I had any clean clothes at that point and it was only the third day of our bloody holiday. Holiday from bloody hell.'

'So that was when you collapsed?'

'Oh no, not yet. I had one more little "moment" to get through. I had a bit of a sleep, got a bit of strength back and we went off for our felucca ride on the Nile. Halfway over my guts went into overdrive and I thought I was going to die. I had to run for a toilet when we got to the other side but guess what? The only one that I could find was locked. But when a girl's gotta go, a girl's gotta go. I had to squat down, hitch up my skirts and just do it right then, right there. I was on the edge of a pavement. Some Japanese

tourists took pictures. Their driver even stopped the bloody
bus. I'm probably on YouTube now.'

It was later that day when Sandi's kidneys finally gave up
on her. 'I ended up in hospital with one plastic tube up my
nose and another one up near where the sun don't shine.
I'm not exactly a great advert for love's young dream, you
know? Anyway, that was when our week was supposed to
be up. They said I couldn't leave the hospital but he had
his return ticket and I told him he just had to use it. I don't
think I've ever seen a man look so relieved or so sheepish.
He said he'd call me when we got home, but you know
what? I'm not going to sit by my phone.' She slows down,
suddenly. She rests her chin on her hands.

'You want to know the worst thing, Ben? I'm lying here
in a hospital bed in a foreign country. I've been critically ill
and I've been chronically embarrassed. I've thought I was
going to die. But what bothers me the most is that if things
had been different, I think that guy really could have been
a contender. Some lucky girl is going to get him. Whoever
she is, she's going to seem such a treat after me that he'll
probably propose within a week. I deserve an invite to their
wedding at the very least, don't you think?'

I can't stop smiling. 'Sandi, I think this guy may still
surprise you. I say we get you home and see if he's called.
Then maybe I can come to your wedding.'

'Well, it'll be my fourth so I'll give you a season ticket.'

Sandi gets serious when I start to examine her. For all the
jokes she knows how ill she has been. The plastic tubes for
the dialysis are digging into her groin and her treatment is
still ongoing.

'The people here have been great but this isn't something
I'd have wanted to happen abroad, Ben. Am I really okay?

Will they have spotted everything? Is there anything they're not telling me?'

I take another look at her notes. She had four hours of dialysis the day she was admitted and another session yesterday. She'll probably need it every two days when she gets home. But there's a high chance that things aren't as bad as they seem. I'd suggest she's in pre-renal failure, so there is a chance her kidneys will recover and she won't be left needing either a transplant or dialysis for the rest of her life. I explain this to try to lift her mood. At the back of my mind I'm remembering an article I read about high levels of Hepatitis C in Egypt which don't make it an ideal place to be sharing a dialysis machine. That is something I keep to myself for now.

'Sandi, I'm going to go over your charts again and speak to your doctors. Then I'm going to check with the London office to make sure everything is arranged for you to go to the hospital in Cambridge. You're going to get through this. We've got flights reserved for the day after tomorrow and I don't think there's going to be any reason not to take them.' I put the charts back on the end of her bed and shake her hand again as I leave the ward.

'Remember, if you see a hot buffet, run a mile,' she shouts after me as I go.

Sandi's lead doctor is an Egyptian lady who spent a year working at the Royal Liverpool University Hospital. Her name is Dr Bari and she tries to get back to Britain for a visit every couple of years. Apparently she likes our curries. She agrees that Sandi is ready to travel.

'She has told me she doesn't have any close family to help get her through this in Cambridge,' she says, 'but I'm not sure that she will be completely on her own. I think that the gentleman who brought her in here will exceed her expectations.'

It seems I'm not the only one who has heard Sandi's hopes and fears over the past few days.

I head back to my crumbly old hotel and call the office on my mobile.

'We're fine for the flight on Thursday but I'll let you know if anything changes,' I say. Then I grab my guidebook and head out into the city.

My first stop is the Museum of Egyptian Antiquities, and a ninety-minute hunt for Tutankhamen. My guidebook, it seems, is not as up to date as it should be. While the death mask itself is far smaller than I'd expected, the colours are amazing and the legend is overpowering. Sandi says she didn't get to see it before her crisis began so I've promised to give her a full report on our trip home. I then head to Islamic Cairo, get some mint tea and find a tiny Arabic café with great rice puddings for dinner.

The sheer buzz of the city is extraordinary. I'm on the edge of the terrace and have a ringside seat for a thousand dramas playing out in front of me. There are people meeting up and saying emotional goodbyes. There's kissing, hugging, shouting, sometimes fighting. There are hawkers selling everything from cigarettes to canaries. Huge waves of hookah pipe and barbeque smoke keeps blowing over me and the whole experience is wrapped in the sound of a thousand car horns hooting. Even the people who normally cause you hassle abroad are a bit of fun here. A little lad who can't be much more than eight follows me around begging for small change.

'Where you from, where you from?' he keeps asking.

'England,' I tell him in the vain hope it might shake him off.

'England,' he repeats. 'I know England. Manchester United. Princess Diana. Queen Elizabeth the Second. Pound Sterling. Lovely Jubbly.'

I'm up at four the following morning – my second pre-dawn wake-up in as many days. This time I see the sun rise over the sphinx which is just a touch better than seeing it rise over Hounslow Central. I get persuaded to pay a ridiculous amount to ride a dodgy-looking camel and forced to walk around a parchment factory with about fifty exhausted Germans. It's all brilliant fun.

There's no medical reason for me to revisit the hospital that evening but I get a taxi over there all the same. I'm on such a high after my day that I want to talk about it with someone who'll share my enthusiasm. Sandi doesn't disappoint. She gets a coughing fit every time she laughs, but it doesn't stop her.

'I could have used some of that parchment when I got the runs on the riverbank,' she says. 'You should have bought some just in case. It can strike without warning, let me tell you.'

Dr Bari comes by Sandi's bed to say that visiting hours are over but that as long as she's with us it will count as a consultation. She turns out to be just as much fun as Sandi. Deep down I wanted to have another night out in Cairo. I'd found a great-sounding place in the guidebook and had planned to go there for dinner. In the end a bit of company, a sandwich from a vending machine and two cans of Coke were just as good. I was still on a high when I got back to my hotel room and scattered the cockroaches. The car horns were still blaring outside and a hundred generators seemed to be buzzing just outside my windows. What an amazing place.

'Sandi, I've got to warn you, the food poisoning didn't get you, but the traffic might.' We're settling into the ambulance before heading off to the airport. 'I suggest you close your eyes. You might even want to be sedated.'

Somehow our driver steers us across multi-lane highways and around vast free-for-all roundabouts without as much as a scratch. There's a bit of fun and games at the airport when everyone wants a bit more cash in return for our pre-ordered wheelchair. At least security is easy. I never know when or if I'm going to get hassle over my med bag. In the past I've had huge rows at security over everything from blades to blood bags. To be honest I can see the security staff's point. Today it seems to be anything goes. The bag goes through the X-ray machine but no one appears to be looking at the screen. The metal detector arch goes crazy when Sandi is wheeled through it. None of the security guards even bats an eye. We shuffle on through into the main terminal.

'Oh, bugger, this doesn't look good.'

I probably wouldn't use bad language in front of most patients but I'm pretty sure Sandi won't mind. Especially as I imagine she's thinking the exact same thing. The terminal is packed. It's totally jammed. I wheel Sandi towards the departure board. When we'd checked in groundside there had been only two or three delayed flights showing up. They'd lied. Airside the screens are a sea of red. It looks like no one has taken off for days. Funnily enough one of the few flights that's not coming up delayed or cancelled is ours. But I've long since learned that for most airlines 'On Time' really means, 'We'll tell you later'.

Doubly annoying is the fact that we don't have access to any business lounges. We're on expensive tickets on a good airline but for some reason whole areas of the terminal have been closed down, including all the nice bits. We carve out a tiny bit of space beside one of the bars and settle down to wait. And wait. 'On Time' soon disappears from our flight line. The half-hour shuffle begins as the old departure time of 10:20 is replaced by 10:50. Then 11:20. Then 11:50. I leave Sandi on her own a few times so I can head to the help desk for an update.

'More like Won't Help Desk' says the angry Aussie in front of me as he turns away. He's not wrong. The delay, I'm told, is caused by 'late running aircraft'. At what point will airlines realise that this statement doesn't really tell us anything? If our incoming plane is on its way then someone, somewhere, must know where it is. But today, in Cairo, no one is telling. I head back to Sandi.

'Can I get you anything?' I ask.

'A matter transporter?' she suggests.

We settle for a Kit Kat.

Four hours into our delay and we're getting close to decision time. Sandi's bearing up but she's looking really pale. She also needs to take her antibiotics three times a day. We dosed her up just before leaving the hospital and she'll be due another set in about an hour. I've got two doses in my med bag. When I pack it I always factor in a long delay and even a divert to a different airport mid-flight. But if we don't get a departure time soon I'm going to have to consider our options. We are surrounded by empty Coke cans and litter. I take a look at Sandi as the shadows start to form outside the terminal.

'Time to look at the boards again,' I say. 'If there's nothing doing we might end up back with Dr Bari for dinner.'

My mobile goes off as I stand up. It's Robbie.

'Mate, we've been tracking your flight and the airline's just told us you're not going anywhere this side of God knows when. So we've got an option for you. There's a Lufthansa flight into Frankfurt that leaves Cairo in under an hour. You can take that and then connect with a BA flight into Heathrow. You'll have fifty minutes to do the connection and both flights are coming up as on time.'

'Genuine on time?'

'That's what we're told. Can your patient handle all that? If not, we can get you into an airport hotel and book you on an early direct flight tomorrow morning. Or you can get her back to hospital for the night. We'll call to alert them.'

I take a look at Sandi. 'What's the total flight time, including the connection?'

'Just under seven hours.'

It's a really tough one. Sandi is so much fun and so full of life that it's easy to forget how ill she is. In the end I decide we should take the flight. No offence to all the great care in Cairo, but I'd rather we ended up in a German hospital if our connection doesn't work out than going back to an Egytian one. I call Robbie back and ask him to try to sort out her luggage. We'd checked it in already, but the airline won't now fly it without us. It will have to be found and couriered back to Britain another day.

Robbie was right, our Frankfurt flight leaves on time. We land bang on schedule and fortunately they don't have miles of Heathrow-style corridors to get down to our next departure gate. The final BA flight starts well. It's basically just me, Sandi and a whole army of tired-looking men in suits. They're probably expecting the same mind-numbingly dull long-distance commuter flight they do all the time. Today they've got a bit of a shock in store.

'Ben, I'm starting to feel a bit bad.' I look across and put my hand on Sandi's arm. 'Oh God,' she says, holding on to her stomach and groaning, 'I think it's back.'

As she speaks she's reaching down to click open her seatbelt and trying to pull herself up out of her seat. 'I'm going to be sick,' she says. I'm ready for it. The first thing I do on a repat is to check the seat pocket in front of me for sick bags. Today there were two and I've grabbed one of them, opened it and lifted it up to Sandi's mouth before she's finished speaking.

'You okay?' Nothing has come out of her mouth. But her face is that awful shade of green. 'You want to get to the toilet?'

She nods her head and is lurching halfway out of our row and into the aisle when the first wave of vomit rises up out of her. Then there's another wave. Then another. Where the hell has all this come from? So much for 'nil by mouth'. Over the rumble of the engine noise all I can hear are disgruntled businessmen choking on their shortbread biscuits.

'Sandi, you're going to be fine, let's go this way, we'll take it slowly. Don't worry about anyone else.'

I try to support her as we edge down the aisle towards the lavatories at the front of the plane. Five rows to go. Four rows. Three. Please can one of the lavatories be vacant. Please.

'Oh God, Ben.' Sandi stops for another wave of vomit.

There's very little room in the sick bag now. It's turning into a very slippery thing to hold. I've got to say that things aren't looking good for the pin-striped men who chose the aisle seats today.

'We're nearly there, few more steps. Can someone please help me?' I'm desperate to pass the bag on to someone so I can get a clean empty one. Funnily enough no one seems to hear me. The man to my right is trying very unconvincingly to look asleep. The man to my left is suddenly engrossed in his *FT*.

'I am so sorry. So very sorry about that, Sir,' I say as I thrust the sick bag at him anyway. He's not fast enough to stop it falling into his lap. That'll teach him. I get the new bag out of my pocket and start to open it up for Sandi. Just a few more steps to go. The lavatory to the left is occupied and the door clicks open the moment we approach. But I can't get the new sick bag to Sandi in time. The man coming out gets the shock of his life. I do hope those shoes weren't hand-made.

Sandi and I both apologise profusely to the cabin crew when we finally reach Heathrow. They've had to do a little more than the usual 'brush and flush' to keep the toilets clean in the past hour.

'It's fair to say I've had more relaxing flights. That includes on Aeroflot,' I tell Sandi as we wait to be guided towards the fast-track immigration line.

'Ben, I don't think I have ever been so embarrassed in my whole life. It was worse than the riverbank in Cairo. This just keeps on getting worse and worse.'

We've been sent a car to take us up to Cambridge. It's a

huge people carrier and we rattle around in the seats at the back. Sandi gets a little bit teary. I've tried to tempt her with some chocolate and Coke but she doesn't want to risk it. I'm guessing that after the events of our flight she's pretty much running on empty. When we get her to hospital she'll finally get the fluid she needs through a drip. In the meantime she has a bit of a doze while I sneakily eat one of the Mars bars I'd bought for her. She wakes up and smiles as I try to hide the wrapper. Then her face clouds over.

'Is it some kind of parasite or tapeworm or something? Is there something growing in me? Is this serious, Ben?'

To be honest, all I can tell her is that the hospital staff will check absolutely everything out. It's true that Sandi's illness has been pretty extreme. But then we all react differently to different bugs. Things we can shake off one year can knock us down the next. I'd say Sandi's just been unlucky. She's certainly worried. She looks out the window as we head up the M11. It's the first time since I met her in the hospital that she's not made a joke out of things.

'I hope the guy calls you, by the way. Let me know if he does,' I say once Sandi has been found a bed and is getting some fluids. I don't often stay in touch with patients but I've given her my card. I would like to find out how this story ends.

It's dark as I head out of the hospital. The office has arranged for a minicab company to take me back down to London. As I sit in the front passenger seat a wave of tiredness hits me. I also notice a pretty nasty smell of vomit. I've got a horrible feeling it's coming from me.

Winter Breaks

DECEMBER

Jackie laughs and then has a bit of a coughing fit when I ring her to pass on the story. 'I don't know if her cystitis or your handing the sick bag to some suit on a plane is the funniest thing,' she says when she gets her breath back. She's had her first few cycles of chemo and says the bad times come in waves. 'If I'm not feeling sick, I'm exhausted. But I'm not letting it beat me,' she says.

'It wouldn't dare, boss,' I tell her.

Back in the office it's all hands on deck. A lot of our freelancers turn jobs down in December so they can stay at home with their families. Even the regulars who don't have kids are unavailable. They're too busy covering all the extra shifts in their main hospitals. It's a time when Jackie would normally pitch in to do a lot of jobs. This year we're tying to get Rebecca to forget her fears and get back out there. In the meantime Robbie has had to dust down his passport to help us clear the backlog.

'Forget the jet-lag, just think of the air miles,' Camilla tells us as she allocates us back-to-back deals. Robbie gets the broken bones. He's collecting a guy who broke his leg quad-biking on a stag weekend in Estonia, followed by a lady who flew into Dubrovnik, tripped up on the lip between the plane door and the air-bridge and broke her hip. Her holiday was over before she even left the airport, which must be something of a record. I've been allocated a businessman who's had major surgery in New York. But before that I've got one quick European trip to squeeze in. I'm off to Lapland to visit Santa.

My patients are a mum and her two children. Apparently her husband waved them all off on a high-speed snowmobile adventure without saying the three little words – hold on tight. One patch of ice and a few very big fir trees later and we've got two broken arms, two fractured knees, one dislocated shoulder, one broken ankle, a bit of concussion and a whole lot of shock to deal with. Plus several black eyes and three missing teeth. All this family wants for Christmas is to get home.

I'd actually asked for the job the moment I saw Camilla tracking it. I know that strictly speaking, Lapland isn't a proper country but it's still somewhere I'd like to tick off my mental list of destinations. I've also got a bit of a soft spot for husky dogs. Where better to see some?

I fly north on a charter flight that's packed with desperately excited children on a vast collective sugar high. My patients were on one of the 'meet Father Christmas' packages and a very worried rep is at the airport to meet me. She makes me sit at the front of the coach with her as we head over to the hotel. The last thing she wants is for me to tell any of the other parents why I'm there.

My patients have been discharged from the hospital and are back at their hotel. I meet and assess them in their rooms. None of them are exactly mobile but the kids still seem to be enjoying themselves. I ask about the huskies and get two gappy grins. The little boy asks if there's any way he can go on a sled ride that afternoon. The poor lad's almost entirely covered in bandages and plaster casts. To be honest I'm sure he'd be okay as long as the riders kept it slow, but I get the feeling that this isn't what his mum wants to hear. I tell him he'll have to wait till next year.

We're booked on to the first flight out the following morning so I get my coat and go for a bit of a wander after saying goodbye to the family. The sun has set and it's incredibly cold. No wonder all the kids get given all-in-one artic suits to wear for the duration of their visits. Apparently it can go as low as minus 35 degrees here. Today it's halfway there and it feels as if ice is creeping into my bones as I walk. The tour rep has given me a huge fur hat, but my skull still hurts in the early evening air. It's a pretty slick operation in a near-perfect setting. There's masses of snow and very few modern buildings. You can almost imagine Father Christmas living here. I feed some reindeers and pet a few huskies till the temperature beats me. After less than twenty minutes I head back inside to warm up. There's a night safari tonight and I think I'll have to find some extra layers if I join it.

Another good thing about this trip is that I don't have to eat alone. I've been granted honorary membership of 'The Christmas Crew' – the twenty-strong bunch of out-of-work actors and performers who create all the magic for the kids. They're all staying in an annexe building and eat long after the children have gone to bed.

'The bosses want to keep us apart to stop the kids from recognising us and destroying the magic. It's brilliant,' an elf tells me in a broad Australian accent. 'It means we can do what we want. Get ready for a party, mate.'

It is a brilliant night. They've got a karaoke machine and

a heavily discounted bar. After a few hot ciders I forget all
about the night safari. Funnily enough the only person I
don't get on with is Santa. He's a very fat fifty-something
Geordie who says he's been an extra in *The Bill* and had
a speaking part in *Silent Witness*. When he's out of his
Santa costume he favours tight black jeans and tonight he's
wearing a T-shirt with the message, 'Screw Rudolph' written
across the front in red letters.

'I'm not going to be doing this job again next year, just
you remember my face,' he keeps telling me. He seems
determined to drink his own body weight in booze over the
course of the evening.

'It makes you sweat, all the padding in these costumes.
The beard, the hood, it all dehydrates you so I need to
drink,' he tells me with another chaser in his hand. I've got a
horrible feeling I might be flying out to pick him up later in
the season.

I can't say I feel that good the next morning. One
of Santa's little helpers had told me that you never get
hangovers in the Arctic Circle. He lied. I feel as if I'm the
one who fell off the snowmobile. I have to hand it to all the
staff, though. They're all there for breakfast, even Santa who
is eating a runny omelette and looks as fresh as a daisy.

I've told my patients that I'll wait in reception for them
from eight, and will come up to help the kids get down if
needed. We've got a car organised to take us to the airport
and a whole row set aside on the flight so the youngsters
have plenty of room to move. To their credit the two injured
children are fantastic all the way home. It's their mum who
spends the whole flight worrying and working herself up.
She's read somewhere that it's not just our feet that swell up
when we fly. She's convinced that the kids' arms and legs

will burst out of their plaster casts any moment. She asks them if their arms hurt so often that they end up saying that they do just to make her happy. Their dad is another unwelcome distraction. He spends the whole trip home sulking.

'We're going on an ordinary flight?' he had asked back at the hotel when he saw me going through the print-outs of our flight confirmation. 'Don't we get an air ambulance? Bloody insurance company. Bloody cheapskates.'

Robbie's sent a long email about the stag party in Tallinn. His patient had a lucky break by ending up in hospital. It meant he was the only one of the six not to get arrested. The group had gone on a massive drinking spree and bashed up a bar. They missed their flights home and had to pay a huge amount for new tickets, plus the costs of the bar and fines for criminal damage. The groom-to-be came to the hospital begging his friend to pay £1,000 towards the bill. He refused and was told he could forget about coming to the wedding. He was the best man. The big day is on Christmas Eve and Robbie wants to sneak in to the back of the church. He reckons it will be better than *EastEnders*.

I get some very good news in a couple of Christmas cards. The first is from the Wallace family. Fiona, the mum who had been in spinal shock after diving into a swimming pool, is recovering just as I'd hoped. Her husband Gavin has written the card. He says Fiona still needs a huge amount of physical and occupational therapy and she's nowhere near back to her old self. She is taking some steps, though. He's enclosed a photo of the whole family. Fiona's standing up in the middle of it. There's an enormous smile on her face and her arms are stretched out around her kids. It's the nicest photo I've seen in ages. The other card is from Sandi. The man from her Cairo holiday didn't call but her kidneys have recovered and she's determined to find love next year.

'I swear I'll be inviting you to my next wedding within twelve months,' she writes. 'My honeymoon will not, however, be in Egypt.'

Rebecca reads the cards while I pin Fiona's picture on our wall. 'Not all the jobs we do are nightmares, see?' I tell her. She's not convinced. Camilla's just told me Rebecca's finally agreed to do a solo job – her first in nearly two months. She's leaving Heathrow for Pisa the day after our office Christmas party. I'm pleased she's going but I'm a little worried about the timing. Because whenever the whole team gets together for a night out all we talk about are the things that have gone wrong.

We've picked a Mexican restaurant in Ealing and the stories come thick and fast from the start. Alan, one of our freelance doctors, is just back from a repat from a safari in Tanzania where an older lady had a mental breakdown.

'She lay down on the tarmac halfway between the terminal and the plane and refused to get up. When I turned away to speak to one of the ground staff she started taking her clothes off. It's always me who gets those patients.' He looks over at Camilla and Christine at the end of the table. 'You remember the time you gave Charlotte and me the sixty-something woman from Sydney? She was logged as having had a mild stroke but she was as mad as a hatter. She went to the loo, refused to come out and when the crew opened the door she was naked and covered in excrement. She got past them and then tried to break into the cockpit before some poor passenger and I could jump her and restrain her. I had to throw our clothes away and buy new ones when we landed in Singapore.' Now he's looking at Maria, one of our accountants. 'I don't think I've had that refunded yet, by the way.'

'It's not always like that, Rebecca,' Camilla says hastily as everyone laughs. 'Most of the jobs are easy, remember.'

'No, they're not,' says Sylvia, one of our other freelance nurses. She's only about five foot three and can't weigh much more than eight stone. She had to give a guy CPR on an American airline back in the autumn.

'The moment it happened the entire cabin crew disappeared into thin air. The guy was huge and I had to move him, do the CPR and deal with all the other passengers on my own. Later on I spoke to one of the flight attendants and I had a bit of a go at her. I asked her why no one had been helping me. She was furious. "I was helping you. I was in the rear galley praying," she said.'

'That's better than my last trip from Madeira,' says Alan. 'My patient collapsed. I got him on his back in the aisle. I'm giving him oxygen and the bloody crew only carry on doing the Duty Free all around us. At one point they bashed me in the back of my leg with the trolley so they could reach over to sell perfume to someone in the next row.'

Bilal then launches in to say how the oldest joke in the medical book backfired on a flight back from St Petersburg with a woman who sliced her fingers in the lavatory door.

'I had to stitch her and bandage her in front of everyone but she was on warfarin so there was a hell of a lot of blood. When it was done one of the passengers came up to me and tapped me on the arm. "I've never seen anything so awful in my whole life," she said. "Neither have I," I said. "And I've been a vet for nine years." She only went and reported me to the cabin service director. I had to get my ID out to prove I was a doctor and not James Herriot.'

I forget that I'm supposed to be making Rebecca feel better and tell my sick-bag story from the Frankfurt to London flight with Sandi. That sets off another round of similar recollections from everyone else. Poor Rebecca looks as white as she did when Mr Cadogan first went into VF.

The conversation gets a bit lighter as we go on to talk about air miles, about sexy or snooty flight attendants and about the most or least effective security measures we've seen. We compete for who has suffered the longest delays or ended up in the worst hotels. By now we've drunk a lot of beer, eaten a mountain of nachos and had all our main courses. Camilla stands up to propose a toast to Jackie. She's wanted to come tonight but is trying to keep her strength up by having a lot of early nights. She has however, left a message for Camilla to read out.

'I've not missed a Christmas party in ten years so I'm very sorry not to be with you all tonight. I hope having my credit card behind the bar is some compensation. Please be kind to it. But seriously, I miss you all, I'm getting stronger every day and I'm going to be back making your lives hell very soon in the New Year. Enjoy your freedom while you can.'

Robbie has made a little banner saying 'Happy Christmas Jackie – See you in the New Year' and we all hold it up for a photo. His mobile beeps when she receives it. 'I'd forgotten how much I love you all. God help the other people in the restaurant' she texts back. But as it turns out we don't stay there much longer. Pretty soon we head to a bar. That's when it all goes a bit hazy.

'Rebecca, you are going to be absolutely fine. Think of your training. You're a qualified nurse. You're good. You can do it.'

It's the morning after the night before. Rebecca's going to Italy via Gatwick, and I'm off to New York from Heathrow. Her job's a middle-aged lady who got whiplash in a car accident. All the medical reports say she's stable and simply needs a bit of help with her mobility. It's the perfect job for Rebecca. If only she could see it that way.

'Get yourself an ice cream at the leaning tower and just enjoy yourself. Call or text me if you have any problems at all. But the worst that will happen will be that she's boring,' I say. I do hope I'm right.

I'm flying on BA and the good news is that I see Hillary on the executive lounge desk and get lots more free coffee and snacks before I fly. The bad news is that the plane is packed and I'm in economy. Right up to the last moment I'm hoping for an upgrade. I'm holding my silver Executive Club card at the gate in the hope that one of the agents spots it and takes pity on me. There's nothing doing. I'm in 44E and the man in the seat next to me is huge and doesn't quite understand armrest etiquette.

'It's not yours. It's ours. We share it, okay?' I want to shout. I'm also horribly aware that it's not just his elbow on top of the armrest that is encroaching on my space. A roll of his flesh is seeping underneath the armrest as well. I can feel it settling against my thigh. I know someone recently sued an American airline for breach of contract. He said the person sitting next to him was so huge he only had half a seat for himself. It got settled out of court. Maybe I could make legal history by taking up the fight.

When my neighbour manages to sleep in that position I give in and get up. Maybe it's not too late. Maybe one of the cabin crew further up the plane will recognise me from another flight and wave me through the magic curtains to a nice fat seat up front. It doesn't happen. But I do get lucky in another way.

'You're a doctor, aren't you?' one of the flight attendants asks when I'm stretching my legs and helping myself to some shortbread in the galley mid-flight. I give a very wary confirmation. This might just mean she's got a rash on her elbow. But there's always the chance someone is giving birth on the upper deck.

'I read your name on the passenger manifest,' she continues. 'I hope you don't mind, but I wanted to talk to someone about medical school.' She tells me she's thirty-two and a trained nurse. 'After about six years of nursing I wanted a new challenge so I started doing this. Unfortunately pushing a meal cart across the Atlantic isn't all it's cracked up to be. Have you seen the older guy I'm working with today?'

'Grey hair, quite big?'

'Yes. His name's William. He's a great friend. He's always saying that when he started flying he put white gloves on to serve people cocktails. Now we wear rubber gloves to pick up empty beer cans. I missed out on the golden age of travel. So I'm thinking about stretching myself again. I want to be a doctor. But I don't know if all the med schools will say I'm too old.'

I eat about four more mini-packets of shortbread while we talk. This lady is really nice and I can totally relate to her having itchy feet. That's why I ended up doing repats myself.

'I don't think you'll have any problems as a mature student,' I say. 'You'll never get bored if you qualify and do this job though. Where are you based?' She's from London. 'I'll give you my number and if you want to meet up to talk about applications or anything I'd love to help. Or maybe we should just meet up anyway?' She promises to call. Her name's Cassie. It looks like I've finally got myself a date.

My vast seat-mate is still looming over the armrest when I concertina myself back into my chair. As the two people in the row in front have both reclined their seats it's an ever-trickier exercise. If you fly economy a lot you don't need to do yoga to keep your body flexible. I watch Cassie do a few circuits with a tray of water and smile. For months now I've been happy to joke with Robbie and the others about being single, but deep down it has been bothering me. I'd started to worry that I'd never get a relationship going while I travel so much. Dating a flight attendant has to be the answer. I can't believe it took me this long to work it out.

I'm also smiling because the flight seems so quiet. A few pools of light show that one or two people are reading in the rows ahead. The blue blur of personal television screens cast other shadows in the gloom. The sound of the engines blanks out any other noises. Apart from Cassie and one of her colleagues hardly anyone else is even on their feet. Nine out of ten people seem to be sleeping. That's just the way I like it.

We've talked about it a lot back in the office and it seems that we're all being called upon to help at a lot more in-flight emergencies. Statistics explain it. A big factor is that more older people are flying, as well more people with pre-existing medical conditions. Then there's the typical make-up of the business and first-class cabins: an army of middle-aged, male executives who have lived too well and looked after themselves too little. Meanwhile the economy cabins include their fair share of sick or injured people who don't have insurance and are going home on their own, or with family or friends. Add in the rich foreigners heading to or from private hospitals in the UK for heart surgery or other specialist procedures, and it's easy to see why things go wrong when everyone's breathing the same thin air for up to twelve hours at a time.

Often it is something small that triggers the call for a doctor. A few weeks ago Bilal was asked to help a little girl who had an asthma attack and had lost her inhaler. Apparently he borrowed one from another passenger, punched some holes in a couple of polystyrene cups and created some kind of DIY alternative to her spacer. Razia, one of our nurses, got lucky when she had to help out on a flight recently. She said she was mortified, sitting next to an incredibly unpleasant man who was rude and abrupt to every member of the cabin crew. They took their revenge. His knee took a hefty bash from a passing meal cart.

'What a terrible accident, Sir,' the steward had said archly. Razia had to check for broken bones and did a bit of bandaging. Then the passenger started throwing his weight around and said he couldn't possible spend the rest of the flight squeezed into his aisle seat in economy.

'Of course you need more room, Sir,' the cabin service director had told him. She upgraded Razia to business so the injured man had an empty seat to his left!

The most depressing type of in-flight emergency doesn't really require much input from a doctor. Apparently the

most recent one happened on a flight from the Middle East
to London. The crew had noticed that a passenger had been
in the mid-cabin lavatory for an awful long time. They'd
knocked and knocked but got no response. So they'd got a
doctor ready when they used their master keys to open the
door. The passenger had hung herself.

Today I get to JFK without any incident – although I
almost trigger my own medical emergency when I stumble
getting out of my seat on my way to another chat with
Cassie in the galley. It turns out we might be on the same
flight back to London tomorrow. She's got an overnight
in New York and is back on duty at eleven the following
morning. If my patient is ready to move I'm hoping to have
him on a flight around the same time. In the meantime we
said we would try to have dinner together in New York. My
patient is in hospital just north of Central Park and I'm in
a hotel nearby. Cassie and the crew are in a hotel near the
United Nations' Building – a twenty-minute cab ride away.
How great is this?

My patient is a portly, but cheery, City banker. His kidney
stones started to gang up on him during a night at the opera.

'The fat lady was singing, I was screaming and everyone
sitting near me was in shock,' he says with a smile from his
hospital bed. He seems the kind of man who takes anything
and everything in his stride. He's fifty-eight, looks a bit
like Henry VIII and clearly lives just as well. His file says
he's got high blood pressure, madly high cholesterol and
has a lifetime of heavy drinking behind him. I'm sure he's
probably got gout too but maybe he's too embarrassed to
say.

What I really enjoy about this repat is the chance to nose
around an American hospital. These come in two distinct

categories. The first are like the ones my lucky banker is in today. It's lavish. Cut flowers and modern art in a lobby that looks like a five-star hotel. Vast, wide, gleaming corridors with yet more art. All the patients are treated in glass-walled private rooms the size of a two-bedroom flat. The medical kit is incredible and there are staff absolutely everywhere, though very few of them are ever actively doing anything.

The other sort of American hospital is a little different. When I was at med school I spent three months of my elective working at a public hospital in Charleston, South Carolina. It would have been great training for practising medicine in a war zone. The uninsured – and possibly the uninsurable – dominated the beds and lined up in all the corridors. Mentally ill patients dominated the wait lists. The staff were permanently exhausted. I tried to patch up far too many gun shots and overdoses and left work each night feeling as if I'd been beaten up. British newspapers are full of stories about the horror of tourists who claim they had to give their credit card details before they got admitted to good American hospitals. They'd do it double quick if they saw the alternative.

In Manhattan my large, opera-buff banker has been getting fantastic care. His doctors have lavished time, as well as all the best equipment, on him. They sit me down in what looks like a fancy boardroom for the hand-over consultation. I wonder if they know I normally do these in corridors or canteens. I get the distinct impression that if I'd wanted to stay there all day discussing our patient then that would have been absolutely fine with them. It's not like we'd go hungry. We've got bagels, almond croissants, vast fruit bowls and other assorted snacks on the table in front of us. Everyone seems desperately concerned that I'm not eating enough and that they should bring in a different selection. Compared to the manic activities of public hospitals – and NHS hospitals – everything here moves at a pace that is positively glacial. I quite like the contrast to the rest of my professional life. But it doesn't really feel like medicine.

'I think your Mr Vadera will recover very well,' the radiologist tells me after wowing me with some near CGI-style graphics that detail exactly what they have seen, what they have done and how they've left things. You can sometimes pass kidney stones spontaneously, which can give you a little bit of a shock but saves everyone a lot of bother. Mr Vadera didn't. So the doctors gave him a nephrostomy – opening up a hole from his back to his kidney so they could pull out the offending stones. Sometimes you are given these in a jar as a medical souvenir. Mr Vadera's appear to have disappeared into some expensive ether, possibly quite literally.

'Now, there are a few other areas we need to discuss with you,' the lead doctor tells me as the croissants get offered around again. 'We noted that his liver tests are abnormal. That's given us cause for concern. It's something that needs to be looked into at some point.'

'What have you seen?'

Quite a lot, as it turns out. It seems Mr Vadera's liver enzymes are high, his platelets are low and his clotting is off. He's got some heavy scarring on the liver itself, which suggests the problems have been going on for a quite a while. I look at their charts and listen to their explanations with a frown. This isn't good. The liver never seems to get the credit it deserves when we talk about how amazing our bodies are. Every drop of blood has to pass through it to be filtered as it travels from our gut to our heart. Blockages are very bad news. They force the blood to go elsewhere, normally into the veins of the oesophagus. If those veins can't take the pressure, which they usually can't, then you really don't want to be around when the system blows.

'So how bad is it?' I ask.

The doctors admit they don't have all the answers. Mr Vadera was brought in for emergency treatment for his kidney stones. The liver results are peripheral to his care.

'We are mindful of the cost of fully examining his liver here when he can arrange his own treatment back in the United Kingdom,' the radiologist says. I don't know why but something strikes me as funny about a man in this lavish consulting room saying he is mindful of any costs at all. We talk a bit further about the kind of on-going treatment we think Mr Vadera will need. It's nice to have such a relaxed conversation that's not about a patient's immediate needs. It's also nice that these well-paid American doctors have so many nice things to say about our NHS. They have no doubts at all that whatever care he needs he will get, for free, at home. One more cup of coffee later we wrap it up. Mr Vadera's liver is an issue for other doctors on another day. I make the call that he's ready to be taken home. Then I grab a cab and head over to meet Cassie.

If you want to really get to know a foreign city then go out for a night with your cabin crew. They're the experts at all the latest, cheapest and best places. Cassie and five of the crew from our flight are heading to a speakeasy in a part of Manhattan I'd never even heard of. I'm invited along for the ride. It's a brilliant night. The first person Cassie introduces me to is William, the older colleague she had mentioned on the plane. He could hardly be funnier. He tells story after story about the 'good old days'. There can't be a

scam he doesn't know about. And woe betide any passenger
who annoys him. Forget the old story about crew members
putting laxatives on meal trays, he's got his very own
version of 'ice and a slice' you need to avoid if you don't
want to spend the whole flight in the lavatory.

Cassie is even more beautiful off duty than on. She's in
a black wool dress that clings just where you want it to.
She's got dark hair, big grey eyes and an incredible sense
of humour. This could be very, very good. It turns out that
we're not on the same flight back tomorrow but we set a
date to meet up when we're both back in London.

Five hours after getting back to my hotel I'm back in the
hospital with Mr Vadera. Four fierce nurses with clipboards
are assigned to us to complete the paperwork on his
discharge and we climb into his ambulance just after six. An
hour later and we are still edging across the Manhattan grid
towards the Midtown tunnel and a morning flight out of
JFK. That's when he turns very pale.

'Mr Vadera, are you okay down there?' He's well enough
to sit, but he chose to stay lying down on the trolley for this
part of the journey. His dark skin has started to look grey
and clammy. He's not really looking at me any more.

'I feel a bit sick, to be honest,' he says. 'Too much
breakfast.'

I reach out so I've got a receptacle dish ready in case he
does vomit. I loosen his stretcher straps so he can lean into it.

The ambulance rolls forward a bit more then really starts
to move. We must have finally caught a green light. I brace
myself slightly as we take a corner and look down at Mr
Vadera again. He's started to look a bit green now and is

clearly feeling very sorry for himself. He flashes me a very
rueful smile and I return it.

'Do you normally get car sick? I can give you something
for it if you want.'

'I feel bloated,' he says. I'd started to reach into my med
bag to check I've got an anti-sickness injection if he wants
it. I pull myself up sharply. Bloated isn't a word I really
want to hear. That doesn't chime quite so well with the
thought of car sickness. It's reminded me about his liver.

'Well, you're in the right place if you're feeling ill,' I say,
trying to keep him calm. 'I can move you on to your side if
you think that will feel better?'

He doesn't speak but he starts rocking his head
backwards and forwards. Things are clearly changing
pretty fast inside him. His eyes are starting to bulge out of
his face. He is cold to the touch but sweat has broken out
on his forehead. I've got a terrible feeling I know what's
going to happen next.

'Oh God, I am going to be sick,' he says. His head rocks
forward and back again as he starts to dry retch. I get the
bowl to him just as the ambulance takes another sharp right
corner. His eyes are really bulging now. Here it is. He's being
violently, horribly sick. But it's not vomit that's hitting my
hands and pouring out across into my lap. It's blood.

'Oh my God.' I can't think anything else as a second
mouthful of hot blood hits me. This is very, very bad.

'Mr Vadera hold on in there for me, I'm going to get you
sorted.' I try to wipe some of the blood off his face and get
him to look at me. His mouth is bubbling, dripping with hot
dark blood. His eyes are wild, terrified, desperate. And this is
only the beginning.

'We need to turn this around. We need to get back to the

Emergency Room,' I yell at our driver. I've had not time to
pull on gloves, let alone goggles or a mask.

'Just don't breathe in, Ben, just don't swallow,' I'm telling
myself as another wave of blood comes towards me.

'We're already on our way, buddy.' The driver shouts back.
It's not as if he could have missed all this. He fires up the
siren on our roof but I don't feel us move. Damn New York
traffic. Damn gridlock. How the hell can we get back to
hospital in time?

'Mr Valdera stay with me.' A new mouthful belches out of
him. It's the bed scene in *The Exorcist* but with blood. Every
time he opens his mouth to retch, more of it hits my arms. He's
weakening every moment. He must have lost a pint of blood in
the first few mouthfuls. More is building up all the time.

'I'm going to move you on to your side,' I say. If he stays
on his back he could choke on his own blood. As I get my
arms around him I'm almost gagging myself now. The stench
in the ambulance is already overwhelming. Blood smells rich
and cloying. It feels even worse. Another mouthful hits me
as I move his head to one side. It's the biggest one since his
first retch. This time it sprays right out and probably hits the
ambulance wall behind me. It's all over my upper arms and
shoulders now. Blood like this clots every so slightly on its
way out of the body. It's warm and surprisingly thick. It looks
like chopped liver. There is just so much of it.

When he's in a safe position I move to get a line into him.
He's got a small cannula in the back of his hand. It would
be fine for drugs but I need to get fluids in to replace what
he's losing. That's going to need something bigger. I drag
my med bag across the horror of the ambulance floor. I rip
it open and grab a large-bore cannula. I pass a tourniquet
across his upper arm.

'Hold on, guys,' the driver shouts back suddenly. We're finally moving but it's just when I need us to be still. Mr Valdera's arm is wet, slippery, filthy. I'm squeezing and kneading the skin inside his elbow, fighting to get access. The more blood a patient loses the harder veins are to find. I brace my legs as we take another hard corner. I feel us brake, then speed up. Where's the vein, where's the vein? I'm breathing as hard as Mr Valdera now. As we take another corner I finally get it. I'm in. I can help him now.

Inside my bag I've got a bag of gelofusin – a plasma expander that will bulk up the rest of his blood. I rip it open and connect it up to him. I'm trying to tape the line to him to keep it still, but when everything is this sticky it's almost impossible. In the end I wind the tape round and round his arm. It will hurt like hell when it comes off. That's the least of his problems right now.

'I'm going to get another drip into you,' I shout over the ambulance noise. I don't really need to say everything out loud. If I was sensible I'd keep my head down and my mouth shut. But I want Mr Valdera to know I've got a plan. I find a vein in his other arm and get it ready for another plasma bag. That's when Mr Valdera says his first words since this all began.

'Help me.' Then his mouth bulges and his body heaves yet again. This is almost certainly a variceal bleed. It's what the doctors and I had talked about in the hospital yesterday. Once cirrhosis has set in, blood can't flow freely from the gut to the heart. It takes a little diversion through the veins in the oesophagus but they can't handle that much blood at that much pressure so they burst. That's what's happened here. Mr Valdera is haemorrhaging into his stomach. Then he's vomiting it all over my feet. Only major internal work is going to stop the process. My job is to keep him alive till we get him to the ER. That has to happen soon. How much blood has he lost already? I'm covered in it. Three pints? Four? His vital organs will soon start to shut down. His blood pressure will slump and he's in line for a cardiac arrest.

'How long to go?' I yell at our driver. Our siren is still screaming overhead but we just don't seem to be moving.

'Ten minutes maximum. We'll be out of traffic in thirty seconds. I'll get you there, buddy.'

Mr Valdera gives another ugly retch over the edge of the stretcher. I look down. He's got tears in his eyes now. His hair is matted with sweat and blood. His skin seems to have shrunk back around his skull. His hand reaches out and holds my arm. He gives one desperate squeeze then lets his hand fall.

'Mr Valdera, I'm going to get you through this,' I say, leaning close. Everything is hot and wet. The air inside the ambulance stinks. My lungs are screaming for clean, fresh air. There isn't any. Another load of ugly blood is building up in Mr Valera's mouth. But maybe, just maybe, we've made it through the worst.

'Let it out, all of it.' I want him to vomit again. 'Now take this.' I slip a mask over his face so he can get some extra oxygen. I watch him take half a dozen breaths. I take the mask off just before he vomits again.

'Two minutes now. I've called us in. They're expecting us,' the driver calls out.

'We're going to make it, Mr Valdera. We've got you there.'

He closes his eyes and vomits one last horrible mouthful of blood.

Ben MacFarlane

'Not nice. Not very nice at all.' A tiny Filipino lady in a very crisp green uniform is checking out the interior of the ambulance after Mr Valdera has been whisked into surgery. I follow her gaze and don't envy her job. Quentin Tarantino could hardly have conjured up an uglier scene. The cleaner probably knows it could have been a lot worse. Vomiting blood from a variceal bleed is one thing. When the blood pours into your gut and makes its equally dramatic exit though your bowel the stench is a hundred times worse. It's called melena, looks like black tar and smells like hell. The first time I dealt with one was when I was in working in a North London hospital shortly after my house officer year. It had hit me, quite literally, towards the end of my shift. I'd been due out with my flatmates that evening. I can remember the call I made from the staffroom.

'I'm going to be a bit late because I'm covered in shit.' The smell stayed for days. I don't wish that on the immaculately clean, white suited paramedics and ER doctors at Mr Valdera's sparkling hospital.

'We can find you new clothes,' one of the orderlies had said as I'd stood in the delivery area with my bag. He came back with scrubs and took me to a locker room with a set of fantastic showers. I bag up my old clothes and dump them. One of the other staff shows me their canteen but somehow I've lost my appetite. The sugar in a few cans of Coke keep me going until I'm able to see a very groggy, very pale Mr Valdera being wheeled out of the endoscopy suite. This time he's on a much higher floor and has a great view.

I've had another long chat with his doctors and been shown his notes. They've banded the burst veins in his gullet and given him a major transfusion. Good for him to

184

be sitting up in bed. After losing so much blood so fast he probably feels as if he's run a marathon. Which I suspect is something he's not done for a long time, if ever.

'You gave me a bit of a shock back there, Mr Valdera. I think that probably trumps your night at the opera story as something to tell the grandkids.'

'So I guess I'm not going home?' he asks weakly.

I smile at him. 'Not today, I'm afraid. Can you imagine what that would have been like at 35,000 feet?'

It's his turn to smile. 'First my kidneys, now my liver. What do I need to do to get the full mixed grill?'

I'm smiling broadly. 'You probably don't want to know. But lightning can't strike a third time. Next time you really will get home, I'm sure.'

I spend a while talking him through what will happen next. I've been rebooked on to a night flight home that evening.

'We'll keep on tracking your progress and then someone else will be sent out to get you when you're ready.'

'Not yourself?'

'It could be me. It just depends on rotas and other jobs. Someone will get you home.'

He smiles his thanks. Then he notices what I'm wearing 'Oh my God, doctor, your clothes. Did you have to throw them away?'

'It's an occupational hazard.'

'Well, how are you going to get home? You'll have to let me buy you new ones. My wallet must be among my things somewhere.'

I hold up my hand to stop him. 'I'll claim it against your insurance company, don't worry.'

He asks me to spell my name for him.

'Please don't write me a cheque or anything. I'd just have to return it,' I say.

'It's not for a cheque. I want to tell my wife and my children who you are.' His eyes are serious, suddenly. 'If you don't come out to pick me up next time then I doubt we will ever meet again. But you saved my life in that ambulance. I have never been so scared in my life. Having the kidney pain was terrible, in its way. But all that blood? The way it looked and smelt? That was like nothing I've ever known. You saved my life. That's what I won't forget.'

I shake his hand and leave. His grip is surprisingly strong. There's a tiny touch of colour in his cheeks again.

'You make sure you buy your new clothes on Fifth Avenue, mind,' he says. 'Screw my insurance company for as much cash as you can.'

In the end I don't spend much money at all on new clothes. I'm not really a Fifth Avenue kind of person. Anyway, the whole of New York seems to be having some kind of mass reduction day. Everything is at least twenty per cent off. I get a bagful of bargains at The Gap and create a bit of consternation when I ask if I can wear my new purchases straight away.

'My other clothes all got covered in someone's blood,' I begin. The assistant can hardly cut the tags off fast enough before waving me into the changing area. She's not listening to the rest of my explanation. When I come back out of the booth she's disappeared and has been replaced by two vast, six-foot-something security guards with very fierce faces. One of them looks to have a gun in his pocket and certainly isn't pleased to see me. I smile briefly and leave the store fast. I've got a horrible feeling I may end up on the evening news.

The flight Mr Vadera and I had been booked on to is now long gone so our logistics team have rebooked me on a red eye leaving just after eleven that evening. I check in, head through security and get a very strange feeling. I'm free. I've no patient to check up on, no complicated boarding procedures to tackle, no difficult small talk to make if delays mount up on the departure board. I leave the sanctuary of the business lounge and get a smoothie and a sandwich on the main concourse. It's busy, but not noisy. There's always something about airports at night that calms everything down. The reflections on the windows make it hard to see outside, so you feel as if you're in a bubble. It's like a step out of the real world. You can't control anything so you just have to relax into it. It helps that everyone's the same. We're all tired. We all want to be somewhere else.

The sense of calm is still with me when my flight starts to board and I head to the gate. But there's something I need to do to stop any new worries entering my head. Just ahead of me amongst the pre-boarders is a pregnant woman. A very pregnant woman. I deliberately edge my way up alongside her.

'Is it your first?' I ask, trying to sound as if it doesn't matter.

'Yes it is. I'm right at the limit for flying but I wanted to be home for the birth,' she says.

'Well, have a nice flight.' I drop back as she walks down the air bridge. That was exactly what I wanted to hear. Second and third babies can arrive a lot faster than a pilot on a transatlantic flight can dump its fuel and divert to a nearby airport. That means the doctor who gets called when the waters break is very likely to have to deliver it and cut the cord. First babies normally take a lot longer – so if this lady goes into early labour all I should have to do is keep her safe till we touch down.

A wave of tiredness washes over me as I settle into my seat. I'm in business so there's plenty of space, but there still doesn't seem to be much air. Adrenaline normally keeps me going when I do a repat. Off-duty I feel totally exhausted. But as I close my eyes I realise I'm smiling. I have forgotten all the stresses of this trip. Now I'm on my way home I'm thinking about Cassie. We've made plans to see each other in the first week of January. I haven't looked forward to something this much in years.

JANUARY

It's New Year's morning and I'm in the office having a chat with Rebecca. She survived her solo job to Pisa but she's still not sure she wants to do many more.

'It was fine because the doctor out there spoke great English and the patient was lovely. She was like my mum, really easy to talk to. But I was still terrified. I was so worried about things going wrong on the flight that I nearly threw up.'

She asks how my New York job went. I lie and say it was just as easy. I'll have to make sure she never sees the full report.

'I know Camilla thinks you should do more jobs,' I say, getting right to the point. 'She doesn't think you should stay on the desk. She thinks you should see the world and make the most of this place.'

Rebecca smiles. 'Part of me wants to, but part of me isn't ready. You have no idea how much you all freaked me out with your stories at the Christmas party. I will try to do a few more hand-holding jobs if they come up in the next few weeks. But at the moment most of the repats are on long-haul flights. Twelve hours with a patient is too much for me. I don't feel confident enough for that.'

We chat a bit more then she's back to the phones and I'm off to pack my med bag. She's certainly right about all the long-haul flights. I've got two lined up. We've been tracking a guy who had problems in Las Vegas, and I'm due to be heading there early next week to collect him. Before that, I'm off to catch a tiny bit of winter sun in Jamaica.

My patient is a real treasure. He's a sixty-seven-year-old man from the West Midlands who had a stroke on Christmas Day when he was visiting his grandkids in Jamaica. He tells me he moved to Britain in the 1960s in search of a better life. He can't quite get his head around the fact that his daughter has now done the same thing in reverse.

'I'm a widower and I'm lonely without them,' he tells me, 'But I can't afford to fly out every week now, can I? She has the kids and the sunshine. All I have is a bit of savings and my state pension. And now I'm a sick man as well as an old man. Don't let this happen to you, my son. Keep your loved ones close. Let me tell you why.'

He starts off on a long, extended series of anecdotes about his family. For all his talk of being alone in Wolverhampton it seems he has at least five other grown-up children. He's also got about a dozen grandkids in England to dote upon. He talks throughout the check-in process and our hour-long wait in the terminal. He talks through the half-hour we spend on the tarmac. He talks through the first hour of our flight. He's still talking when I get a tap on my shoulder. Out of courtesy I'd already identified myself to the purser as a doctor. He says there's a problem at the back of the plane.

'You'll be okay without me for a few minutes, Mr Walcott?'

'I'll be fine. You go do your best, Doctor Kildare,' he says. I reach into the overhead locker for my medical bag.

'Is it the usual?' I ask the purser, deliberately vague as it's clear all the other passengers are straining to know what's going on. He nods and shakes his head in resignation. So it's drugs. The Jamaica to London route is one of the world's hottest corridors for smugglers. A few years ago a report said one passenger in ten had swallowed condoms full of drugs and washed them down with constipating pills before boarding their plane. Medical staff picked up one woman who had tried to swallow 160 little packages. She'd given up at ninety. She'd been trying to raise money to look after her kids. She ended up in jail in South London. At least she didn't die. Too many others do when the condoms burst or when the whole payload obstructs their intestines.

The purser leads me towards the back of the plane. I'm frowning, suddenly. It all seems much too quiet. If a condom full of cocaine has burst inside a passenger then there's likely to be some serious agitation going on. I'm ready for a really physical task getting him or her safe. But all is still. I'm led to a young girl in an aisle seat. She's unconscious. That's not normal.

'Hello, can you hear me? Are you still with us? Can you hear me?' The girl is so young and she's out cold. Her face is pale, her breathing is shallow and she's unresponsive.

'How long has she been like this?' The man in the next seat says five minutes, maybe ten.

It seems the girl is travelling alone. No one else seems to have noticed when we lost her. I lift her eyelid with my thumb. In a cocaine overdose I'd expect her eyes to have rolled back into her head. Here I can see tiny pinprick pupils. This girl's had an opiate overdose. Heroin. I wasn't prepared for that on this route but I'm pretty pleased. This is something I can tackle straight away. I zip open my bag and find the drug box at the bottom. I tie a tourniquet round the girl's arm and get a butterfly needle into the back of her hand. I'm slowly injecting naloxone. It's the drug that kicks drug-users right back to reality in a matter of seconds. I know from my hospital days that it's not a treatment most drug addicts want. It saves their lives but when they come round, it's instant cold turkey. They often turn on the A&E staff in fury. Did't we know what they had to do to get that fix? Did't we know how good it was going to be? How dare we have ended it? Who the fuck do we think we are?

On our 747 over the Caribbean things don't get that heated. The girl comes round. It's incredible to watch. She snaps back to us as if she's never been away.

'How are you feeling? Can you tell me your name?'

She won't. She's wide awake, she's not stupid and she thinks I'm the police.

'I'm a doctor. You were unconscious. Are you okay to talk about it with me?'

Her eyes are rich, dark and scared. There's sweat on her brow and she's shaking. Now I look closer I put her age at no more than sixteen. Maybe that was the problem. Had she agreed, or been persuaded, to carry far too much? Just how loaded is she? I don't find out. She won't talk and she starts to cry when I ask again. I stand up. I'm not the police. I've done my job. I head back to my seat.

'Doctor, she's gone again.' It's not much more than twenty minutes later. The purser is back at my seat when I'm talking to a sad-looking Mr Walcott about the events in economy.

'Too many people are dying in this world. They're throwing everything away. You stop them, doctor,' he tells me.

The trouble is I'm at the end of what I can do. With this follow-up injection I've used my last dose of naloxone. If the girl needs more then we're out of luck. She is well aware of what's going on. This flight connects in Miami. We'll be on the ground there in half an hour, but she won't be left to wander around the terminal with the rest of us. The pilot has radioed this incident in and the medics and police will be waiting for her.

'You have to say I'm okay. You have to say it was nothing,' she says, clinging on to my arm. 'I need to get to London. You don't understand. I have to get there.'

But when the fasten seatbelt signs click on I have to pull my arm away and leave her. This is no longer something I can control. I can hear her crying as I head back to Mr Walcott. She's so young and it's already game over

We have a ninety-minute stopover in Miami. I have to speak to the police and explain what happened on board. I never see the girl again. In the terminal poor Mr Walcott starts to get very low. Back on board he becomes even more emotional. Lots of people get this way when they fly – it's supposed to be something to do with the oxygen levels. I remember reading about a tough guy comedian once who said he cried so much watching the cartoon version of *Tarzan* on a flight that he practically needed help getting off the plane. Mr Walcott's not quite that bad but he's close. I've told him about the girl and he can't get her out of his mind.

'Why do these people waste their lives with drugs?' he keeps asking. 'Look at me, I'm sixty-seven and when you've got me home I intend to live to be ninety. Or maybe a hundred. I saw the first man walk on the moon. I've seen the whole world change. Does no one else want to see how it's going to change in the future? It's guns and drugs and knives and gangs, doctor. Easy money and no respect for the Lord. Maybe I don't want to be one hundred after all.'

'Well, I want you to be one hundred. You're a good man, Mr Walcott. You go out there and tell people what you've told me.'

He says that everyone will call him an old fool. 'Maybe I am,' he says. His eyes are filling with tears now. I realise that he's been holding onto my arm. He has one hell of a grip.

'You're one of the good guys so don't forget it. I want to bump into you on a plane again in ten years' time. Maybe when you're on your way to visit your great grandchildren. We can all make a difference, Mr Walcott.'

He says he doesn't believe me anymore.

Robbie cheers me up when I get back to the office. He hands me an article he's just spotted in the medical press. It's about Paris Syndrome, when super-polite Japanese tourists are so shocked by the rudeness of French shop assistants that they have a mental breakdown and need doctor-led repatriations back to Tokyo.

'God help them if they ever take a trip over to Bluewater in the January sales,' he says. 'I was there yesterday and it was carnage. It was every man for himself at the checkout in Marks.'

He has got one bit of good news though. We've had a medium-haul trip come in and Rebecca's very reluctantly agreed to do it. It's a middle-aged man needing a pick-up from Cyprus.

'Camilla's spoken to the hospital to make sure there are no hidden nasties. They swear it's just a simple broken-bones case. I've told Rebecca that the worst that can happen is that his wheelchair won't be waiting back at Gatwick.' I remind him that on the air ambulance trip I'd said the worst that could happen was a bit of vomit. A horrified look passes over Robbie's face.

'Oh God. I just hope it's you that's jinxed, not her. Because I don't want her to quit on us. She's too much fun.'

I sign my bag back into the storeroom, finish the paperwork and head home for a shower. Cassie's leaving on a Boston flight in the early evening but we talk on the phone for nearly an hour before she has to get ready to leave. We're meeting up in four days' time. By then I'm expecting to have a very funny story to tell her. I'm flying to Las Vegas tomorrow to collect a married businessman who's been a very naughty boy.

'Hello, Mr Olin.' My patient had been staying in a vast, fountain-view room at the Bellagio hotel when his business trip took a big turn for the worse. He's a forty-seven-year-old company director who dialled 911 and was rushed to hospital with a ruptured abdominal aortic aneurism – what we call a 'triple A'. I've got more than a medical report on this one. I've had a few extra clues from the police report that had to be filed alongside it. It seems my patient had been out having a few drinks and a little bit of fun. He met a lovely young lady at a bar and invited her back to his room. Everything went well for a while. But when her clothes came off, Mr Olin realised she wasn't a lady after all. He lashed out. His companion hit back hard. Mr Olin took a serious blow to his stomach. As he's a life-long smoker with a cholesterol problem his arteries didn't like it. His guest left and Mr Olin's next nightmare began. The internal bleeding was building up as he tried to get into the shower. His blood pressure dropped through the floor and he collapsed on to the tiles. If you ever wonder why anyone needs a phone in a hotel bathroom then ask Mr Olin. Having a phone next to the loo saved his life.

I check out what happened once they got him into the emergency room. They scanned him then carried out major vascular surgery to replace the aorta with an artificial graft. Then they'd patched him up and left him to recover. He looks weak and pale when I greet him in the hospital.

'This isn't quite how I thought my stay in Vegas would end,' he says.

'It's not quite the Bellagio, is it,' I say. Though looking around it's pretty close. If you've got money or insurance then this class of Vegas hospital is the place to be. Mr Olin has his own room, which patients almost always seem to get in America, and it's gleaming and well appointed. Just like my last businessman in New York he's also surrounded by some seriously good kit.

'I'm guessing that you know I ended up in a bit of a fight,' he says. His file says he's married and I'm guessing that's how he's going to describe things to his wife as well.

'I'd like to say you should see the other guy but, well.' He trails off. Maybe that line is a little too close for comfort.

'Well, you've certainly been in the wars. It's good they got you here as quickly as they did.'

'They have been extraordinarily efficient. I didn't have much idea what was going on when they got me in here but they've spent an incredible amount of time talking me through it all afterwards. They've got more staff here than I have at home and I run one of the biggest call centres in the country.' That seems to be another line he regrets the moment he has said it. Bearing in mind the circumstances, perhaps he's wary of telling me too much about himself. His eyes fall on the folder in my hands. He must be wondering how much information I've got.

'Everything about this whole episode is confidential, isn't it?' he asks.

'Of course it is. All I'm here to do is get you home safely, which I think we're planning to do tomorrow. I'll examine you now, if you don't mind. Then if you feel up for the journey I'll see you in the morning.'

After a final chat with Mr Olin's doctors I'm free to go. I'm effectively off duty for the next eighteen hours. I'm in Las Vegas. How can Rebecca not love a job that gives you days off like this? I leave my medical files at my hotel near the hospital then get a cab down to The Strip. I love this city. Forget the gambling and the shows. I just love looking at the people. How do so many Americans get so big? Where do they buy jeans? How do they fit into an airline seat? I pay my driver outside Caesar's Palace and I'm immediately surrounded by a group of people who must all weigh more than a family car. I thank my lucky stars I'm paid to get Brits back to the UK. Sure, we've got an obesity problem. But we're not in this league just yet. I have absolutely no idea how American repat doctors get their clients back to Florida, or Texas or wherever they're from. I love reading articles in the medical journals about the new hospital beds and ambulances they need to buy to cope with ever-larger patients. Apparently paramedics in Vegas need to call for additional manpower at least twice a

week because their patients are too heavy for a single crew
to move on its own. Dealing with patients weighing more
than thirty-five stone is no longer unusual, they say. To be
honest I wouldn't want someone that heavy on my flight,
let alone in my care.

On the plane out one of the stewards had told me that
Vegas has had snow this winter and it's still surprisingly
cold. It's also as mad as ever. I leave Caesar's and head to
the indoor canals at The Venetian. On the way I see three
Elvis impersonators. One of them even looks like him. I
don't think I'd want to stay here for more than a couple of
days. For a flying visit like this it's just about perfect.

Mr Olin and I get a half-hour delay leaving Vegas the
following day but the captain says we've got a strong tail
wind so we'll easily make up the time. We're in premium
economy and Mr Olin is looking good. As usual I'm just
planning to check his vitals every now and then. I'm not
expecting any surprises. He actually looks fit enough to be
travelling alone. The cabin crew can't seem to do enough for
everyone. Mr Olin and I both watch a couple of movies then
he has a doze while I read. When he wakes up he smiles,
stretches and rubs his face. That last bit was a mistake.

'Ow. I think I've given myself a nose bleed,' he says a few
moments later, rummaging in his pocket for a handkerchief.
I pass him over a napkin from my meal tray. A few more
moments pass.

'Have you got another one?' he asks. I pass it over as well.
Both are soon soaked in blood. So is the tissue he found in
his pocket. This really isn't looking good.

'Do you get nose bleeds very often?' I ask, though it
doesn't really matter. The fact that he's on blood-thinning
drugs means this will be the worst he's ever had. A flight

attendant stops next to us before Mr Olin has had a chance
to reply.

'That doesn't look nice. I'll be right back,' she says. She
heads off to get paper towels and some ice while I stand
up and get my med bag down from the overhead locker.
By now Mr Olin looks like he's been in a car crash. He's
wearing a pale blue polo shirt. It's starting to look like a
painting by Jackson Pollock.

I zip open my bag and glove up. I'm aware that all the
passengers near us have stopped watching TV and are
staring in horror.

'Is everything all right?' One of the male flight attendants is
at my side, just as his colleague returns with the towels and ice.

'We're going to be fine. My friend here just needs a little
help.' I pinch the bridge of the guy's nose, aiming to squeeze
what's know as the Little's area.

'Do you want me to hang around or leave you to it? I'm
not great at the sight of blood but I'll help if I can,' the
steward says.

'Would you hang around? Just to stop anyone else getting
freaked out by this.' He stands between us and the next row
of anxious passengers.

'It'll be over in a moment. Happens all the time up in
the air,' he tells one of them. But I'm still struggling. We
get some of the ice in a towel and hold it over Mr Olin's
forehead and face. Freezing cold can constrict the blood
vessels, but it doesn't do the job now. People don't believe
it, but in hospital a surgeon might paint a bit of prescribed
cocaine on the lining of the nose to stop a bleed. I wouldn't
be surprised if someone on a Las Vegas flight has got a stash
of the drug somewhere but I'm not going to ask. Desperate
times call for other desperate measures.

'Mr Olin, I've got one last idea but it's not going to be very comfortable. Are you ready to try it?' He nods. An air bubble pops through the blood oozing out of his nose as he breathes his approval. I wipe my gloved hands down on one of the stack of paper towels and reach into my bag. I pull out a urinary catheter. This is unorthodox, to say the least, but I reckon it could do the trick.

'I'm going to get this in your nose, Mr Olin,' I say, pushing the balloon end into his nostril. I ease it as far back as it can safely go. Then I get a syringe and draw up some water from a sterile vial. I inject that into catheter valve. The water then does its thing and starts to inflate the balloon. I hold it and watch. With luck the balloon will create enough pressure to stop the bleed. In the meantime I block off the other end of the contraption to stop blood dripping on to the seats.

'Let's just see how this is doing,' I say, wiping Mr Olin's nose and the outside of the catheter. I let a few moments pass. Then a full minute. No blood. 'It's an unusual solution, but I think it's done the trick,' I tell him. He tries to smile. The steward, who had already admitted to being squeamish, pulls a face.

'I thought I'd seen it all,' he says. 'I'll clear up some of this mess.'

Ten minutes later all the bloody hankies have gone, my patient's nose is still dry and the cabin has settled back down to the more usual in-flight entertainment.

'So what the hell is this thing?' Mr Olin asks as the end of the catheter rests on his chest. 'What's it normally used for if not for this?'

'Trust me,' I say. 'You don't want to know.'

'Did you have fun in Vegas?' Jackie calls me at the office the following day.

'I did. And not just because I ended up putting a catheter up a guy's nose.'

'Do tell me it was a patient.'

'Of course it was a patient.' I tell her the story.

'What was he in hospital for?'

I consider medical confidentiality for about a second. Then I spill the beans. It's my medical director who's asking, after all. She can get the gossip by reading the files in the office if she wants. Anyway, the thought of a guy having a few drinks with a transsexual prostitute might cheer her up. It does. It's great to hear Jackie laugh.

'How are you getting on? You sound a lot more chipper,' I say.

'I'm feeling it. I had a bit of a bad time at the end of last month. Did you hear I had an episode of neutropenic sepsis?' That's when your bone marrow takes a hit, your white cell count gets very low and you fall prey to a host of fevers and infections.

'I did know. Camilla told me, in confidence.'

'That was four weeks and two cycles of treatment ago. It's just a bad memory now. Today I'm just dealing with hot flushes, embarrassingly enough.'

'So you're feeling stronger?'

'Much stronger. It's a walk in the park. I'm thinking of doing a few days in the office at the end of next month. You guys can't get rid of me that easily.'

'Well good. People like Camilla are running wild without you. Christine and Robbie are practically feral.'

'You know what, Ben? That's exactly what they said about you.' She asks after Cassie. I tell her I'll have a lot more to say soon. I'm seeing her tonight and we've both got the day off tomorrow.

We meet in a cool bar in Acton Town. I'm still in shock that there is a cool bar in Acton Town. But I've already realised that this is the beauty of dating cabin crew. If there's a good place to go within a forty-minute radius of an airport, they'll know about it. I ask after William and the others I'd met in New York. She asks about Vegas and I tell her all about my patient - though I don't mention his name. We get some food in the bar and consider going to see a film, but suddenly it's gone midnight and we haven't even left our chairs. Cassie knows her work schedule for the whole of February so I write it down and hope I can work my trips around a lot of it.

'We should try to get on the same flight sometime,' she says. As we head out into the night, things are looking promising.

I don't want to wave Cassie goodbye and go to work two days later. It's the first time I've felt that in ages. But at least I've got a good trip lined up. Less than a week after Las Vegas I'm booked on to a flight to Nice. I'm off to pick someone up from Monte Carlo.

The client sounds as ordinary as Mr Olin. His name is Peter Randall, a forty-four-year-old, married father of two from Maidstone in Kent. The so-called 'presenting complaint' is very ordinary: chest pains. The location is a bit more exciting: the casino of the Hotel de Paris. I read through the few lines he gave the doctors at the Princess Grace in Monaco - a great hospital where they may even outspend America on the latest kit. Then I check the patient's past medical history. Appendix out at twenty-two, attacks of gout from thirty-six, diagnosed with diabetes at thirty-nine and with hypertension two years ago. I hardly need to check his height, weight or family history. I already know he's pretty much your classic middle-aged male time-bomb.

There is one unusual detail in the file. We've been faxed his ECGs and the full doctor's report so we can see just how much damage has been done to his heart. If he had got the Princess Grace quick enough, then there wouldn't be much to see. But there is. I'm guessing he must have stayed in the casino and put up with several hours of extreme chest pains before calling for help. It must have been quite a winning streak. The final page of the file has the financial details of the man's case. He's been in hospital there for six days and that's probably been building up bills of up to £4,000 a day. No wonder his insurance company is ready to pay us to get him home. That way it can hand him over to the NHS and close the file.

'Ben, there is one potential problem you need to know about,' Camilla says just before I leave the office. 'French air traffic control is threatening a set of one-day strikes starting on Wednesday. We're being told they're likely to back down so you might as well go tomorrow anyway. But if the airports are closed you'll have to wait till it all sorts itself out.'

I smile at her. Cassie's got a run of back-to-back shifts coming up so I've no other plans.

'An extra day in Monte Carlo? They can keep the strike going all month as long as I'm in a nice hotel. If I owned a dinner jacket I might even think about hitting the tables myself.'

'Well remember me if you break the bank,' Camilla says. 'I've been booking you nice hotels for over a year now. Just remember that nothing says thank you quite like a new BMW.'

Over in Monte Carlo Peter Randall is pale and seems very worried. He's also got company. A much older lady is sitting next to his bed. She stands up and holds out her hand when I arrive and introduce myself. She speaks in a soft voice with a light French accent. But she doesn't say who she is or why she is there. Neither does my patient. Curious.

'Now, Mr Randall, I'm going to do some checks and go through your medical history one more time if that's okay with you. We can do it in private if you prefer?' I nod my head towards his companion to give him a bit of a get-out clause but he doesn't seem to get it. She listens intently as I run through all the forms in his file. Then I get him to repeat his symptoms and tell me exactly what happened. Reading between the lines I work out the truth. He didn't put up with those chest pains for so long because he was winning. He stayed so long because he was losing. Is that why he's not alone at the hospital? Could this lady be Monaco's version of the heavy mob?

I get my stethoscope and I check my patient's heartbeat is regular with no murmurs and his lungs are clear. I do his blood pressure, peg his finger to check the oxygen levels in his blood, and then pass him as fit to travel. I also need to check that the planes are still flying. The cardiologist at the Princess Grace shrugs and says it's a classically French strike. Foreign airlines seem to be grounded but Air France planes are taking off and landing as normal. I call the office and find we've already been re-booked on to Air France from Nice. We can leave on schedule that afternoon.

'We've got a private ambulance coming to pick you both up in two hours,' Camilla says. I tell her it looks like there might well be three of us, but that I'll give her all the gossip later. I'm right about my patient's new best friend. She's right there in the ambulance with us, undoubtedly the most fragrant passenger it's had in some time.

'Doctor, I need us to make one short stop before we leave Monte Carlo,' my patient says, sitting slightly shame-faced on the scoop stretcher in the back of the ambulance. 'I know I've had a heart attack and I know it's not exactly very orthodox but I need to stop at a bank. They wouldn't let me out of the hospital before so this is the only way I can think of to do this safely.'

I get the message that I shouldn't really ask what he means by 'this'. So we stop at a branch of a bank I've never heard of. The driver and I help our patient out of the ambulance and watch him walk across the pavement and though the bank's big double doors. His companion goes with him, but about five minutes later he comes out alone.

'Just us, now?' I ask.

'Just us.'

Our driver nods and pulls out into the traffic. He hasn't so much as turned a hair and I get the feeling this sort of thing might be perfectly normal in Monte Carlo. It's all a far cry from Hounslow. It's no surprise that Mr Randall seems too embarrassed to talk much as we zip out towards France. I sit up front looking at the last of Monaco's high-rise blocks and wonder why they all look so shabby. Maybe at night or in the right photographs they look glamorous enough. But in the winter sunshine it all seems a little tired. Are they

really full of billionaires? I'm thinking that if my patient is
a casino regular he must be able to tell me. Even if he is, it's
clear he has other things on his mind today.

Fortunately, we don't have hours together trying to make
small talk once we've arrived at the airport. Our plane has
only the shortest of delays on the runway and Mr Randall
closes his eyes and pretends to be asleep for most of the
flight. I check his pulse and blood pressure every now and
then. As usual, it's a fine line between checking things too
often and panicking patients, or checking them too rarely
and missing something. With Mr Randall I think I get it
right. All his signs look good. I even have time to eat my
meal and read a bit of my book.

'I think my wife will be meeting me at Heathrow.' The
words come out of nowhere as the seat belt signs come
on and we start our descent. I'm guessing that's code for:
'Please don't mention the other woman. Or the trip to the
bank.'

'That's great,' is all I can think of to say. Of course I won't
land him in any trouble at home. But I'm looking forward
to meeting this lady. I want to try and guess who wears the
trousers in this relationship.

'There she is.' We've just made it into the arrivals hall
and my patient is almost talking to himself. His wife, a tall,
similarly aged lady with glamorous hair, rushes over. Mr
Randall holds her very tightly, for very long. It's nice, but
it almost gets a bit embarrassing. Then he turns round and
hugs me, which is a bit of a surprise.

'I cannot tell you how glad I am to be home,' he says.
'From now on everything is going to be all right.' I sit in the
ambulance with my patient and stare out the window as we
head down to Kent. His wife is somewhere behind in the

family car. In Maidstone the bed manager is expecting us, and he is admitted quickly and moved on to a ward straight away. I'm free to go.

'I haven't spotted anyone delivering a shiny new BMW. So I'm guessing you didn't win big?' Camilla asks when I come in to the office with my report.

'If I'd had a dinner jacket I think it would all have been very different. I don't think they'd have let me anywhere near the tables in my cargo trousers. Anyway, I don't really think Monte Carlo is my scene. A lot of strange things seem to happen out there.' I tell her about my patient's companion and his trip to the bank.

'I think we should all just stick to scratchcards,' she says.

We talk about Jackie for a while. She's within sight of her final few cycles of chemo but she's still not letting anyone visit her. While she's hoping to do more admin work from home soon, she's not given a definite date for coming back to the office.

'This is the time of year we could really use an extra pair of hands,' Camilla says. She looks up at the red-dot matrix board that runs along over the back of the office saying how many calls we're answering and how many other people are trying to get through. Then she looks at the jobs board that lists which doctors and nurses are where, and the jobs that are waiting to be allocated. None of it looks particularly good.

'It's the ski season,' Camilla says. 'I hope you're full of energy. Half term's around the corner and it looks like you're going to be busy.'

FEBRUARY

One year I'm hoping to have time to ski on a winter repat.
Not this year. As we're so busy Camilla and Christine
are trying to arrange as many fast turnaround jobs as
possible. I start out with an airport pick-up for a lady who
dislocated her shoulder and got a bit of concussion in
Chamonix. The hospital has sent her to Geneva airport and
she's waiting in an ambulance for our trip back. She's very
pleasant, affluent and pleased to have help getting home.
I soon discover why. She has a vast amount of luggage –
the curse of ski repats. We check in two suitcases, a pair
of skis and a boot bag. She's in a wheelchair and she has
a handbag and a huge carry-all bag on her knees as I try
to get her to passport control. It's not easy. Trying to steer
her through a sea of luggage trolleys is a nightmare. One
guy near us turns around to speak to a friend forgetting
he's got a bag of skis over his shoulder. He nearly takes my
patient's head off. One day, I'm sure we'll get a repatriation
job for someone who survived the slopes but didn't make it
through security.

When I get back from Geneva I have an overnighter for a
patient who was in the Dolomites when he did the double -
getting two major injuries on the same day.

'I thought I was just winded,' he tells me of the first. He had taken a tumble just before lunch and broken four ribs, though he still managed to store his skis, join his friends for lunch and have a couple of beers. Back on the slopes in the afternoon (when, statistically speaking, the vast majority of ski accidents happen) he got breathless, lost his balance and screwed up his elbow and knee. He needed a snow-stretcher to get him off the mountain and an ambulance to take him to the hospital. Once he got inside he had an early lesson that emergency services overseas don't always run the way they do at home.

'The only English the driver seemed to speak was "We only accept cash". He handed me a bit of paper saying I had to pay 200 euros for the journey. He stopped outside a bank cash point and made out that I had to give him my pin number. I refused to give it so he folded his arms and refused to drive on. By then I think every inch of my body was hurting. I thought I was going to vomit and collapse again so I said I'd get the cash myself. The driver supported me as we slipped along the pavement to the machine so I could get the money. I still can't believe that happened.'

'You should get the money back from your insurance company.'

'That's not the point. What kind of person does that to someone who's injured? I'd practically broken my knee. My lung was about to get pierced by my rib. Does he steal your wallet if you're in a coma or something? I don't think I've ever met such a git before and I'm an estate agent.'

Sadly for Mr Patterson, his troubles aren't over. The first problem is that he hasn't got any proper clothes. The hospital staff had to cut him out of his ski kit and left him in a pair of boxer shorts and a T-shirt for the rest of his stay.

I don't know if his friends took his luggage home or if the hotel just bagged up his belongings when his week's holiday ended. Either way, no one thought to bring Mr Patterson anything to wear. I've barely packed a change of clothes for myself, so I've next to nothing to offer him either. The poor bloke only has his hospital gown to hide his modesty when we arrive at the airport. That doesn't stop the security staff from treating him like a known terrorist. Once he's staggered through the security arch he's taken aside for a secondary search. I watch as he's patted down very roughly. I feel his pain as the guard's hands move over each broken rib in turn.

'Mr Patterson, I'm afraid we don't have access to a lounge of any kind here. I'll try to find us a quiet corner where we can get away from the crowds,' I say. I don't succeed. Airports are always jam-packed in the ski season. The only bit of spare space seems to be at the end of a bank of seats near one of the departure gates. When I wheel Mr Patterson there I find out why it's vacant. The glass door isn't properly closed and an arctic gale seems to be blowing in through it. We could hardly sit there even if Mr Patterson wasn't half naked.

'I think we'll freeze to death here. Let me look around again.' The best I can find this time is a bit of space just below the main departure board. My poor patient has become a one-man tourist attraction. A steady stream of kids come over to check out his clothes and his casts. Several people don't stop at taking photos of us with their phones. One group of teenagers appear to be making some kind of video.

Over our heads I can see ever more 'delayed' messages clicking up on the board. For this poor man's sake I hope our flight doesn't join them. It does.

'I'm sorry, but it looks like we'll be here a bit longer,' I

tell him. 'They've put us back forty-five minutes.' All Mr
Patterson does is smile.

'This holiday just keeps on getting better,' he says. When
we get another ninety-minute delay he says nothing. All
around us other passengers are necking lager and getting
alternately rowdy and angry. The budding film directors
seem to have moved on, but every half-hour or so another
wave of hopeful travellers come through security and stare
at Mr Patterson anew. This must be how street performers
feel. If we had a hat to put down in front of us we could
probably collect a fortune.

When our flight finally gets called we board first and
leave last. Mr Patterson wisely closes his eyes as the other
passengers walk by. At Heathrow he gets his first bit of good
luck. I'm allowed to wheel him past the snakes of EU and
non-EU passport holders at immigration and through a 'staff
only' area for our checks.

'Nearly there, now Mr Patterson. At least we don't have
to wait for any luggage.' Then things go wrong one last
time. A private ambulance is supposed to be waiting for us,
but it went back to base when our flight was delayed. I call
Camilla who calls the company.

'They're on their way back to you now. Can you wait
another forty-five minutes to an hour?' she asks. 'Is the
patient okay?'

'He's okay, but he's hardly got any clothes on, poor sod,' I
whisper, hopefully out of his earshot. A few minutes under
the hour later I finally get to load Mr Patterson on to his
ambulance.

'This hasn't been a great journey, I'm sorry,' I tell him.

'I'm just glad to be getting home.' He shakes my hand.
'I'm sure all your patients tell you they're never going skiing

again. I mean it. If you ever see me at another airport in the spring you've got my permission to shoot me.'

The jobs are still coming in when I get back to the office. Rebecca's been persuaded to do one – and it's gone well for a change.

'It was Gstaad in Switzerland,' she tells me. 'I stayed in an amazing hotel. It was wall-to-wall fur coats on the streets. Shops like you wouldn't believe. I couldn't have seen all that on £19,000 a year if I'd stayed with the NHS. Maybe you and Camilla are right about this job after all.'

Robbie's on the road as well. He's been to Tignes in France and he's packing a bag for a trip to Canada that afternoon.

'Business class to Vancouver, Ben. Read my air miles statement and weep,' he says as he heads to the med storeroom. I head into the main office with a coffee. Christine has just ended a call so I join her.

'Why couldn't I have done Vancouver instead of Robbie?' I ask, pretending to sulk. 'I've just done three short-hauls in a row. It's not fair.'

Christine won't look me in the eye. 'Ben, if you're cross about that then you'll be furious when you see what I have given you.' She clicks a job up on her screen. It's a fifteen-year-old boy with two broken heels, a broken hip, a fractured tibia and a crush fracture of his spine. It looks bad, but not that bad.

'Why wouldn't I want to take that?' I ask.

'Because it's a school trip.'

'So?'

'Ben, trust me, nothing good comes out of accidents on school trips. Don't you remember the story Razia was telling

at the Christmas party?' A few bells start to ring in my
mind. Something about harassed, neurotic teachers. About a
head teacher terrified about lawsuits. About parents running
out of people to threaten lawsuits against. And about
teenagers. Crowds and crowds of teenagers.

'Oh dear,' I say. 'I'll have a word with her.'

Razia doesn't exactly reassure me. I think her exact words
were: 'I'd rather boil in hot oil than do another school trip.
If they ask you to do one then run, resign or both.' But it's
too late now to try and get reassigned. I fly out to France
the following day just after lunch.

The accident happened in Les Arcs, but not on the slopes. The
boy, Austin James, fell out of a fourth-floor window and landed
on the rubbish bins behind the hotel. He was taken to hospital
in Bourg St Maurice and has been there for five days.

'He says he was sleepwalking, but we all know he was
climbing over to the balcony of the room next door. He
wanted to check out the barmaids through their bedroom
window. Randy little sod but full marks for effort,' is his
head teacher's verdict. He is a young-looking man with a
very old-fashioned moustache. He certainly doesn't seem
that worried about lawsuits.

'Are his parents here?'

'They're going to wait at home. We've kept them fully
informed. My view was that if they came out it would just
make matters worse. Better that the boy recovers in a bit of
peace and quiet. It's given him the chance to get his story
straight if nothing else.' Wow, I could have used a head
master like this when I was at school. He leads me through
the hospital at a cracking pace.

'Austin, this is Doctor Ben MacFarlane. He's here to check you out and look after you on your journey home. I know you'll thank him and treat him with respect.'

When he says hello and shakes my hand the boy, God bless him, refers to me as 'Sir'. This all seems to be very different to the school poor Razia was working with. It feels as if I've stepped back in time. It's actually rather nice.

'So you fell out of a window? It's not quite as good as hitting black ice when you're winning the slalom, is it?'

'No, Sir.'

'At least the report I've got says you're going to live. I just need to check you out and then get you home.'

'Thank you, Sir.'

I check his pulse, his blood pressure and listen to his lungs. All fine. His legs are both plastered up, the left one hiding the wound where they opened him up and screwed a plate into his tibia to hold it all together. There's not much anyone can do about the honeycomb of his spine. Compression fractures are painful but in time they ought to heal themselves. Part of my job is to make sure Austin doesn't make matters worse by jolting himself on the trip home.

'You should have some pretty cool scars there when all this is over,' I tell him, looking at his cast again.

'Thank you, Sir.'

I take a look at his drug charts and feel even more impressed with this boy. He's dosed up with a hefty amount of morphine. He must have been in a lot of pain – he probably still is. You wouldn't know it from the way he looks or anything he has said. He's strong. It turns out he's also looking ahead.

'Will I be able to ski again next year, Sir?' he asks as I turn the final pages of his notes.

I'm glad to have good news for him. 'You know what, Austin? This could have been a lot worse. You didn't land on your head, for starters. Do you do biology at school?' He nods a yes, to the obvious approval of his head teacher.

'Well, you've been scanned and your skull, your brain and internal organs all survived unscathed. Your bones are going to mend. You might not win an Olympic medal but I reckon you'll be back out here next year.'

'If my parents let me.'

'If I let you, more to the point,' his teacher chips in. 'One day we'll have to have a proper chat about exactly what you were doing on that window-ledge in the first place, remember?'

'How will you actually organise the journey?' Austin's head teacher asks as we walk towards a consultation room for a final chat with his pupil's doctors. 'Call me Mr Hoggard,' he added, clearly the height of informality in the British public school system.

'I think it should be very routine. We'll have him wheel-chaired out of here and an ambulance will get us to the airport in Lyons. We'll be able to pre-board, we'll have plenty of room and the crew will give us plenty of time to get settled before anyone gets in our way. Austin's on a high dose of painkillers, but even with delays it should be no more than a two-hour flight so his body shouldn't bother him any more than it is at the moment. I'll have a bag full of kit in case anything goes wrong. When we land we'll have another wheelchair booked and we'll be met by an ambulance at Gatwick to take him on to his home.'

'At which point his parents will want some proper

answers. They're both lawyers. They're what we call
"very committed" parents. I don't think they'll buy the
sleepwalking story for a moment. I think before you leave
tomorrow I should pop in to wish young Austin some luck.'

Young Austin certainly proves to be a hit with the cabin
crew. We board first and he apologises for interrupting the
last of their pre-fight break. He smiles bravely, says 'please'
and 'thank you' at every opportunity and that he'll only
have a glass of water 'if it's not too much trouble'. We're
in the first row and he copes well with being the focus
of around a hundred people's attention as the rest of the
passengers board from the front and walk right past him.

I check there are sick bags in our magazine rack as we get
ready to taxi towards the runway. Austin has so many drugs
rushing around his system he can't fail to feel nauseated.
But he survives the take-off and every time I ask him how
he's feeling he says he's fine.

'So is this what you do full-time?' he asks early on in the
flight. 'I thought doctors worked in hospitals. This must be
quite cool, isn't it?'

Funny how doctors get so used to asking other people
questions you get taken unaware when one of them returns
the compliment. Especially when it's a teenager.

'It is quite cool. I've been doing this for almost three years
now and I've not got bored yet.'

'What's in your medical bag?'

'Pretty much anything I might need if a patient has a
problem on a flight. I could probably deliver a baby, cut
someone's leg off or do a bit of heart surgery with the kit
I've got in this one.'

'Cool. So what's the worst thing that's ever happened to you on a plane?'

Where to start?

'Are you sure you want to know? I can be pretty gruesome. I don't want you passing out or throwing up on me.'

'I cut up a rat in biology last term. We dissected a cow's eyeball as well. I think I'll be okay. I might do medicine when I leave school. I wanted to be a pilot till they got rid of Concorde so I'm up for some new ideas on a career.'

I decide to go for it. I tell him about Toby, the eighteen-year-old whose lungs collapsed mid-flight last year.

'Cool,' is all he keeps on saying. I describe what it's like in an air ambulance. I get the same reaction, but with even more enthusiam. Then one of the flight attendants comes over and joins us.

'I've been listening to you and I can beat all that. We had a guy on a flight out of Bucharest. He projectile vomited across five rows of the cabin when we hit some turbulence.'

Austin is captivated. It's probably breaking some sort of rule to freak him out like this but it's passing the time. Gory stories can't cure back pain but they're clearly taking Austin's mind off his troubles.

'So what's the worst thing that could have happened to me on this trip?' he asks. 'Aren't I a bit boring compared to all that?'

'You really want to know?'

'Yes. It's not going to happen so it doesn't matter.'

I flash a look at our new flight attendant friend. She's leaning against the lavatory wall and shrugs. 'Come on. He can take it. Scare the heck out of him,' she says.

'Well, if bacteria in your wound got into your blood you could get septicaemic shock. Or you could have blood clots

breaking off from your legs and heading to your heart. Or
you could develop DIC.'

'What's that?'

'It's Disseminated Intravascular Coagulopathy. Basically
your blood stops clotting and you bleed internally and
externally until, well, you're dead.' Austin wriggles a bit in
his seat and looks out of the window.

'That's all really, really cool,' he says. 'The bit about the
disseminated intravascular thing is the best. If my parents
have a go then I think I might tell them it happened.'

Our flight attendant smiles and heads back up the plane.
'This boy is going to be Prime Minister,' she says as she
passes us.

Austin's parents make me think she may well be right.
They're concerned without being obsessive. They care
but they're not going to make a drama out of a crisis. No
wonder he's so level-headed.

'Thank you very much and we hope he didn't cause you any
trouble,' his dad says with a military handshake at Gatwick.

'Thank you, Sir,' Austin says, formal again now we've
got an audience. I say goodbye to them all with a smile. If
Austin is working on a tall tale to tell his parents then I'm
working on one of my own for the office. Doing a school
holiday repat was supposed to earn me a lot of credit. I can't
imagine I'll get much if they find out just how easy this one
has been. Maybe Austin's plan of claiming he developed
DIC mid-flight isn't such a bad idea after all.

Fortunately, Christine and Camilla have already taken pity
on me. We've got plenty of ordinary jobs coming in, amidst
the ski-season rush. Not only have they allocated me what

sounds like a very relaxed hand-holding job, they've booked me into business class on one of the big Asian airlines. I'm flying to Borneo and along the way I'll get to wallow one of the widest seats in the sky.

'I'll buy you both chocolate for this,' I say as I leave the office. I can hear Camilla saying something about preferring a Mercedes Benz as I walk through the door.

I'm flying out of Heathrow but I've cut things a bit fine so I've only got a few moments in the airline lounge before boarding. That's when it gets a little creepy. I can't believe I'm saying this, but the flight attendants – almost exclusively female and all porcelain doll pretty – seem too keen to please. To me, it's attentiveness bordering on the obsequious.

'Is it all right if I top that up for you, Sir?' 'Is it all right if I take that glass from you, Sir?' 'Is it all right if I clean that rubbish up for you, Sir?'

I look around the fellow passengers in my lavish business-class cabin – interestingly enough almost exclusively male and all middle-aged or older. They all seem to be loving it. I can't help but feel it's all just a little bit much. But, oh boy are the seats comfortable. If I could buy one of these and have it in my living room I would.

On the first half of my return trip the crew are just as attentive and I have to admit I was wrong to think they are only there to woo high-spending businessmen. They are adorably kind to my patient, an eighty-nine-year-old Miss Marple of an old lady called Mrs Dean. She's a widow and had been on an escorted tour to Borneo to visit the orang-utan sanctuaries. She had what we call a 'TIA' - a Transient Ischemic Attack, which is a mini-stroke. It occurs when a clump of platelets temporarily blocks the blood supply to part of the brain. The clump breaks down and things should sort themselves out within twenty-four hours. The only worry is that the event may signal a forthcoming major stroke. That's why I'm with her.

Like so many of my patients this is the first time Mrs Dean has been out of the economy cabin. She loves it.

'You could fit six of me in this chair. You'll lose me in it,' she says after we pre-board. She isn't entirely wrong. At just five foot one and no more than seven stone she can't get her feet even close to the floor. If I hadn't been there then getting the in-flight magazine from the seat back pocket in front of her would have involved a short walk.

'I'll take a glass of water, if I may. That's just lovely, my dear,' she says to our attendant when a drinks tray comes round long before anyone else has boarded.

'I feel like royalty,' she whispers at me. For the next five minutes she is treated that way as well. One of the attendants approaches and gives a little bow.

'My name is Florence. Madam may wish to visit the lavatories before any other passengers arrive?' she asks, holding out her arm in invitation. What a very kind thought, and what a clever way to articulate it. I watch the pair of them as they step very slowly up the aisle. They are both so tiny it's hard to work out who is supporting who.

'There are fresh flowers in the loo and the most wonderful skin creams,' Mrs Dean coos when Florence brings her back to me. I'd got ready to try and impress her even further by showing her where our armrest televisions are stowed. But something in her eyes makes me pause.

'Mrs Dean, is everything all right?' I reach over and put my hand on hers very lightly. It's cold, worryingly so. I look up at her and she's shivering and starting to fight for breath.

'I've got a blanket for you right here and I can have them turn off the air,' I say. 'Mrs Dean, what's the matter?'

Out of nowhere this lovely, optimistic old lady is crying. Great waves of tears are flowing down her face and her tiny body is shaking in distress. She lets out a sudden gasp that somehow breaks my heart. What is this? What's happening to her? I take both her hands in mine. They're soft, but still so cold. Then I try to reach across between our two seats to actually hold her. I have no idea how, but I've sensed that this isn't medical. I don't need to feel her pulse or check her blood levels. This is a strong, proud but desperately sad lady. She's a long way from home, she scared and she's lonely. She doesn't need medical care. She needs friendship, companionship, family. Instead she is marooned all alone on some vast airline seat with a man she barely knows.

'I'm so sorry, so very sorry,' she is trying to say between gasps. I can feel her tears now on my neck. She is holding me much tighter than I'm holding her and she won't let go. The tears go on and on. The sobbing gets louder. It's as if I've got an infinitely fragile wounded bird in my arms. I look up slightly and see that what seems to be the entire cabin crew has surrounded our seats. It's extraordinary but almost all of them are crying too. Big clear tears are falling down perfectly made-up faces. Florence has both hands clasped to her temples in shock. Her immaculate black hair is falling down the side of her face. She looks distraught – and as I catch her eyes she sparks into action. She has just looked ahead of her. The first of the other passengers has stepped into the cabin. Several hundred more are right behind him.

'No one boards. No one boards!' she shouts, a tiny spitfire of a figure rushing towards this intruder. 'Please, sir, nothing

to see. Five minutes, please. Please don't come on board.' I
look around and see her practically pushing the man back
around the edge of the door and hissing at the ground
staff in their hi-visibility jackets. She guards the door like
a tigress to protect my patient's privacy. When she catches
my eye again I can see she's still crying. I've got a horrible
feeling that I am too.

'Mrs Dean, you're setting us all off now, you're making
me look like a big girl's blouse,' I say. I pull back just a little
so I can look down at her. 'I'll do whatever I can to help
you. Do you want to leave the plane? Are you feeling ill or
is there anything else I should know?'

'I'm so sorry, just so sorry,' she carries on repeating. She's
breathing deeper now, clearly trying to pull herself together
and focus her thoughts. She closes her eyes tightly, forcing
a final river of tears down her face. When she opens those
eyes again she has moved her head back and is looking right
at the crowd of cabin crew in front of her. They all flinch –
desperate to help but terrified to intrude. One is holding a
glass of water, another is holding a blanket and pillow and a
third, unaccountably, a small vase of yellow flowers.

'What have I done?' Mrs Dean says. 'What a fuss I've
made.' She looks up at me. 'I think it suddenly just dawned
on me that I really was going to get home. I suddenly felt
overwhelmed by how kind everyone has been to me, the
people on the tour, the people in the hospital, the people
here on the plane, yourself, of course. I've spent my whole
life looking after young people. Now all you kind young
people are looking after me. I think it just got a bit much for
me. I'm just a foolish old woman and I'm so sorry.'

'Mrs Dean, that's the last time I can let you say sorry
for anything. It's just us and the crew on the plane, no

one else is on board so no one else has seen anything. The crew all just want to help you. I just want to help you.'
A handkerchief has appeared from nowhere and is being offered to us from the aisle.

'Thank you so much, my dear,' Mrs Dean says. She dabs her face and mops up the edges of her eyes. 'I was always told a lady never blows her nose in public but I think I will have to make an exception.'

She does so, very gently, and somehow this is our signal that everything will be okay. The crew edge away towards their stations. I see Florence whisper an instruction to a colleague at the door before she approaches us.

'I can keep people away as long as you need,' she says. 'But we do have to get the plane ready and start boarding soon. What would you like me to do?'

Mrs Dean takes a very deep breath then forces the ghost of a smile. 'I think, my dear, I would like to try some more of those hand creams in the lavatory. If I could stay in there until the plane is full then that would be just wonderful. I imagine I look an absolute sight. I don't want to put your other passengers off their dinners.'

Mrs Dean and Florence are almost inseparable for the rest of the nine-hour flight into Dubai. She brings Mrs Dean's meals ('Madam, I've brought you less than the gentleman but there is plenty more if you are hungry'). She is constantly offering, plumping or removing pillows and tucking in blankets. I swear Mrs Dean only needs to even think of the lavatory and Florence is at her side to lead her up the aisle towards it. Woe betide any other passenger who might even want to stand in a queue while Mrs Dean is inside. Florence ushers them to another part of the plane to preserve her new friend's dignity. If the rest of the crew are annoyed at having to do more work while Florence focuses all her attention on us then they certainly don't show it. I've never seen so many concerned looks or kindly faces. Our male, middle-aged passengers are quite put out.

I've decided to scale down my checks on Mrs Dean. As ever, there's a fine line between making sure she is okay and reminding her how vulnerable she is. The last thing I want is to make her cry again. We're on a night flight and just after our meal the blinds are pulled down and the lights are turned off.

'I think I might read for a while,' I whisper across to Mrs Dean, twisting my shoulder light into position and clicking it on.

'Please don't stay awake on my account,' she replies.

I won't sleep when I've got a patient next to me - at least I've never done so before. Two hours later I wake up with a start. Fingers of light are tugging around the edges of some of the blinds. The wall of sound from the engines still surrounds us. The cabin is still the usual night-time mess of bodies and blankets. And Mrs Dean? She's sitting upright in her vast chair. Florence is sitting opposite on the companion seat. They're playing what looks like gin rummy. I smile across at them.

'Good morning, young man,' says Mrs Dean.

'We will bring you some tea,' says Florence giving a nod to a crew member who must have suddenly appeared behind my seat.

'Please don't tell me I snored,' I say.

'Then we won't tell you that you snored,' says Mrs Dean. 'How are you feeling?'

'Absolutely fine, thank you. Florence has been telling me all about her family in Singapore. It's been an absolute education. After my earlier embarrassment I've had the most marvellous flight.'

Unfortunately for Mrs Dean, this was just the first leg of her trip home. We have another eight long hours on a different plane out of Dubai. She's resigned and ready for it now. There are no more tears, no other crisis. As usual the young, fiercely cool buggy driver at Heathrow is charm itself as he helps an exhausted Mrs Dean on to the back of the vehicle and straps her in.

'I feel like Elizabeth Taylor,' Mrs Dean whispers as he steers us through the crowds towards the immigration desks and on to the arrivals hall.

'There won't be anyone to meet me,' she says, slightly apologetically as I scan the crowd for our driver. There's no one to meet her at her hospital in Reading either. She's admitted straight away and the last I see of her is a frail little figure in a big bed, sitting up bravely but all alone.

'She's a lovely lady, will you look after her for me?' I ask one of the nurses as I leave the ward. The nurse is a large blond girl of about twenty-five. I hope she's another Florence.

Outside the hospital I need a bit of cheering up so I ring Robbie.

'I've just left Mrs Dean and I'm on my way back down with my bag. Anything going on over there?'

'Funny you should ask,' he says. 'One of us has had a bit of a 'mare.'

'You?'

'No, for once it wasn't me. It was Rebecca.'

'Not again. What's happened to her now?' It's clear Robbie is desperate to tell the story.

'Everything's quiet now but she sure can pick them. I love

her to bits, but maybe she really is jinxed. It was supposed to be a quick pick-up from Portugal. The hospital had sold it as a simple hand-holding job but when she got to the ward the guy was clearly unstable. She got him to Faro airport with his wife and he pulled his trousers down at check in, crapped on the floor and wiped his bum with his boarding pass. His wife burst into tears, ran into the loos and wouldn't leave. In the end they had to get security to get her out of there. Meanwhile Rebecca declared them both unfit to fly but no one else would help her. It took her about an hour in the disabled toilet to get the guy cleaned up enough to leave. It then took her another hour to find a taxi driver who was prepared to take them back to the hospital where, guess what, they refused to readmit him. We had a Portuguese speaker on the desk that day and through her Matt had to practically threaten an ambassador on the place before they found the guy a bed. Rebecca came back on her own the following morning and we've got poor old Bilal flying out there tomorrow for round two. She was finally getting into this job a week ago but I've got a feeling she might now have been put off it for life.'

'Bloody hell. So much for simple hand-holding jobs.'

'Well, there is one other thing that might cheer you up. You've had a fancy hamper from Fortnum and Mason delivered as a thank you from the family of the schoolkid who broke all his bones.'

'Nice. What's in it?'

'What *is* in it, or what was in it?' Robbie asks. I should have known.

'Tell me what's left then tell me what I've missed.'

'We've left you a couple of bags of dried fruit and some Turkish Delight. There's a sort of hollow shape where a bottle of champagne and some red and white wines used to go. I think there was some smoked salmon, some chocolate and lots of other goodies as well but it all disappeared in about twenty seconds flat.'

'Well, thanks for fighting for me, Robbie, I'm sure you did your best.'

'You're joking, right?'

'Of course I'm joking. You've probably only left me the Turkish Delight because no one bid for it on eBay. Frankly I'll be amazed if the hamper itself still exists by the time I get back.'

'No bids so far, buddy, so fingers crossed.'

'Put me through to Camilla before I get you fired.'

'How was Mrs Dean, Ben? After Rebecca's troubles I really need to hear that it was uneventful,' she said.

'It was. We had a lot of tears on take-off but she got through it. She's fine, a really nice lady. She's tucked up in hospital now and I'm on my way back with my bag.'

'Excellent. Now, I've got an update on Jackie to give you. Do you want to hear it now or when you get here?'

'Is it good news?'

'It's very good. I'll tell you now. She rang in to say she's about to finish chemo. She's opted to have radiotherapy as well. It'll last four weeks. She says the doctors are cautiously optimistic.'

'Do they mean it?' Like every doctor I know the phrase 'cautiously optimistic' can mean just about anything.

'I don't think Jackie would sugar coat it for us. I don't think they'd dare lie to her, either. She reckons she'll be back sooner than she'd hoped. Maybe at the end of next month. Oh, Robbie wants another word.' I hear the phone being passed back over.

'Did you hear that about Jackie? If she's coming back

next month you'd better get your hair cut. We all think you've let yourself go since you fell in love. Anyway, I've got you another job lined up. It's not a good one, I'm afraid. Are you seeing Cassie tonight?'

'No. She's in Atlanta.'

'Good. So you won't mind getting up for a 5:30am flight out of Stansted. It's the only flight we can get and it's a job we need to clear. It's a psychiatric case in Toulouse. You'll be back the same day. I promise I'll find you something better next time. How's that sounding? Hello?'

The Toulouse job doesn't turn out to be too bad. It's a twenty-two-year-old guy with schizophrenia who stopped taking his anti-psychotic medication when he left the country. The local hospital have stabilised him and I get him home without any incident. Without, to be honest, much more than a few grunts. He's physically well and he's easy to care for. But he certainly doesn't want to talk. I sign him in to hospital in North London and head home for a shower. Cassie is due back this evening as well and we're going to suffer jet-lag together. Better still we get to see each other for each of the next five nights. She's taking a week's holiday and I'm due to do my first set of office shifts in nearly a year.

When I started this job Jackie told me to book the occasional week on the logistics desk. You don't earn as much in the office as you do on the road, but a break from flying keeps you sane. It lets you re-set your body clock and catch up on laundry. It's also a good opportunity to get your passport up to date. Some countries are bureaucratic nightmares. We might just be flying in to pick a patient up at the airport. We might not be on the ground for more than a few hours but we'll still need a valid visa, which might require a personal visit to an Embassy in London. I flick through my passport on my first desk day and work out which visas I should renew. When I started the job I'd had a standard passport. As the stamps built up I soon ran out of pages and had to upgrade to a forty-eight pager. Now that's filling up as well. If I stick in the job I can't see it lasting the usual ten years.

'My paperwork's up to date. What do you want me to do now, boss?' I ask Camilla. She wants me to take calls for the rest of the week. It's actually a lot of fun. I speak to travel insurers, big businesses, and occasionally embassies and wealthy private individuals. I try to get as many details as possible and assess whether or not the patient needs help getting home and when they should be well enough to travel. I see how much care costs overseas – and just how much of a bargain we get on the NHS. Next up come the travel arrangements, which can involve having seats open on a variety of airlines on several different days. Finally I hand over the task of booking a nice hotel to Camilla so she can earn some more chocolate.

Working on the desks has taught me some of the patterns of holiday emergencies. Forget Friday the 13th, for example. Statistically Monday the 27th is the worst day for accidents abroad. It's also good to know that if you make it to day three of your holiday you've got a decent chance of getting home okay. Apparently the vast majority of serious illnesses happen in the first forty-eight hours of a trip. So do most of the deaths. For older people, many are triggered by the stress of packing, worrying about an empty house and actually travelling. For middle-aged businessmen the reasons are a little different. Too many executives hit the hotel gym or pool and go crazy trying to keep up with younger colleagues. We get the call when a heart attack cuts the competition short.

I see Cassie every night I'm on my five-day office stint and at the end of the week she comes down to Hounslow to have lunch with the whole team. They love her and I go back to the office that afternoon with a huge smile on my face.

Then I get some bad news. I'm sorting the logistics on a job for Bilal. He's got to get a patient back to the same hospital in Berkshire that took in the lovely Mrs Dean. I make sure the bed manager is expecting him and ask after her. I get put on hold. A few moments later someone comes back on the line. She informs me that Mrs Dean died two days after they'd admitted her. No one had come to collect her stuff. I call her local authority. In the absence of any known relatives it had arranged what's called a 'public health funeral'. It put an obituary and funeral notice in the local paper beforehand. No one turned up on the day. I've never been to a patient's funeral before. I wish I'd gone to Mrs Dean's.

Spring Sun

MARCH

Cassie's got a theory about cabin crew and colds. She reckons they catch every bug going in their first year of work. Then one day they wake up immune to it all. They've got used to breathing recycled air in planes, airport terminals and hotel bedrooms. They can fight off viruses from every corner of the globe. They're invincible.

'And you want to get into medical school with crazy theories like that?' I ask her with a smile. But a tiny part of me thinks she might be right. I had a constant cold when I started this job. I got a new one the moment each one finished. Then I woke up one day feeling fantastic. It was roughly a year after I started doing repatriations. I've hardly sneezed since. Until today.

'Five days working on the ground and my body has packed up. I was supposed to be recharging my batteries. The office has killed me.'

Cassie makes some comment about man-flu. I pretend I can't hear her. She looks great. She's showered, in her uniform and ready for Heathrow. We're going there together. She's flying to Boston at ten thirty. I'm going to New York at eleven.

'Eight hours in an economy seat and you'll be right as rain,' she says.

I tell her she's got a terrible bedside manner. We say goodbye at security and I head off to buy some paracetamol. I'll save the really hard stuff in my medical bag till later.

My flight isn't great but I manage to sleep through most of it. Maybe eight hours of recycled air is just the cure I need. I struggle a bit getting through US immigration – repatriations never quite fit either the business or pleasure box and today my border guard asks a lot of questions before letting me through. I'm feeling a little better when I leave JFK and head into Manhattan. Unfortunately, I get a relapse the moment I meet my patient. His name is Dr Tom Moore. He's a fifty-six-year-old Harley Street man who had a heart attack six days ago. I had a feeling he might be a pompous old bore. I'm right.

'You'll want to read my drug charts,' he says after I've introduced myself to him. I'm actually holding his drug charts but this doesn't seem to have registered with him. He rattles off a list of the medication he's on, spelling the names as if I might never have heard of them, let alone be able to read them. At one point I look up to see if he might be joking. He's not.

I start my examination. At every stage he tells me what I should be doing, what I should be looking for and what I should find. He informs me what his pulse should be, what his blood pressure should be and what his chest should sound like. He even tells me what I should say when I go to speak to his attending physician. I've got a feeling the physician will have plenty to say about him. Still the instructions flow.

'On the flight tomorrow you'll need to keep a very close

eye on my rhythms and make sure that I don't go into a pulmonary oedema,' he starts.

And if you arrest, should I await for instructions from you before defibrillating? Or will you be okay if I use my own training and save your life? I want to ask. And if you know so much about heart pains how come you went out without your GTN spray in the first place?

'So what were you in New York for?' I ask instead, trying to get a conversation going, rather than just stay on the receiving end of a long series of instructions.

'A cardiology conference,' he barks, not quite spotting the irony. 'Waste of everyone's time. Now, if I were you, here's what I'd take with you tomorrow.'

The tone doesn't change on the plane the following day. 'Below sixty, that's what you want it to be,' he says when I check his pulse. 'Now I don't want you to wake me if I'm sleeping but you will need to keep an eye on me. Here's what I think you should do.'

He goes on and on. I'm finding it hard to focus. My cold seems to come back overnight. I woke up with my eyes gummed together and a nose that dripped like a tap. Just before take-off I clip the oximeter on my own finger to see how much oxygen's getting round my system.

'Just testing it,' I tell Dr Moore. My reading is worse than his. I swallow a couple more ibuprofens in the lavatory and stare at my face in the mirror. I look as white as the plastic walls. God, the lights in here are bright. I click open the lock on the door. You're always supposed to look better when you do that and the lights dim. Not today.

Back at my seat my patient is in the mood to talk.

'So, been doing this job long?' he asks. He barely gives me time to open my mouth before he answers the question for me. 'If you've been doing it for a year then that is too long. What you want is to get into a teaching hospital and get your name known. Get something published. That way you can go private as quickly as possible. You earn by the hour doing this job don't you?'

'By the block of hours.'

'That's ridiculous. That's a dreadful return on your education. You probably get no pension rights or any other benefits. You're throwing your life away.'

'What if I enjoy it?'

'You can't take enjoyment to the bank. You can't spend it in any shop. So where did you go to med school? Where did you do your house jobs? Have you got your MRCP yet?'

The flight seems to have turned into some kind of job interview. I thought he was planning on going to sleep. Instead he starts talking through various patient scenarios. I detail some of the cases I've dealt with on planes and in ambulances overseas. Obviously, I only mention the most dramatic and heroic incidents. After a while I get the feeling I might actually be winning him over. I get the feeling that I do more on my uneventful repatriations than he does in his private clinic. He's a classic Harley Street man. His clients will be the 'worried well'. He's a cardiologist but I bet it's been ten years since he got his hands dirty and did anything other than write private prescriptions.

'Take my card,' he says as we finally approach Heathrow. 'I'm always looking for good people at my clinic. If you ever want help getting a proper job then call me.'

I'm still reeling from that one as I head back to the office with my bag. A proper job? What does he mean, a proper job? I'm furious. But for some reason I keep his card in my wallet.

My nose has dried up a bit as I get off the Tube in Hounslow but I obviously haven't got much colour.

'My God, Ben, you look a sight. It's breathing in all the bad air on the planes that will have done it,' Christine says as I head to the logistics desk.

I start to explain that it's the office that's made me ill but I give up. Christine doesn't seem to be buying it and I'm too tired to argue.

'Well, I've got a quick job that should perk you up. Maybe it's not that hot there yet but we've got you an overnighter in Barcelona. I went there last year for my wedding anniversary and it's my favourite city in Europe. If a trip to Barcelona doesn't make you feel better than nothing will.'

She hands me the paperwork. 'It's a bit of a sad one, I'm afraid, but hopefully they're nice people. I spoke to the girl's parents on the phone. They're scared, but they sound lovely, poor souls.'

It's a private job, which is why the patient's parents have been involved. Their daughter took too many drugs at a party. She was in Barcelona for a long weekend and didn't have any insurance. She's nineteen and has spent two days in intensive care and a week on a high dependency unit. The initial reports suggest her future is bleak. If she's got one at all.

I get a good night's sleep at home then fly out to Spain early the following morning. Christine's not wrong about Barcelona. How can you not fall in love with it? All I do is get a taxi from the airport to the hospital but I still feel excitement in the air. Even the people who empty the bins in the hospital look like they could be models. It's easy to see how you can get carried away if you go partying out here. My patient, Gemma Spencer, is the barely living proof that it can all go wrong.

She probably looked good when she flew out. Today she's got a tube going into her stomach to feed her and another hanging out of her nose to drain her secretions. She has facial droop. Her right leg can barely move and is going to wither away. Her right arm is just as useless. She won't dance again for a while, if ever. Inside her body I'm guessing that the situation is even worse. I'll read her notes in a moment to check on that. Before then I want to say hello. It seems she doesn't want to say hello back.

There are two teenage girls and a boy at her bedside. She's been sharing little jokes and laughs with them ever since I walked into the room. None of her friends seem to have any idea of how serious this is. All three of them seem to find it funny.

'Babes, your knight in shining armour is getting annoyed with you,' the first one says as I stand by the bedside. Her voice reeks of aggression and sarcasm.

'Are you going to get her home in a private plane?' asks another.

The third simply looks a little too closely at my medical bag. There's a very knowing, very calculating look in her eye.

'Gemma I think I should speak to you on your own before I examine you,' I say. No one moves. 'I need some privacy with my patient.'

'You want to watch him, babes. I had a doctor who wanted some privacy with me once. He touched me up for half an hour when I was too tied up with tubes to move.'

What should I say to that? I genuinely don't know. I'm
ashamed that I stay silent while the trio finally kiss and
fist-bump their way out of the room. They're white, rich
kids who like to think they're gangsters. All I know is that I
mustn't let this cloud my thoughts about my patient.

'Gemma, let's start again. I'm Doctor Ben MacFarlane.
Your parents have arranged for me to come here to help get
you home. I know that you've had a stroke. Can you tell me
how you feel?'

Gemma's blue eyes seem to sink even further into her
head. She's not said a single word so far. 'Gemma can you
hear me? Can you understand me?'

Nothing. She moves her head to lean away from me so
she can look out towards the other end of the room. The
right-hand side of her face is like an ill-fitting rubber mask.
We're at an impasse.

'Gemma, I will need to examine you to check you are
ready for the flight. Do you understand that? I'm going to
need to check your pulse, look into your eyes, your ears and
your throat. I'll need to get your blood pressure and check a
lot of other things as well. I need to know how mobile you
are and what you do and don't understand. Will you help
me with that?'

Nothing. Her eyes stay fixed on the wall opposite.

'Gemma I know how hard this is, but I am here to help
you. I'm going to speak to some of your doctors now but
when I come back I will have to start that examination.'

Outside the room her three friends are waiting. They
swagger back in as I walk away. I can hear Gemma telling
them not to leave next time. The stroke hasn't robbed her of
the power of speech, just good manners.

Gemma's doctor talks in clipped, concise English. He is

clearly a man who has seen more than his fair share of drug-related problems.

'People leave their brains behind when they come to Barcelona,' he says. 'They think the normal rules of life do not apply. Then this happens. Always cases like this happen.'

He talks me through Gemma's story. It began with cocaine but she probably branched out with other things as well. Maybe she got the high she wanted but she also got a surge of blood pressure that caused one of the arteries in her brain to burst. Gemma collapsed. She was comatose and convulsing when they got her to hospital. The doctors managed to control the fits with medication and they stopped the bleed into her brain. But that's it. She's got a severe neurological deficit – in simple terms, brain damage. She's hemiplegic, which is why the right side of her face and body is in such bad shape.

'She had another problem when we were caring for her,' the physician says.

She inhaled some food, something that happens a lot with stroke patients who lose their gag reflex. It gave her a nasty aspiration pneumonia that have could have killed her. Since then she's been fed through tubes and has fought that illness with the help of intravenous antibiotics. She's stable now but it's going to be touch and go for an awful long time.

'Maybe the best thing you can do for her is to take her away from her companions,' the doctor says. 'Have you met her parents?' I haven't. 'They have been here three days. They are good people. Perhaps it is not too late for them to help her. They need to find her different friends.'

I meet Gemma's parents as I walk back to her room. They are a pleasant-looking couple, probably in their early fifties, dressed in sober, conservative clothes. Her father is greying and tall. Her mother is petite and dark. They are standing in the corridor, seemingly intimidated by the people in their daughter's room. I shake hands with them both.

'Thank you for coming,' Mrs Spencer says to me. 'We're so sorry you've had to come all the way out here. We've never been involved in anything like this before. Thank you for helping us.'

'Can we go somewhere to talk?' her husband asks. We head to a waiting area that has a few spare seats. It's a busy room but everyone else is speaking in Spanish. Somehow that makes it feel as if we've got a bit of privacy.

'Steve can get you something, but I'm sorry I don't want to drink another cup of coffee for as long as I live,' Mrs Spencer says as we sit by a vending machine. It's the second time she's said sorry and the second time she's thanked me in the space of two minutes. She doesn't deserve all this. I'm fine without a drink so we get down to business.

'I know how worried you must be about your daughter but the first thing I can say is that she's been well looked after. I've met her doctors and I've seen the records of her treatment. She really couldn't have been in better hands.'

'Could she have died, doctor?'

'She could have done. People do, that's the saddest thing about all of this.'

'Bloody drugs,' her father blurts out.

His wife suddenly looks close to tears. He doesn't look at her but he reaches out across an empty chair. He instinctively finds her hand.

'You're not seeing the best of her, you know,' he says, a desperate, angry defiance in his eyes. He stands up, suddenly. 'She's a wonderful girl, the very best daughter we could have.

She's funny, bright, charming, beautiful. If you met her in any other place, doctor, you would be captivated. There's nothing in this world my daughter can't do. You should not be seeing her like this.' Then he slumps back into his chair. This time it is his wife's hand which somehow finds his.

'Tell us what happens next,' she says a few moments later. 'Please tell us she's going to be all right.'

The three so-called friends are still there when I walk into Gemma's room for her examination. I hold the door open and tell them they need to leave. This time they take even longer to say their shallow goodbyes. There is aggression in three sets of eyes as they strut past me. In their minds I'm the enemy. No wonder Gemma's poor parents are too scared to approach them.

The good news is that Gemma is ready to be moved. We have reservations on a scheduled flight out of Barcelona International Aiport the following morning. I talk her through how we'll get her to and through the airport, how it will be on the journey and what I'll need to do to keep her safe. I ask if she understands. Still there's nothing. She's still refusing even to look at me.

Her parents are outside the door. They always seem to be outside that door.

'Can I ask you something?' I say, edging them a few paces down the corridor. 'Your daughter hasn't said a single word to me so far. I think she's been talking to her friends though. Has she talked to you?'

This nice ordinary couple's utter embarrassment gives me the answer. 'She isn't well,' her mother says in the end. 'She doesn't mean to be cruel. She doesn't know what she's doing. When we get her home it will be different.'

They are still out in the corridor when I leave the hospital and head back to my hotel. I'd thought about heading into town. As it turns out I just stay in my room. It must just be the tail end of my cold. I feel totally wiped out. I've not eaten anything but I can't help feeling sick.

We get Gemma back to Britain the next day. The trip is a blur. Medically speaking I'm prepared for almost anything, not least a further, catastrophic bleed into her brain. I'm also ready for a nasty surprise at customs. I had seen real cunning in the eyes of one of Gemma's friends that morning. I wouldn't have been surprised if she hadn't slipped something into one of her bags. That way they might have all had something to use or sell back in Britain. As I wheel Gemma through the EU channel at customs I'm willing us to be taken aside for a search. If they find something I know who to point the finger at. I'd love to see those three people in court.

'You need to take it one day at a time,' I tell Gemma's mother in the ambulance. We're heading through the traffic to the stroke unit at the family's local hospital in Surrey. Medicine is full of such clichés. They cover a multitude of less attractive truths. Gemma simply lies on the stretcher next to us. She's saying nothing. The whole right side of her body is still drooped and useless.

'She'll get stronger every day. My daughter's going to be back to her old self in no time,' her dad tells me from the front seat. All I can do is nod and smile.

He's a decent man. The longer he believes that the better.

Jackie has left a message on my answering machine at home. 'I want to invite you and Cassie round for dinner on Monday if you're free. I've got a surprise to spring on

Tuesday and I want you to be the first to know.' I return
the call and ask about the surprise. Apparently I have to
wait and see. I look at Cassie's rota. She's on a layover in
Chicago next Monday.

'As she can't make it does that mean you can tell me the
surprise now?' I ask. Apparently not. Four days to go. At
least I'll be away for two of them. Less than twenty-four
hours after getting back from Barcelona I'm on my way to
the Canary Islands.

My patient fell off a balcony in a nightclub at 2:30am. The
notes we've been given are confusing. He's in a small medical
clinic and no one there seems to speak much English. We
always have plenty of language students working shifts in
our offices to translate documents and make calls for us. But
even the Spanish speakers haven't been able to make head or
tail of the information. In theory, every hospital in the world
should use the same basic format when they record a patient's
presenting complaint, medical history and so on. That way
any doctor can pick up the case and run with it straight away.

Here the system seems to have broken down. I'm on a
charter flight to the islands with very little idea of what I'm
going to find. This kind of job would probably be Rebecca's
worst nightmare. I'm looking forward to the challenge.

Camilla's booked me into a simple but nice hotel. I've got
a white-walled room with a big balcony that looks out over
what appears to be a long-forgotten building site. I stand in
the sunshine taking deep breaths of dry, dusty air. There's
not a single person in sight anywhere. It feels fantastic.

Things aren't quite so idyllic at the medical centre. In
many ways it resembles the building site opposite my hotel.
It's like stepping back in time. Everything's crumbling.
Nothing looks clean. The equipment looks as if it should

be in a museum. And where is everybody? Nobody stopped me when I arrived and I've walked around freely ever since. Most of the beds are filled with tired-looking elderly people. No one's watching over them. This is not where I'd want to end up after an accident on holiday.

'Buenos días. Soy medico. Soy aqui por un paciente, Andy Tyler.'

My Spanish is always something of a gamble but it seems to have got the message across today. I'd spotted a nurse sitting in the sunshine just outside a ward and she's leading me through to my patient.

He's asleep. The nurse leaves me with him and disappears. There are five other beds in the room, four are occupied and everyone in them is sleeping. I try to push the implications of that out of my mind for the moment. The notes I have on Andy Tyler show he's thirty-three and has had a lot of broken bones and injuries in the past. Looking at his upper body I see tattoos and a lot of bruising. On his shoulders and upper arms it's hard to see where one stops and the other begins. This little episode looks set to add to his already impressive collection of scars.

There's a file at the end of his bed and I take a look. There's not much there, but what I do see is puzzling. My Spanish is good enough to tell me that they've noted a skull fracture. But there's no record of a CT scan. The file says he's on oral antibiotics but I'm not sure what they're supposed to be tackling. It's time to wake him. 'Mr Tyler, I'm here to have a chat with you. Can you wake up?'

He does, with a start. 'Who the hell are you?' he asks.

'I'm the doctor who's been sent over from Britain to get you home. You've been here quite a while now. Are you okay to talk about your injuries?'

He is. Though bearing in mind that he can't speak Spanish and hardly anyone in the hospital speaks English he doesn't have much information to give me. I start to examine him. His ribs are a worry straight away. Several are fractured, but this wasn't mentioned in the case notes. It's also clear he's got a severe chest infection, though the antibiotics they've got him on are unlikely to clear it up. My call is that he needs different medication straight away – preferably intravenously. My other instinct is that it's too soon for this guy to travel. There are a lot of tests I'd like to be done before I can be confident we know how vulnerable he is. Putting him on a plane before his chest infection stabilises would certainly be a bad move. Then I look around me. This place is incredibly basic. This is more of an evacuation than a repatriation and Mr Tyler will have a tough journey ahead. My call is that if the alternative is to leave him here then it's a risk worth taking

I do another self-guided tour of the hospital and finally find someone to speak to about my patient. The doctor speaks faltering English and he's extremely keen to please. It's not his fault he's working in a medical dark age. I call the office on my mobile and get one of our Spanish speakers to ask him some other questions so I know a bit more about Mr Tyler's care.

Then I ask to be put through to someone on the logistics desk. I get Robbie. 'We want to be on the first flight you can get,' I say.

'First thing tomorrow okay?'

'Sounds perfect.'

'You know he's got his girlfriend with him? I'll give you her name, it's Aileen Barham. The insurer's paying for her as well. I'll text you the exact times when I've had them confirmed. It'll be about seven-thirty in the morning. We've got you taking them on to Leeds Bradford after that. Is everything okay out there?'

There's not much I can say in front of the local doctor. 'It's fine. The guy just wants to get home. I'll maybe see you tomorrow.'

I head back to my patient's bed. He's looking a bit confused, all of a sudden, which is yet another thing to worry about. For a moment I don't think he remembers who I am. When I ask him about his girlfriend it takes him a while to reply. 'She'll be here later,' he says, finally. Then he just stares down towards the floor.

I write our probable flight times on a sheet of paper and put my name and mobile number at the bottom of it. 'Does Aileen have a phone?'

'Of course she's got a phone.'

'Well, get her to call me when she arrives and I can talk her through how we'll get home. It's going to be an early start and a long day.'

I don't want to go to a restaurant on my own so I buy some food in a little supermarket and eat dinner on my balcony. Not everyone would like my dusty little view, but I find it restful. It's so quiet. I'm amazed Mr Tyler found a nightclub at all round here, let alone one with a balcony to fall off.

I meet Aileen just before six the following morning. She's a slight, nervous-looking girl in her early twenties. She's dragged two big suitcases to his bedside and she's sitting next to him staring at her hands. When I introduce myself to her she can barely look at me. Her eyes keep darting towards her boyfriend's face. She seems far more nervous than the situation demands.

When we're sitting on the plane a couple of hours later
I get my first clue about why. She's reaching up to get
something out of the overhead bin. As she does so her
pale blue shirt falls down to reveal a black sleeveless top.
She's got her own collection of heavy bruises all over her
shoulders and upper arms. There are also a few wounds that
look suspiciously like burns. She blushes as she sits down.
She pulls the shirt back around her. Her boyfriend is on my
left, wide awake. Do I say something? I have to.

'You look like you've been in the wars yourself. You didn't
fall off the balcony as well, did you?' I'm trying to keep it
light. She looks panic-stricken.

'I'm fine. Just fine,' she keeps saying. Her hands hold her
shirt even tighter round her shoulders.

An ambulance takes us to the medical centre at
Heathrow. I give Mr Tyler another intravenous shot of
antibiotics, the type he should have been having all
along. What I can't do is get Aileen on her own. She
won't leave her boyfriend's side. I can't say a word to
her without him hearing. After an hour we head back
to the terminal to fly on up to Leeds Bradford airport.
She sticks to her man like glue. I hand them over to the
orthopaedic registrar at the hospital in York and get a
train back to London.

I've just remembered that Aileen's phone number will
be in my mobile. I don't know quite what I'm going
to say. But I won't sleep unless I make the call. At the
office we have contact details for dozens of counselling
services and medical support groups we can give to
patients and their families if they need them. We don't
deal with this kind of thing every day but we know
where Aileen should go if she needs help. I'll pass some

numbers over tomorrow then leave it up to her. I hope she takes advantage.

I don't know what to expect when I ring Jackie's doorbell on Monday night. She hadn't wanted anyone to see her since she started her treatment. I think her exact words had been: 'Don't take it personally but if anyone comes round I'll set the dogs on you.' Her exile ended last week. Camilla had gone round for dinner on Thursday and Christine went for coffee on Saturday. They'd both said how well Jackie looked. But you never know. I'm ready for anything as the door opens. 'You look amazing,' I say. I mean it. She really does.

'Thank you for coming all the way out here. I don't feel ready to brave the restaurant scene in Hounslow.'

'Good idea. It's hard to believe, but none of our usual places have won a Michelin star while you've been away. Jackie, I am so pleased that you're looking so well.'

'I told you it would take more than a few rogue cancer cells to beat me. Now have a drink. I've become obsessed by juicing but if you fancy something stronger take your pick.'

I have a beer and sit opposite Jackie in the living room.

'The kids are all still awake so I don't want to talk about any medical things till they're asleep. If you don't want to talk about them at all then that's fine. So tell me a bit more about your latest jobs. Christine said you were in the Canaries. Any dramas?'

'None, apart from a health centre that was practically medieval, a skull fracture that no one seemed to care about and a battered girlfriend who wants to stand by her man.'

'Fabulous. You have no idea how much I've missed all

this. Talk me through the whole trip. As well as everything else you've done this month.'

We carry on talking shop for about an hour. I'm slightly aware that all my stories are a bit grim. Drug overdoses, domestic violence, irritating private practice doctors and lonely old ladies. But Jackie wants to hear every detail. Her kids come in at one point to say goodnight. I've not met them before and they're just as well behaved as I'd expected. I look around a bit while Jackie's upstairs. There are family photos all over the living room. There are swings, slides and bikes out in the darkness of the back garden. My Harley Street doctor was wrong. You don't need a private practice or a fancy pension to build a great life.

'So what do you think of my hair?' Jackie's back. Good for her for facing up to the elephant in the room. She'd decided not to wear a cold cap for her chemo so she lost her hair over the course of the treatment. 'The best gift I got was a clothes brush. When you wear black like I do you need to pick up a lot of hairs,' she'd told Camilla last week.

'You look great. Very chic,' I say. She does. Her hair's grown back a lot straighter and shorter and greyer than it was. But it looks healthy and it suits her. If anything she looks younger, though I'm sure she'd laugh at me if I said so. Instead I tell her she should have had it cut that way years ago.

'Thank you. I was worried I might scare the horses. Now, time to eat. It's not posh cooking, I'm afraid.'

I follow her into the kitchen and she heats up some soup and makes some pasta. Back in the living room it's good to see her appetite is back. 'You know the best meal I've had so far this year was in first-class on Emirates. This beats it by a mile,' I say as I eat.

'There's no finer compliment than that. I can't wait to get back into any first-class cabin.' Jackie pushes her empty plate away from her.

'So, you're still going to do repats?'

'Of course I am. You try and stop me. I've done a lot of thinking over the past six months. One thing I'm sure about is that this is the best job in medicine.'

'I wish you'd spoken to my Harley Street man. He made me feel as if I'd screwed up my whole career by doing this. I had a real wobble for a few days when I tried to work out if he was right.'

Jackie smiles. 'Ben, we all have wobbles every now and then. I had a bad patch when I'd done a year or so of repats as well. I got spooked by the thought of all my med school colleagues calling me a trolley dolly behind my back.'

'So what happened?'

'I got over it. I quite liked the idea of being a trolley dolly. I always thought I'd look quite fetching in a little hat and scarf combo.'

'I'm serious. Why did you stay?'

She smiles. 'Because the job's in my blood. Yes, I worried about the money for a while. Yes, I got fed up of the jet-lag, the airline food, the airport coffee, all the delays. I started to hate all those crack-of-dawn trips down the Piccadilly line and the times I didn't get back to my front door till past midnight. But you know what? If I had a week at home I'd walk past a kebab shop and just the smell made me want to be in Istanbul. I'd see a Chinese lantern in a shop window and I'd want to be on a street in Hong Kong looking at a thousand of them. I'd think of all the places I still wanted to see. I couldn't bear to work in the local medical centre and just have a few weeks of annual leave. Plus I worked out I could get promoted, pick and choose the best trips and still take my kids to school most mornings. I've missed this job so much over the past six months. I don't want someone like you to take it for granted.'

We carry on talking till about ten. It's like old times and it's great. I'm getting ready to go when I remember my other reason for being there. 'What's the big surprise?'

This time Jackie's really smiling. 'I don't want to do my first job back on my own. I want to ease into things. So I asked Camilla to let me know when a relatively straightforward air ambulance job comes up.'

I think I've guessed what might be coming next. 'Well I'm doing an air ambulance trip tomorrow afternoon. I'm picking up a guy from Abu Dhabi. I'm travelling with Rebecca.'

Jackie is clapping her hands together in excitement. 'Not any more you're not. Camilla and I swore Rebecca to secrecy. She's having three days off and I'm taking her place. I'll see you bright and early tomorrow morning because you're travelling with me.'

APRIL

Jackie gets a round of applause when she arrives at the office just after midday to collect her med bag. I get a stern talk from Robbie while everyone is crowding around her.

'You make sure you look after her, all right,' he tells me. 'Don't let her lift anything, don't leave her on her own anywhere, don't let her out of your sight. Remember you nearly scared the life out of poor Rebecca when you took her on an air ambulance job. We don't want any dramas with the boss.'

Things certainly start well. There's no traffic and it's a smooth taxi ride to Biggin Hill in Kent. The airport is great. Apart from Heathrow and Gatwick it's the only place in southern England where your pets can fly in with you from abroad. If you hang around long enough you get to see the country's most pampered pooches trot down the steps of private planes. There's also some brilliant people-watching, from harassed executives to rich teenagers who have no idea how lucky they are.

Our pilot is all uniformed up and greets us with a smile and a handshake. There really is something very cool about being led across a terminal building by your own pilot, even if everyone else is doing the same. When we get outside

we head across the tarmac towards our plane. It could be
a coincidence but I'm guessing that Camilla, Christine or
Robbie pulled some strings to get us something this good.
It's a Lear jet. It's just as flash as it sounds.

We settle down in our big leather seats. 'I've been told
this is a special flight,' the pilot says to Jackie. 'One of your
colleagues said something about tracking me down and
haunting me if we have even five minutes of turbulence.'

'That must be Robbie,' Jackie says.

'One of your other colleagues arranged for full catering,' the
pilot adds.

I'd guessed as much. We normally buy our own sandwiches
for air ambulance trips. Camilla had told me not to bother
today. The food we get must have cost a fortune. There's tea
and scones for just after take-off. We have canapés a little
later. Then smoked salmon, salad, quiches, breads, cheeses
and all sorts of other nibbles for a light dinner, and coffee
and cakes for pudding. Before we start on all that Jackie and
I open a mini bottle of champagne. We toast the office as we
reach cruising altitude.

'This is even better than I remembered it,' says Jackie.
'How many other people get to fly in a plane like this for a
living?'

Northern France is spread out beneath us as we start on
the scones. Jackie picks up one of the small glass jars of
jam and smiles. 'You know the last time I used one of these?
I was on holiday with the kids. I answered an "Is there a
medical doctor on board?" call on a flight from Orlando. We
had a diabetic in economy who'd gone hypo. I got them to
do another tannoy call to see if anyone had any glucagon.
No one came forward. So I stormed into first class and
grabbed a pot of strawberry jam off some guy's tea tray. By

the time I got back the passenger had passed out. I grabbed the back of his head, pulled his jaw open and smeared the jam on to his gums.'

'Did it do the trick?'

'Straight away. But I nearly gave everyone else a heart attack when I headed to the loo to wash up. The steward let me jump the queue. He told the others I was a doctor who'd been treating a fellow passenger. There I was with all this red stuff all over my fingers. They thought I'd done open heart surgery.'

We laugh away talking about other jobs. I finally tell Jackie about the time I was offered a kidney on a trip back from Pakistan. 'I'd only done three or four jobs so I wasn't sure if this sort of thing was normal. I think they saw my med bag and reckoned I could get through customs without a proper search. They must have planned to buy it off someone in some village out there and transplant it to someone in London.'

'Where did they approach you?'

'In the hospital. A little group of them scuttled after me as I headed back to my hotel. They said they needed to talk about business.'

'Were they doctors?'

'I don't know. No one challenged them about what they were doing there. They were deadly serious about it all. I could have put down a deposit on a flat with the money they were offering. They said if it worked out I could do one every few months.'

Jackie shrugs. 'Some idiot will take them up on an offer like that one day. Which is stupid because you don't need to break the law to get rich doing this. Before you joined we lost two freelancers to a big Saudi family. They'd done a couple of private hand-holding jobs for them and got offered full-time positions – on crazy salaries. I saw one of them a year or so into the job. He flies around the world with the family and lives in the most incredible houses. All he really does is clear up some STDs on the men. Plus twisting a few arms so the death certificates always say "cardiac failure" or "pneumonia" when one of the uncles dies of cirrhosis of the liver.'

'Incredible.'

'Isn't it? Fingers crossed we get that kind of job offer in Abu Dhabi.'

The plane is fantastically comfortable and incredibly quiet. We snack on our dinners, read a bit, doze a bit and talk some more. We also run through the details of the man we are flying out to help. Con Porter is a twenty-six-year-old financial adviser who broke his neck in a kite surfing accident.

'What exactly is kite surfing?' Jackie asks as we read through the file. I'm not the world's expert but I explain it as best I can. 'It's hard to see how you can do that *without* ending up paraplegic,' she says when I've finished. 'He must have a bloody good insurance policy.'

Mr Porter has been in intensive care for five days breathing with the aid of a ventilator. He's now had a tracheotomy – not nice but at least he can breathe for himself. We'll just need to suction the tube every hour or so to clean out the secretions. He's also lost control of his bowels and bladder so we'll need to keep an eye on that. He's being fed through a tube and will need regular turning to stop him getting bed sores. I seem to remember Jackie saying she wanted this job because it looked 'relatively straightforward'. She always did like a challenge.

We refuel in Cyprus and it's just before midnight when
our pilot tells us we're starting our descent into the UAE.
I'm guessing we'll be tucked up in our hotel beds within
the hour. But that's not quite how it works out. We land
smoothly and taxi towards a quiet corner of the airport.
'Good sleep?' I ask Jackie.

'I always sleep well on planes. I'm lucky,' she says. 'But
I'm still looking forward to my bed at the hotel. Camilla
reckons she's booked us in somewhere really special.'

I look at my watch. We're due to collect the patient in ten
hours time. I want to get to the hotel soon so we have a bit
of time to enjoy it.

Our engines shut down and we wait for the ground staff
to come over and do their checks. Nothing happens for ages.
Our pilots come in to apologise.

'They said they were ready for us, but something must
have come up,' one of them says. After about half an hour
a little crowd of uniformed staff finally arrive. It's hard
to know if they're customs or immigration workers. It is
clear that they're all in a very bad mood. They walk round
the plane then huddle outside and start some long mobile
phone conversations. Then they come on board. No one says
anything as they begin what looks like a fingertip search of
every inch of the plane. Then they open our medical bags.
That's when it gets noisy. Several long conversations in
Arabic begin. Many more phone calls are made from inside
and outside the plane. Still we don't get any clues as to
what's going on.

'Can we help you at all? We're doctors. We're here to collect
a very sick patient and fly him back to England,' Jackie
says. 'All the correct paperwork is here. Everything has been
arranged officially from London.' The men ignore her.

It's the same when they demand our documentation. 'We want your passport,' one of them says to me. 'Now, the other passport,' he says when he wants Jackie's. He won't take it from her when she offers it. She has to hand it to me so I can give it to him.

'Is something going on?' I ask our pilot at one point. He shrugs but doesn't speak. There's a slightly resigned look on his face. Maybe this happens all the time. The most difficult moment comes when a new set of officers arrive. Our medical bags are once more the subject of an argument.

'We need to take these,' one of these newcomers declares.

'We will need them at the hospital,' I say. I point at my watch. 'Ten o'clock, at the hospital. We will need our equipment. We're doctors.' I don't get any response.

Finally we are led out of the plane and into a Range Rover that takes us towards one of the terminal buildings. It's still hot in the night air and the smell of plane fuel quite literally takes your breath away. Jackie and I are led to different desks where we stand while yet more officers begin a forensic examination of our passports. All I can think is that two months ago Jackie was undergoing chemotherapy. This should not be happening to her. Of all the trips she could have chosen, why on earth did she go for this one?

It takes more than forty-five minutes for the immigration staff to finish discussing us and allow us into the arrivals area. Several members of the airport staff follow us as we head towards the taxi queue. When we get into a cab we discover we've got company. A police car has pulled up just behind us and follows us all the way to our hotel.

'This is absolutely amazing. I've never had a single problem coming out here before,' Jackie whispers. 'I've made it through that airport in ten minutes on other jobs. I think it must be you, Ben. You're dragging me down.'

Things don't get much better at the hotel. The receptionist wants to hold on to our passports but we want to keep them with us. He speaks to the policeman who has just walked in. After a few moments he hands them back to us with our room cards. 'Well, let's try and get some sleep. I'm going to go down for breakfast at eight and we can leave to see the patient at nine,' Jackie says.

'I'll see you at breakfast,' I reply. 'I don't think either of us will have any trouble getting to sleep tonight.'

Unfortunately I'm wrong. I've been given a gloriously large suite with a view out over a vast swimming pool. I find out later that Jackie's room looks out on an inner courtyard and is the size of my bathroom. Both of us have visitors every hour, on the hour. 'Your passport, please,' a security guard asks. I refuse to hand it over and when he's gone I ring Jackie's room. She's going to do the same. An hour later the guard is back at my door. Once more he asks for my passport, once more I refuse to hand it over. I call Jackie. I hear her doorbell ring while I'm on the line. It continues like this all night. By 7am the routine is running a little stale, so I shower, shave, gaze out over the pool and head down to breakfast. Jackie joins me shortly afterwards.

This is the best part of the trip. There are only about ten other guests scattered around the hotel dining room and there's enough food to feed about a hundred of us. There are amazing bowls of fruits as well as every type of bread and pastry. Half a dozen chefs are standing at different tables ready to prepare any type of hot food we choose. It's overwhelming. After forty minutes we go up to our rooms to get our stuff and check out. I chat briefly to the bell hop while I wait for Jackie to join me in reception. He tells me the city is having a heatwave. It's humid and it's already thirty degrees – far hotter than it should be on an April morning. I can't say I mind. I step out into the sun and feel it bleach all the tiredness from my bones. No wonder people retire to hot countries. Last night feels like a distant memory already.

The hospital is world class. Our patient's been well looked after though it's clear he's going to need a lot more care when he gets back to the UK. We chat to him, examine him and speak to his doctors.

'What do you think?' I ask Jackie out in the corridor.

'He's going to keep us busy. It won't be an easy one but I'm confident about him. I say we do it.'

We finish off the paperwork and Mr Porter is trolleyed out to an ambulance. The great thing about private planes is they can leave whenever you want them to. We call the pilots and confirm we're on our way. With a bit of luck we'll be in the air within an hour. 'We've got a very nice plane lined up for you, Mr Porter,' I say as we sweep down an avenue of palm trees. 'You're going to be travelling in style.'

We've been approved to clear security in the ambulance and to drive out on the tarmac to our plane. That's when it all starts to go wrong again. A group of uniformed staff argue with our driver before we are let through the first of the perimeter fences. The same officials who hadn't liked seeing us arrive appear just as unhappy now we want to leave.

The ambulance pulls up close to our plane but we're not allowed to board it. We open the back doors but a uniformed guard won't let us get out.

'There's probably just a bit of paperwork to do then we'll get you on the plane, Mr Porter,' I say.

Half an hour passes and nothing happens. I ask the guard what's going on and he just shakes his head. After another fifteen minutes a group of customs staff approach. They talk to our ambulance driver then board our plane. Another half-hour passes. Every few minutes the roar of a landing or takeoff rocks our vehicle. The smell of air fuel is even stronger than ever.

'Do you know what the problem is?' Our driver simply shrugs. I climb out of the ambulance, but the guard won't let me step away from it. It's incredibly hot in the sun.

Finally, something is happening. The first set of customs officers leave our plane and are joined by another set of men who have driven up in a 4x4. They approach our driver and he hands them some paperwork. The guard again raises his hand when I move to step forward. My Arabic doesn't extend much beyond hello, please and thank you. All I can hear is a wall of words that could mean anything. Meanwhile the temperature and the humidity are rising.

'Is there any way to put on any air in here?' I climb back into the ambulance. Jackie is fanning our patient with a laminated card. We're effectively in a small metal box on a big concrete runway in the middle of a desert. It's nearly midday and the sun is almost directly overhead. I also look at our patient. If he gets seriously dehydrated he could go into renal failure. Then it really could be all over.

Jackie must be reading my mind. She looks at her watch then she looks up at me. 'Right. That's it. It's over,' she says. 'Keep an eye on the patient, Ben. I'm sorting it out.'

She climbs out of the ambulance. She ignores the armed guard who's put up both hands and is telling her to stay where she is. She marches across the runway to the group of customs men.

'I am a doctor,' she says, hands on hips. I can see them all desperately trying to work out what to do. They can hardly ignore her now. 'I am in charge of a seriously ill patient. He is a very sick man. I need to get him into this plane and I need to get him home to the United Kingdom. I demand that you let me do my job.'

The men start to argue amongst themselves. Jackie's not having it. 'Excuse me. I demand that we are allowed to get on this plane. No discussion. No argument. Right now.'

She turns on her heel and marches back to the ambulance. 'Right, let's get moving.' We lower Mr Porter's stretcher to the tarmac and wheel him to the open door of the plane. Our pilots help lift him aboard. The last thing I see as we climb up the steps are eight burly men looking open-mouthed at this wildcat of a lady who has broken all their rules and got away with it.

'Thank you,' she says to them, from the plane's doorway.

We set up a saline drip for our patient and start making him comfortable. 'You don't take any prisoners, boss,' I say.

'I've beaten cancer. I'm not going to be beaten by a bunch of jobsworths on an airport runway,' she says.

She's glowing. She's back.

Robbie looks at me in horror when I tell him what happened. 'I told you not to let her lift anything. I thought keeping her away from armed guards went without saying,' is his verdict. 'Just for that I'm allocating you the worst job we've got. I'm sending you to Bulgaria.'

I pretend I'm upset but I'm actually quite pleased. Bulgaria is one of the few European countries I've never visited. I'm glad I'll finally be able to cross it off my list.

When I get to the hospital in Sofia it looks as if I'm going
to have a particularly easy ride – the managers have found
me an interpreter. She's an unlikely mix of charm and
ruthless efficiency. We head off through a Pentagon-style
set of concentric corridors at a heck of a pace. As we march
I realise it wouldn't just be the language and the hospital
layout I'd struggle with on my own, simply identifying a
doctor here looks tricky. Everyone seems to be dressed alike.

'I have not met your patient before but I believe he should
be in this next ward,' my interpreter says.

I spot him the moment we walk in. He's a thirty-eight-
year-old engineer. No one else in his ward is under eighty.
Several of the other patients are women. The poor sod must
have woken up and thought he'd been put on a geriatric
ward. 'You're Mr Bawden? I'm Doctor Ben MacFarlane. I've
been sent to get you home.'

His hand is shaking slightly as he reaches out to meet
mine. 'Thank you,' he says, again and again. 'Thank you for
coming.'

'I will go and tell the doctors you are here,' my interpreter
says.

'Are you okay, Mr Bawden?' I ask as she leaves.

He's breathing very fast. 'Can you tell me what day it is?'
he asks.

My heart suddenly goes out to the guy. When you come
round in a hospital thousands of miles from home how do
you know if you've been there a day, a week or a month?
When everyone around you is over eighty you probably
think you've been there even longer.

'It's Thursday,' I say. I give him the date as well. 'You've
been here for seven days. After you were admitted you
had surgery on your gall bladder so they put you under a

general anaesthetic. You also had a follow-up operation
the next day. You've been sedated and you've done a lot of
sleeping. But you've recovered well. Do you want me to talk
you through what's happened to you?'

He does, so I open his file. The presenting complaints
when he was admitted to the hospital were pain, fever
and vomiting. A gallstone had become lodged in his bile
duct, his gall bladder was seriously inflamed and on the
point of rupturing. The pain, at that point, must have been
excruciating. He'd had emergency surgery to remove the
inflamed gall bladder. What they hadn't realised was that
another stone had dropped and was blocking the outlet of
the pancreas. This was becoming just as seriously inflamed
so they needed a second operation to remove dead tissue
and the second stone. He was on an intensive care ward
for four days and has been recovering now for a week
and a half. No wonder he's disorientated and wants to get
home.

He listens to everything I say and starts thanking me all
over again. He asks if I can charge up his mobile phone, but
I don't have an adaptor. 'Do you want me to call anyone?' I
ask.

He shakes his head. 'I do, but I don't know anyone's
number. They're all on my SIM card. I've tried to remember
some in case I ever got to a pay phone but I can't. I haven't
been able to speak to my girlfriend, my dad, my boss or
anyone since the day I got admitted. It's like my whole life's
been turned off since then. It's like I don't exist.'

I pull my own phone apart to see if I can get his SIM card
into it. I can and it works.

'Call away. I'm going to get myself a coffee and then
speak to your doctors. I'll see you in half an hour or so.'

What a transformation. Mr Bawden is no longer shaking when I rejoin him.

'I spoke to all of them. They've all been going spare. The insurance company kept telling my girlfriend that I'd be back soon but she didn't believe it. She had the hospital's phone number but she couldn't get past the switchboard because they didn't understand her. Am I really going to get home tomorrow?'

'That's the idea. I spoke to your doctors and he's ready to sign you out. I'll just check you over now then I'll call the office and confirm our flights. The plan is for me to be here about midday tomorrow, we'll get to the airport by ambulance and we fly in the middle of the afternoon. It's about three and a half hours to London. When we get there we should have another ambulance to take you to hospital in Milton Keynes.' I don't think I've ever seen a grown man look so happy.

'I'll see you tomorrow,' I say and shake his hand. The job's not yet done but this looks like one very happy customer.

He's still smiling when we get to the airport bang on schedule the following day. It's crowded and it's not easy to get his wheelchair past all the luggage trolleys at check-in. Security is tight as well. The staff won't let him go through the security arch in his wheelchair, which is fair enough, though they won't let anyone support him as he stumbles through it on his very weak legs. Lots of hand-luggage is being opened after going through the X-ray machine. My med bag gets a thorough examination and they spot a lot of things they clearly don't want on a plane. A supervisor is called over and I'm led away to an interview in a screened-off area at the end of the room. It is never good to leave a patient unattended. I cross my fingers that the interview

won't take long – and that the only rubber gloves involved
will be the ones in the sealed packs in my bag. I get lucky.
The supervisor and his boss spend a long time looking at my
passport and paperwork. One man leaves the room with one
of the print-outs from the local hospital. A few minutes later
he's back, nods and shrugs at his superior. I'm guessing he
called the hospital to check we're genuine.

'Doctor MacFarlane, have a nice day,' the boss man tells me
in the most serious of voices. I'm free to go.

Outside a man has been found to push Mr Bawden's chair.
He's a very smiley, gap-toothed man of about sixty. The only
word that he can make us understand is his name: Gavril.
We're let into an executive lounge and I look the other way
every time Gavril slips another mini Kit Kat or packet of
pretzels into his pocket.

When our flight is called Gavril pushes Mr Bawden on
towards our gate. We have to go through a second set of
security arches and metal detectors there. Gavril stands aside
and shakes our hands to say goodbye. But the staff still give
him a pat down and a security screen with their wands. I've
never seen that happen before. I'm glad they didn't confiscate
his Kit Kats.

We are given a hot meal on the flight and Mr Bawden
wolfs it all down in about a minute. I can see him eyeing
my bread roll hungrily. I pass it over to him. How do airlines
make bread rolls that weigh almost nothing? He practically
eats it whole.

'It has to say something if the best food you've had in
seven days is an airline meal,' I say.

'You have no idea. All I had in the hospital was soup. It
came in three different colours, on rotation every different
mealtime. I couldn't identify the flavour of any of them.

I thought if I ever got out of there no one at home would recognise me. I'd be like a bloody skeleton.'

'Would you like more water, Sir?' The flight attendant is at our side.

'If this man would let me I'd like a beer,' he says.

'Sorry mate, no can do.'

'Water then,' he tells her. 'But if you wanted to slip something stronger in my glass I wouldn't mind for a moment.'

As we fly on Mr Bawden asks for more details of his illness. He really has been in the dark for the past week. I talk him through what gall bladders are, what they do and what had gone wrong with his. Then I decide he's relaxed enough for me to tell him a bit of medical school folklore. 'Statistically speaking gall bladder problems normally hit people who match up to the six "Fs",' I say. 'You're more likely to be affected if you're fair, fat, female, forty, fertile and flatulent.'

He moves around just slightly in his seat. 'I'm one of those, doctor. I'll leave you to guess which!'

Rebecca has surprised everybody while I've been in Bulgaria. She's volunteered to do another job. It's a two-hander and it's with me. Robbie, for one, is aghast.

'I told her she needs her head examined,' he says to me. 'I said that in Abu Dhabi you made Jackie walk in front of a tank like in Tiananmen Square. I said you were a liability to medicine. But she's adamant. I think she's losing her mind.'

I'm quite flattered, to be honest, but I am a bit worried. Statistically speaking I must be due an incident-free two-hander. I'm just not sure it will be this one. We're flying to

Ben MacFarlane

Madrid to pick up a twenty-eight-year-old long-distance lorry driver from Carlisle. He was taking a nap in his cab just outside the city. He was also having a sneaky cigarette and the two activities don't really mix. When his blankets caught fire he suffered major burns requiring immediate skin grafts. Smoke inhalation means he's also suffered severe heat damage to his throat. It's a full stretcher job to get him home and our man will need a lot of watching.

'It's great that you want to do this,' I say to Rebecca when we're getting our med bags ready at the office.

'I've got an ulterior motive, I'll tell you later,' she whispers. I can't say I like the sound of that.

One of our regular taxi drivers takes us to Heathrow and Rebecca doesn't want to talk in front of him. She opens up when we settle down on a sofa in the executive lounge.

'I'm leaving,' she says. 'I was hoping you might write me a reference.'

'Where are you going?'

'You'll laugh. But I've applied to work on a cruise ship.'

'I won't laugh. We'll miss you if you do that.'

She smiles. 'I'll miss everybody. I've never worked with such a nice group of people. We have such a good time on the desk there. But I know that if I stay I'm wasting my nursing skills.'

'So do more jobs like this one.'

'That's what Camilla keeps saying. I've tried so hard. But I don't think I'll ever get enough confidence. I know it's ridiculous. I just feel so vulnerable when I'm on my own with a patient. I'm even scared on two-handers like this one. I was fine in a hospital where everything was to hand. I just can't relax when I know something could go wrong halfway round the world. I have nightmares about a whole plane

270

full of passengers staring at me expecting me to know what to do. I just crumble. You know that story Bilal tells about making an inhaler for a little girl out of polystyrene cups? I don't have that kind of inventiveness.'

'So why cruise ships?' Rebecca's face softens.

'You probably don't remember but I did do one successful job earlier in the year. A lady who broke her hip falling off a bar stool on a cruise ship in Palma.'

It's my turn to smile. Our nurses do those jobs all the time. Bar stools on cruise ships should carry health warnings.

'I went on board to collect her. The doctor gave me a little tour of his medical centre. I met two of his nurses. Ben, it was incredible. They had an amazing amount of kit. They were a team. They all seemed to get on really well – as well as we do at the office. I could imagine them all supporting each other in an emergency, knowing where everything is, being really efficient and just getting the job done. It tempted me.'

'So did they offer you a job?'

'I wrote the guy a letter. He wrote back and told me who I should speak to at head office. Now I'm having an interview. I can keep Camilla happy by seeing the world this way. But I won't be so bloody terrified all the time. It has to be the right thing to do.'

I get us a couple more coffees while I think about what to say. The others will be devastated if Rebecca leaves. But I can see why she wants to. 'Shouldn't you ask Jackie for a reference?' I ask, playing for time.

'I would, but she hardly knows me. She's been off almost all the time I've been with the company. You were there when we saved Mr Cadogan. You know what I can do if I've got the right support. So will you do it?'

'Of course I'll do it. Only when we get back from this trip, though. I want it to be so good you change your mind.'

We get to Madrid on time. A taxi takes us out into the suburbs to his hospital where our patient has been recovering for nearly two weeks. For Rebecca's sake I'm hoping he's a decent bloke. He seems to be – though the heat damage to his throat rules out any long conversations.

Rebecca and I share the initial examination. We peel back a few of his bandages. The skin graft looks like it's taking well but a lot of fluid is still weeping out of it. It's not just the parts of his body that got burned that need taking care of now. The graft donor site will be just as sensitive.

As with all burns patients one challenge on our flight home will be to keep Mr Crawford's fluid balance right. He's on intravenous fluids so we can control what goes into his system. He's got a catheter so we can measure what's coming out. Just as importantly we need to manage his pain levels. Even now his whole body will be screaming at him. The hospital has had him on slow-release morphine but we'll need to top him up now and then – especially when we move him. The bad news is that we'll need to do this twice. None of the carriers who fly direct to London are offering us stretcher space. We need to change planes in Germany. It will be a long day, even if every flight leaves on time.

'Are you up for it, Rebecca?'

We've talked through all the things that could possibly go wrong and all the kit we've got in our bags and in the airline's bag.

'I'm as ready as I'll ever be,' she says.

So off we go to the airport. Our German crew are brilliant. They offer us a coffee while the ground-staff get Mr

Crawford's stretcher lifted up into the plane. He gives a bit of a groan as he's edged into his new bed.

'It's as small as the cabin in my cab,' he says in a low voice. 'It feels like I'm back at work.'

Rebecca buys him some yoghurts and a banana at Frankfurt airport. At Heathrow we get him ready for a very long ambulance ride north. No internal flight was prepared to carry him.

'So do you promise to give up smoking?' Rebecca asks him as the ambulance staff strap him in.

'I promise to give up smoking in bed,' he says.

Rebecca and I head back into the terminal while we wait for a car to take us back to the office. We'd had a nice dinner out the previous evening and our hotel had been decent, though nothing special. I've got a feeling it's not been enough to change Rebecca's mind.

'Do you still want the reference?' I ask.

'Yes please. I need it quite quickly. My interview is tomorrow morning.'

MAY

One of my old friends from medical school ended up
specialising in liver disease. He reckons his patients are
colour coded.

'If they go walkabout and end up in the wrong part of the
hospital the nurses only need to look at them. The rule is
that if they're yellow, they're mine,' he says.

My next patient could certainly use his expertise. He's
sixty-seven and was taking his children and grandchildren
to Disney World with his wife. He's got a bunch of balloons
and a pair of Mickey Mouse ears hanging on the back of
his hospital bed. He tells me his kids and grandkids have
been visiting him every day. There's a mixture of pride and
sadness in his voice.

Apparently he began changing colour just after they
arrived in Orlando. For a day or so the family thought he
was tanning. When the whites of his eyes went custard
yellow they had to admit that this wasn't normal. He
had jaundice – and a lot more besides. They got him to a
hospital and the CT scan showed up a tumour at the head
of his pancreas. His notes explain what happened next.
The doctors performed what's called an ERCP – using a
telescopic camera to put a plastic pipe in his bile duct. That

gave temporary relief to his jaundice. But ultimately the effect will only be palliative. Mr O'Sullivan has inoperable cancer of the pancreas.

I smile and chat a little after examining him. Then I make some silly joke about the mouse ears and the balloons and head off to see his doctors. They're suitably sober. They say Mr O'Sullivan's options for chemotherapy are limited. The consensus is that I'm taking him home to die.

The poor man struggles to settle on our flight. Jaundice makes you itchy as well as nauseated. But he's looking forward to getting home. He has a theory about what will happen there.

'The NHS is going to sort me out, I know that,' he says. 'Those doctors were good but it's all about the money in America. They were all doom and gloom because they know my insurance company won't pay for all the treatment I need. I'll get it at home. I've hardly been ill a day in my life, doctor. I'll shake this off, you just watch.'

'With an attitude like that you've got more chance than anyone else.' I say.

I can't work out if he knows the truth. Maybe, just maybe, he'll prove everyone wrong. The trouble is, inoperable tends to mean what it says. You can have all the money in the world and still die of cancer. Not even the NHS can save everyone.

'You know, we never got to Sea World,' he tells me a little later when he sees a set of pictures in the in-flight magazine. He's wearing a Disney World T-shirt. He reminds me of my own grandfather, all of a sudden. He's embracing life, even though he's so close to death. At one point I walk him to the lavatory. It takes a long time and he's breathless by the time we reach it. I'm sure there is no way he would

have been this frail on the flight out. He must know how
weak he has become, and how fast. I get him back to his
seat and wait for him to catch his breath. When he does it's
to make me a promise.

'I ruined the holiday for everyone by getting ill. Doctor,
I swear to you we're going to come back to do it properly
next year.' I mumble something at him and smile. I hope he
doesn't notice me wipe my eyes.

I'm on a bed-to-bed deal with Mr O'Sullivan and I drop
him off at a hospital in Romford in Essex. It's a place we deal
with relatively frequently but I don't want to hear from them
in the next few months. I learned my lesson with Mrs Dean.
In my mind Mr O'Sullivan will beat the odds and get back to
Florida next spring. I don't ever want to learn the truth.

I wrote the reference for Rebecca the night we got back from
Spain. It got called in two days later. That must have been a
formality. The next day I'm in the office to get the notes for
a trip to Greece. She tells me she's got the job.

'I start next month. I'm not on the ship I visited, I'm
on an even bigger one so I'm part of a larger team. There
are two doctors and four nurses. I'm joining the ship in
Gibraltar. I just know I'm doing the right thing.' Her words
are rushing out. It's great to see her look excited rather
than terrified.

'So have you resigned?'

'I'm going to see Jackie later on this morning. I'm not
on a contract or anything so it's really just a formality. The
worst bit will be telling this lot.'

We're at the back of the office near the medical supply
room. She's looking over towards Camilla and Co.

'They'll miss you. But I think they'll agree you're doing the right thing. I'm proud of you.'

Am I also just a little bit envious? I'm in the back of the car taking me to Gatwick. I quite like the idea of being in charge of my own floating medical centre one day. I certainly wouldn't miss all the delays, the feral kids and all the discarded fast-food wrappers at the South Terminal. Then there's the money. Rebecca's not being offered much but she reckons the money she'll save living on the ship means she'll be able to put down a deposit on a flat in a year or so. I've been renting in London for far too long. Maybe I should follow her lead. I gaze out of the cab window with a real frown on my face. I've felt really settled since meeting Cassie. But all of a sudden everything seems up in the air again.

I cheer up a bit when I get to Gatwick, which isn't something anyone says very often. It's midweek and it's surprisingly quiet. I don't have access to a lounge but I've got the timing right and after a quick coffee I pretty much walk straight through on to my flight.

Athens is fantastic. Camilla's booked me into a central hotel and I have time to dart around town for an hour before getting a cab out to my patient's hospital. His name is Luke Allen. He's a gap-year traveller who's done Latin America, Australia, New Zealand the Far East and now Europe. He's been on the road for eight months. He reckons he hadn't had a single problem in seven and half of them. No stomach upsets, no colds, no crises, not even sunstroke. Then he got hit by a car on his way back from the monasteries in Meteora.

His external damage will heal. His internal problems have been a little trickier. He lacerated his liver and ruptured his spleen. The doctors stitched the former and removed the latter. Then he got a post-op wound infection that needed a long course of antibiotics. Ten days on he's still in a lot of pain and he's barely got the energy to move. His drug charts show he's on some powerful painkillers and I check I've got enough to top him up on our journey home.

'Tell me about your trip, mate,' I say as we settle into our seats on the flight.

He asks me to get his camera out of his bag. He's got about a thousand pictures on the memory card. Fortunately, I'm one of the very few people in the world who genuinely likes looking at other people's holiday snaps. Despite his coughing fits he has a story to tell on each of them. He's done a bungee jump, been paragliding, snowboarding, scuba-diving and kayaking. He's trekked, camped, worked on a farm and climbed a few mountains.

'After all that I can't believe I got hit by a car while I'm waiting at a bloody bus stop,' he says when he clicks off the camera and we head back down to Gatwick. We've been in the air for just over four hours. His meds are probably wearing off. I'm sure that's why he's suddenly got tears in his eyes.

It's the end of the month and with a bit of luck everything is going to come together. Rebecca's big leaving do is planned for Friday night. I'm flying over to Phoenix, Arizona on Wednesday morning and I'm on target to be back in time to make it. Better still, Cassie is flying with me.

We've been trying to get on the same flights for months. She has her schedules planned out well in advance and I keep looking for a job that might match them. It's finally happened. We have a great night out with her crew in Scottsdale. Then it's back to work. My patient, Tamsin, is a twenty-three-year-old tennis coach who'd been at a training camp just north of the city. She'd broken a bone in her leg and got a huge gash in her arm playing volleyball on the beach. At this point her first mistake was to wait until she got to the ER before having the wound cleaned properly. Her second mistake was to tell her doctors her tetanus was up to date when it wasn't. That's why she got lockjaw.

'It was the most terrifying experience of my life,' she says when we meet at the hospital. 'I had a fever, I was sweating, I felt like crap. Then I got these spasms over my whole body. It was like I was possessed by something. I couldn't control it. What it does to your face is like your worst nightmare. I thought lockjaw was something that went out with Dickens. I thought it was a made-up illness. But I could feel it freezing down my face. I could feel my jaw being pulled into some death mask thing. I didn't know what was going to happen next. I thought my lungs might freeze, or my heart would stop. I thought my own body was going to kill me.'

'That's lockjaw.'

'All because I didn't have a tetanus jab. It's unbelievable. I'm going to kill my mother when I get home. I can't believe she didn't make me keep that kind of thing up to date.'

Tamsin has been dosed up with antibiotics to get rid of the lockjaw and the fever. She's also had some serious surgery on her leg. To be honest, I'm not that keen on the results. Her leg is held steady with external fixators rather than a traditional cast so I can see the incision area clearly. The skin looks very red and feels a little too hot. I'd say her stitches are a touch too tight as well. Getting these concerns across to the local doctors isn't easy. I get the feeling they think I'm some uppity Brit who wants to pick fault in their care and score points against them. The attending physician seems to get more defensive with every question I ask. In the end I decide I'm only making things worse. Tamsin's leg might still be a bit of a mess but her life's not in danger. I make the call that she's ready to come home.

Cassie's working the cabin behind us and she comes over to say hello once she's finished the 'greet and seat' back there. She shakes hands with Tamsin and wishes us a good flight. We have one. At least at first.

'Ben, I don't want to be a pain, but my leg is really starting to hurt. Is that normal? It feels really hot. Is there something I could take to calm it down?'

We're about six hours into the ten-hour trip. The map on the TV screen in front of me shows the plane as a tiny dot in the middle of the Atlantic. This is the worst possible place to be if Tamsin's in trouble.

'Is it itching? Or are there shooting pains? Let me take a look.'

I click off my seat belt and ease into the space between us so I can examine Tamsin's leg. We're in business class so there's plenty of room. Tamsin's in loose sports clothes, having cut off the right leg of her tracksuit bottoms. Her face has gone grey and I notice she's sweating a little and breathing deeply. My eyes dart to the sick bag in the seat back pocket in front of her. I suddenly get the feeling she might need it.

'It feels numb, like it's swelling,' she says.

Her leg certainly looks inflamed. I'm kneeling on the carpet now and my heart is starting to beat just a little

bit faster. Tamsin's skin is stretched tight. It's hot to
the touch. I can see why it's bothering her but I've got
something else on my mind. However bad this is, it's not
really Tamsin's leg that's in danger. It's her foot. 'Can you
feel this?' I ask. I stroke the sole and heel of her foot and
touch her toes.

'No I can't,' she says. I don't think she'd noticed that
her foot had gone numb. I stroke it again. 'I can't feel that
either,' she says, panic in her voice. I feel between her toes.
We've all got a strong pulse there. It should be really easy to
find. There's nothing.

'How long have you been feeling like this?' I ask.

It doesn't really matter. If there's no feeling and no pulse
then we're up against the clock already. If I don't get blood
to her foot soon then tissue will start to die. It's called
'compartment syndrome'. When it's triggered by a leg wound
like this there's only one way to tackle it. Unfortunately, it's
pretty gruesome.

'Tamsin, the swelling in your leg has stopped the blood
getting to your foot. We need to get it flowing again.
I'm going to need to open your leg wound to relieve the
pressure.'

'What do you mean open my leg wound?'

'I'm going to have to take your stitches out.'

'Here?' She's looking around us in the cabin. It does
suddenly look a very grubby place.

'Yes, here. But it's going to be okay, I promise you. Give
me just one minute to speak to the crew.' I stand up and
head back to the galley. Cassie's sitting on a silver food
trolley having a coffee. She's about to say hello when she
stops herself. She can read my face and she must have
guessed there's no time.

'What's up? Is it your patient?'

'I need to do some work on her leg. It might freak some of the other passengers out. Can I get someone to hang around and keep things calm?'

'I'll do it,' she says. 'Just let me call it in.' She picks up the white phone and I head back to Tamsin.

'I need to keep your leg raised. I'm going to lift it back on to your footstool. 'It's going to be okay.'

The fasten seat belt signs ping on as I reach into the overhead bin for my medical bag.

Cassie is heading down the aisle towards me. 'It's not for you. I got the captain to put it on to keep everyone else out of your way,' she says. 'I'll take the bag if you want. Just tell me what you need.'

I turn back to Tamsin. 'I'm going to give you something to relax you and make it a little easier. So I need to get something in your arm first.'

I snap on some gloves, look for a vein in Tamsin's arm, slide in a cannula and tape it on. I'm just drawing up some midazolam – a type of sedative - when a man's voice comes over the plane's PA system.

'Ladies and Gentlemen, if we have a medical doctor on board today's flight could he or she make themselves known to a member of the cabin crew straight away.'

The steward sounds panicked. I look at Cassie.

'Is that for us?' I ask. Has someone decided I need help? Cassie has no idea.

'I'll check,' she says. Less than thirty seconds later she's rushing back down the aisle. 'It's a problem at the back of the plane. With a baby,' she says.

'Has anyone answered the call?'

'Not yet.'

I look at Tamsin. Her leg has to be tackled fast but I can't ignore a baby. I hold off on the injection, snap off my gloves and grab my med bag.

'Tamsin, I have to go. I'm going to be right back.'

Cassie leads me down the plane. We go through the rear business cabin and the first economy section. As we reach the last few rows it's clear that something is up. It's a night flight but no one seems to be sleeping. Everyone's eyes are on Cassie and I as we pass. Whatever it is, it must have been pretty dramatic to worry so many people.

'They're in the bulkhead seats in the middle just here. I'll go back to your patient up front.' Cassie steps aside into the galley to let me pass. Ahead of me a thirty-something man and a woman are kneeling on the cabin floor in those few extra inches of space in front of the galley wall. Between them is a baby. I slam my bag down into the aisle.

'I'm a doctor. You're the parents? What's happened?'

No time for niceties. With a baby you need to act fast. You also need to calm the whole situation right down. The more businesslike you can be the less likely to parents are to panic. That stops things getting worse.

'He's having a fit. He's not conscious.'

'He's burning up. He's dying,' the mother says frantically.

The baby's skin is very pale and tinged with blue. His body is stiff, he's thrown his head back and his legs and arms are jerking every few seconds. I put my hand on his face. He doesn't respond. He's not with us but I'm certain we won't lose him.

'It looks like a febrile convulsion,' I say. 'They look so much worse than they are and they end very quickly. How old is he? How long has this been going on?'

'He's seventeen months. It's been going on for ages. Ten minutes. Maybe more.'

I look into the mother's eyes. If she's right then this is serious. But scared parents aren't the best judges of time. For them two minutes will always feel like ten.

'Doctor, it's been three or four minutes.' A flight attendant is kneeling next to me. She looks calm and in control.

'Thank you. Can you get me the oxygen?' She stands up and moves fast. 'Your baby will be fine in no time,' I tell the parents. 'I'm going to cool him down and he's going to get better straight away.'

Getting his clothes off is a bit of a struggle as his limbs are still so stiff and keep jerking. His ears are red and he still feels very hot indeed. I'm looking at his skin when the attendant arrives with the plane's oxygen canister and mask.

'I can't see a rash so I don't think it's meningitis,' I tell the parents. 'He's cooling down and I'm going to give him some air. It's going to help.'

That's the exact moment something wonderful happens. The baby fights it off. Somehow I can sense the crisis passing as I stroke his forehead. His legs stop twitching and the stiffness fades ever so slightly out of his body. He's lying still on his blanket now. He looks natural again.

'Look at him, he's calm, he's getting through this,' I say. 'His eyes are open. He's your little boy again.'

His mum and dad are close to me. They're both in tears and they're shaking. I squeeze the too large oxygen mask over their son's tiny face.

'Do you have any family history of fits?' I ask as I rock him. 'Does he have any medical conditions? Where are you travelling from?'

Every answer reassures me a little bit more as I pass the

baby back to his mum. A one off, first-time attack like this with no complicating features can come and go in a matter of minutes. This baby will be fine.

'Some calpol could help to keep him cool,' I tell the flight attendant nearest me. 'If there's anything else at all just come and get me. But we've got another patient with a problem at the front of the plane. I'll back as soon as I can but I have to go.'

I leave the baby in his mother's arms. He looks grizzly but sleepy. My guess is that it will be his parents who take longer to relax.

I power my way up the aisle towards Tamsin. Thank God there are no meal carts in the way. Tamsin's leg is now very red indeed and her foot is turning white. There's still no pulse between her toes. I can't believe how much time we've lost. This has to be done quickly. I finally inject the midazolam and get some sterile scissors out of my bag.

'Oh God, this is going to hurt, isn't it?' she says very quietly.

'You'll be fine,' I say. I look up at Cassie. 'Can you get us some blankets? Two or three of them?'

She pushes the med bag out of the aisle and heads towards first class. I'm hoping this has put Tamsin's mind at ease. With a bit of luck she thinks I want blankets to make her more comfortable. In fact I want to be ready in case there's blood.

When Cassie gets back I position the blankets around Tamsin's leg. 'Close your eyes, Tamsin, I'll tell you when it's over,' I say. Her leg is a horrible colour now, the skin stretched out like a human balloon. I spray the wound liberally with antiseptic solution. Then I get going. There are a couple of dozen stitches running down it. I start with the ones at the top. Snip. I cut it and move to the next. Snip, I've done the second one. Then the third. At this point the wound starts to open up. It gets wider as I move down the line. Snip, snip, snip. Cut, cut, cut. I'm halfway through and so far there's been next to no blood.

'Nearly there, Tamsin, keep your eyes closed. It will feel better when it's done.' I can see clenched fists at her side, though the thought of what I'm doing is probably bothering her more than the reality of it. Hopefully the worst she can feel is a tickle.

'A few more to go.' Then I'm finished. Tamsin's whole leg wound is laid bare now. In a couple of seconds the blood will finally get back through to her foot.

'Can you get me some gauze and some bandages?' Cassie passes me a sterile pack. I cover Tamsin's wound as gently as I can with the gauze swabs and hold them in place with a roller-bandage. There is a real risk of infection in opening up an injury site like this. It's a risk worth taking as long as I've saved her foot.

I'm back on my knees feeling for the pulse between her first and second toes. It's called the dorsalis pedis pulse. This time I can feel it. I close my eyes for a split second in relief. I find myself automatically calculating Tamsin's pulse. It's 100. That's fine.

'Can you feel this?' I ask, stroking the sole of her foot. She can.

'Can you wriggle your toes?' She can. Tamsin looks down at her newly messed-up leg while Cassie smiles broadly at us.

'We didn't even ruin your carpets,' I say.

I pull off my gloves and tell Tamsin I'll be back in a moment. I rush off to the back of the plane to check on the baby. He's in his mum's arms and he's asleep.

'He's still calm,' she says, almost crying. 'Other people have been so kind. The stewardess says she's seen it happen before and some other mums have come over to ask if they can help. One of them said her little girl had a convulsion when she was Barney's age and she was fine straight afterwards. He is going to be all right, isn't he?'

'Get him checked out in hospital as soon as we land but if I'm right and it was a febrile convulsion then there's nothing long term to worry about. I can talk you through it a bit more now, if you want. Or just try and relax till we get to London. A paediatrician will be able to give you much more information and put your minds at rest. Your son looks very comfortable, right now. How are you both feeling?'

Mum and Dad looked wiped out.

'I'm still in shock, I'll never forget it,' she says. 'It happened so quickly. One moment he was fine, the next he was unconscious and his body looked as if it might break. I was so scared and being up here made it feel so much worse. Thank you so much for coming to help us.'

'I'm glad I was here. I'm glad it ended as quickly as it did. The crew can come and get me if you're worried about anything else at all or if you want to talk about it again. Did you say he's called Barney?'

'Yes.'

'Well, Barney looks more relaxed than anyone right now. Call for me if you need me.'

Cassie is waiting for me when I get back to my seat.

'I'm guessing you'd quite like a beer but would settle for a coffee,' she says. 'I'm brewing a fresh pot and I'll bring some right over.'

I give Tamsin a dose of antibiotics and check her leg again. It's red raw and weeping. She'll need it all re-stitched when she gets to hospital on the ground - and it will be even longer now before she can get back on a tennis court.

After all that's happened it's little wonder that Tamsin is soon dozing. I head back to chat to Cassie and after a few moments the cabin service director joins us.

'The couple at the back are very grateful to you,' he says. 'The father says they'll never be able to thank you enough. They're a nice couple. You must be completely exhausted.'

Cassie heads off on a water run while I wander back to Tamsin. She's still sleeping and her wound looks stable so I head back to the galley again.

'I've been thinking,' Cassie says when she rejoins me. 'When we go on holiday together, let's not fly. I think life will be a lot less stressful by train.'

I have to tell her she's wrong.

'One of our freelance doctors says that's what his wife thought. She got so fed up of in-flight emergencies she booked them on Eurostar and the TGV to the South of France. He got called when a little boy broke his arm in the automatic doors. We can't escape it.'

I go back to sit with Tamsin for the rest of the flight. The last thing I want is for her to roll over in her sleep and damage her leg, though even in business class rolling over is a lot easier said than done. We land at Heathrow almost exactly on time though we have the usual half-hour wait for a gate that drives everyone mad. Tamsin and I leave the plane last and Barney's parents come by to say thanks and goodbye again. The little lad is still sleeping and still looks very relaxed. They're going straight to hospital but my guess is that they've nothing to worry about. Tamsin and I then get a buggy through to passport control and beyond. She's checked in a couple of bags so I know Cassie will end up beating us through the terminal. She's heading home to get ready for Rebecca's leaving party. I'm taking Tamsin to a hospital in Winchester before going back to my flat to do the same.

I call the office from the ambulance. Camilla sounds very pleased to hear from me. 'Ben, we're in a bit of a panic. We've just had another long-haul job come in for Monday morning. No one else is around – are you up for it?'

'Where is it?'

'It's South America.'

'Wow. Then yes, I'm up for it!'

Jobs down there don't come up very often. What a stroke of luck that no one else was available. Camilla talks me through this one very quickly. It's an elderly couple who were injured in a coach crash coming back from the Iguaçu Falls in Brazil. She's getting all the medical details now but it's likely to be a simple hand-holding job. I hang up, thrilled. Brazil is somewhere else I've always wanted to go. What a treat to be offered a job like this out of the blue. I reckon I'll be the only person in the country going to work on Monday morning with a big smile on his face.

In Hampshire the A&E department is jammed with patients. Somehow the doctors are on good form.

'I'm sure there was nothing wrong with the old stitches, you just wanted to give me something to do,' the orthopaedic surgeon says. 'Because as you can see, I've been twiddling my thumbs all afternoon.'

I apologise one more time. They must be pretty close to breaking waiting time targets there and the atmosphere is already tense. I wouldn't want to be there on the next shift when the Friday night drunks come in to make things even worse. I hand Tamsin her copy of her file, say goodbye and look at my watch. It's only three o'clock. Plenty of time.

We're back at the Mexican restaurant where we had the Christmas party. Credit to her, Rebecca's attracted almost as many people. Camilla, Christine, Robbie and Matt are here. Jackie's here. Bilal is due, Sylvia and a group of the other freelance nurses are on their way. Alan's sent his apologies, but he's got a pretty good excuse as he's on his way to Hong Kong to collect a businessman with a perforated ulcer. Some of the language students are here, as well as one of our accountants. Partners have been invited so there's less danger of us talking shop all night. Though as Bilal is married to an A&E nurse and Robbie's partner works as cabin crew, it's pretty likely travel and medicine are going to figure highly in most conversations.

Jackie makes a little speech just after Bilal and the nurses all arrive.

'As you all know I interview a lot of people for a lot of jobs.'

'Only the finest survive,' interrupts Robbie.

'You slipped through the net,' adds Christine.

'I interview a lot of people,' Jackie continues. 'Above all else I look for medical competence. Then I look for empathy. I need people who can look after people when they are very scared and very far from home. But in every interview I hope I'll find something else. I hope I'll see a spark in someone's eyes. A feeling that they will love the adventure of travel as much as I do. And not just for the air miles. I want them to be open to the world, ready for all the excitement it can offer. I don't see that spark quite as

often as I'd like. I saw it when I interviewed Rebecca last
summer. I was thrilled when she did her first shifts for us.
I was looking forward to working with her. But as you all
know I then disappeared for a while. Rebecca, I don't think
we spoke to each other from your first week right though till
I came back last month. I regret that.'

'I'm sorry too,' she says.

'I also regret that I wasn't around when you had some bad
experiences with us.'

'Oh God, the man who crapped on the floor in Portugal,'
Robbie calls out.

'Exactly. I know my team tried to see you through this but
in the end you've decided this job isn't for you – at least not
right now. So, all I want to do is say three things. First, you
will be missed. Second, you will be welcome back anytime.
Third, you might need this.' She reaches under the table.
We've had a whip-round and bought a leaving present. It's a
rubber ring.

Rebecca stands up at the table after opening it and
throwing the wrapping paper at Robbie's head. There's quite
a lot of Friday night noise in the restaurant now. It's not
really the place where people make speeches, especially
people as nervous as Rebecca. She gives it a go.

'All I want to say is thank you and sorry for not sticking
it out. I didn't know I had a spark in my eye, but Jackie
is right that I love the idea of seeing the world. I'm sorry
I couldn't do it in this job. I hope we can stay in touch. I
promise that every bar stool injury I have on the ship will
come right through to you.'

She sits down to applause as the waiter comes over for
our orders. Cassie whispers something in my ear. She thinks
my colleagues are even nicer than hers. Three hours later

and more than half of us are ready to make a night of it.
Jackie left after the meal because she's still not doing late
nights and Camilla's heading home because she's working
the weekend. Bilal and his wife are the other early birds.
She's working from eight in the morning while he's on a
plane to Innsbruck at ten. Christine, however, is well up for
a session because she starts on nights tomorrow and reckons
this will get her body acclimatised to them.

'What do you think?' I ask Cassie as we get ready to leave
the restaurant. The overnight Miami flight is a killer for jet-lag.
We've probably been awake for nearly thirty-five hours now.

'I'm up for it if you are,' she says. She still looks amazing.
We follow Rebecca and the others into a bar. Christine is
wearing the rubber ring and we must look like some very
mixed-up hen party.

'Let's drink to flying doctors,' Rebecca shouts when we get
our first round of drinks.

'And to floating doctors,' adds Christine pretending to do
the breast-stroke.

A little later I head to the bar to get another round – and
that's when I find it. Lost behind some euros and dollars in
my wallet is the business card the Harley Street doctor had
given me back in March. Proper job indeed. Why on earth
would I ever want to work for him? I look around me in the
bar. I already work with the best people in the world. I meet
the most amazing new people every day. And I'm going to
Rio on Monday. I should have thrown the card away weeks
ago. Now I tear it up, leaving the pieces in a soggy little pile
on the bar.

'What was that?' an eagle-eyed Robbie asks when I get
back to the group with the drinks.

'Nothing. It was nothing at all.'

AUTHOR'S NOTE

I'll never forget my first repatriation job. I was overseas, on
my own and without any of the support and back-up you
get in a hospital. Sitting beside my patient at 35,000 feet, I
couldn't believe that some doctors and nurses chose to face
this kind of responsibility every day. Then I realised I had
the travel bug and loved the excitement of the unknown. By
the time our plane landed I was ready to do it again.

Today I look back on my time doing repatriations as a
deeply challenging and rewarding experience. I'm very
pleased to be able to share some of those memories in this
book. I am also grateful for the recollections, comments
and suggestions from Jane, Richard and other colleagues
who have carried out dozens of repatriations over the years.
Most full-time repatriation doctors and nurses can carry
out as many as eight jobs a month, the majority of which
are incident-free. In this book I hope I can be excused for
focusing on the most exciting or unusual events I faced. Out
of courtesy and medical confidentiality I changed the names
and other details of each case. But the actual medical events
and emergencies are all based on real events that happened
– and will no doubt happen again, as many of them are
quite common – in holiday locations and on planes around

the world. I've also tried to capture the camaraderie I
felt in the repatriation office. Again, I've re-imagined
conversations with my colleagues and friends so the result
is a mix of fact and fiction. I hope it shows how many great
people are involved in the different repatriation agencies
and how hard they work to help people who are stranded
overseas.

I want to thank author, Neil Simpson, for helping me put
all this down on paper. He went through my diaries, asked
the right questions and managed to turn the events into a
proper narrative. I also want to thank his agent, Andrew
Lownie, for putting the idea for the book in front of the
right people at Hodder & Stoughton. First of all that means
Heather Rainbow who was enthusiastic from the start and
who helped sharpen the narrative and improve it every step
of the way. I also want to thank Rowena Webb, Kerry Hood
and Lucy Hale at Hodder for their enthusiasm and support
from our first meeting onwards.

I work in a hospital now, but I've still got the travel bug
and I still do the occasional repatriation job as a freelancer.
I know that no one reading this book will really want to see
me on their holiday. If you do, it normally means you're in
trouble. But I hope the book shows that you will get home
in the end.

Ben MacFarlane, London, Spring 2009.

ABOUT THE AUTHORS

Ben MacFarlane graduated in medicine from Imperial College, London and started carrying out medical repatriations in the spring of 2001. He has also worked as ship's doctor and now works full-time in a London teaching hospital. HOLIDAY SOS is his first book.

Neil Simpson, who collaborated with Ben MacFarlane on HOLIDAY SOS, is a London-based journalist, author and biographer. www.neil-simpson.com